PRIVATIZATION AND INVESTMENT IN SUB-SAHARAN AFRICA

PRIVATIZATION AND INVESTMENT
IN SUB-SAHARAN AFRICA

Edited by Rexford A. Ahene
and Bernard S. Katz

PRAEGER

New York
Westport, Connecticut
London

Library of Congress Cataloging-in-Publication Data

Privatization and investment in sub-Saharan Africa / edited by Rexford
A. Ahene and Bernard S. Katz.
    p. cm.
   Includes bibliographical references and index.
   ISBN 0-275-93374-1 (alk. paper)
    1. Privatization—Africa, Sub-Saharan. 2. Investments—Africa,
Sub-Saharan. 3. Investments, Foreign—Africa, Sub-Saharan.
I. Ahene, Rexford A. II. Katz, Bernard S., 1932– .
HD4338.P75 1992
332.6'73'0967—dc20   91-37511

British Library Cataloguing in Publication Data is available.

Library of Congress Catalog Card Number: 91-37511
ISBN: 0-275-93374-1

First published in 1992

Praeger Publishers, One Madison Avenue, New York, NY 10010
An imprint of Greenwood Publishing Group, Inc.

Printed in the United States of America

The paper used in this book complies with the Permanent
Paper Standard issued by the National Information Standards
Organization (Z39.48—1984).

10 9 8 7 6 5 4 3 2 1

*Dedicated to Frances, Linda
and our family of friends.*

Contents

III Prospects and Alternatives

Figures and Tables

Preface

The recent history of the economic development of sub-Saharan Africa is disappointing. To a large measure this fact has been due to a series of inefficient investment choices by the African nations as well as their dependence on the growth of the world economy.

Over the past twenty years African national governments dominated the direction and role of the use of investment capital. The record has shown that while well-meaning in intent, domestic and foreign resources were not utilized to their most efficient function. In seeking an equitable distribution of income as well as increases in economic growth, investment patterns were directed toward both public enterprises and investment sectors that were protected by official policy. This investment design realized neither equity nor efficiency for sub-Saharan Africa. Events outside the control of governments also mitigated against the desired national ends.

The 1970s witnessed a number of significant global economic disturbances that further hindered the development of the developing nations. The sub-Saharan African economies were wracked by dramatic oil price increases, then by global economic recession. As a result of the economic downturn, raw material prices in international markets dropped precipitously. This decline in revenues for the primary product-exporting nations of sub-Saharan Africa rendered the payment for interest and principal payments for borrwed foreign capital unbearably burdensome, resulting in a reorientation of national economic development policy for the 1980s and 1990s. It is toward this new perspective and experience that this volume is directed.

This volume does not seek to reexamine the paradigms of economic development; rather the focus is on the more recent experiences of contemporary Africa. The emergence of support for free enterprise is viewed as an attempt to move African nations to a more sustainable growth path. However, private investment cannot be expected to carry the entire burden of growth and development. To this extent we have included essays that support the continued intrusion of government into the marketplace to prescribe the direction of the African economic environment.

The editors have designated four main categories of analysis. The Introduction presents the statistical record of the African public enterprises as they have dominated the economic environment of Africa, and the changes that have, and are, taking place. Part I, "Privatization and Investment Incentives," categorizes in greater detail the arguments for changes as well as the debate for the continuation of governmental influence in the marketplace. Part II, "Strategies, Structure, and Practices," specifies the micro-economic arguments that highlight the erroneous policy experiences of national African governments. These chapters provide the foundation for the privatization experiment now taking place within the sub-Saharan nations. The Part III, "Prospects and Alternatives," addresses alternate policy solutions to the problems of investment and to the maintenance of continued growth in Africa.

We, the editors, believe that the array of essays in this volume provides a well-balanced and interesting series of readings for those interested in African development.

We would like to thank Carolyn Lee and Carol Riffert for their assistance in the preparation of this manuscript.

PRIVATIZATION AND INVESTMENT IN SUB-SAHARAN AFRICA

Introduction: Public Enterprises in Sub-Saharan Africa

BERNARD S. KATZ

This introduction to the subject of investment in Africa highlights privatization and the operations of the African public enterprises, and provides a necessary statistical background to the magnitude and operating characteristics of these state enterprises. The chapter begins with the African perspectives that established the basis for the proliferation of public enterprises, and concludes with the recent African experiences toward privatization.

The independent sub-Saharan African states undertook extensive public enterprise investments to ostensibly augment their economic growth upon their independence in the 1950s and 1960s. The states' policy choice for growth was conditioned by their previous colonial status, a zenophobia of multinational influence, observed market failures extant within less developed nations, and the inequalities of the income and equity effects that may have resulted from a pure market-directed development. Thus the states sought a more egalitarian style of development.

In addition to their philosophical perspective, the African economic leaders recognized that there were shortages and scarcities in the supply of the factors of production necessary for a broad-based private sector development. Technical skills, both industrial and entrepreneurial, were seen to be in short supply; the scale of the investment necessary for modern technology exceeded the financial ability of the indigenous private sector; and domestic private investors lacked the required international borrowing power. The economic leaders accepted the conventional wisdom that even if funds for investment had been available, the small size of domestic markets would not have yielded sufficient returns to attract the private investors.

With both market and resource factor constraints, and with an income redistribution goal, the governments of the sub-Saharan African states adopted a program of widespread state intervention in the development process. This policy choice promulgated an extensive array of state-owned public enterprises aided by a wholesale listing of import restrictions.

The broad encroachment of the public sector into the domain of private sector activity was met with relatively little resistance as substantial benefits were realized by diverse groups. The state-owned enterprises provided for stable employment as they were inured against bankruptcy by treasury financing. Consumers reaped lower-than-cost prices, and specified business sectors were protected against foreign competition. Despite the commitment and worthy objectives of the development plan, it began to unravel by the mid-1970s.

The latter part of the 1970s and the decade of the 1980s was an economically wrenching period for the nations of sub-Saharan Africa. The oil price increase of the early 1970s and the ensuing world inflation of the latter part of the decade precipitated reliance on further international borrowing for continued growth as well as to protect the existing level of living. The problems of the African nations were compounded by their experience of a decline in both their terms of trade and export volume. Moreover, the public enterprises proved to be a heavy drain on the nations' resources and government treasuries.

The operations of the state-owned companies did not become contributors to government coffers. In fact, these enterprises continually required state subsidies to maintain operations. Without the discipline of market competition the public companies, often with monopoly powers, were labor heavy and inefficient. Moreover, the widespread import restrictions proliferated the misallocation of scarce resources throughout all sectors of the economy.

In their attempts to deal with their mounting problems, the African nations appealed to the International Monetary Fund and the World Bank, as well as to official lending agencies for the rescheduling of interest and principal debt payments. These efforts were successful, but relief came with strong remedial recommendations as the IMF imposed strict stabilization policies and the World Bank required structural economic adjustments, particularly with respect to public enterprises.

To meet the recommendations of the international lending agencies, the African nations began a program of rationalization and retrenchment for their proliferated public enterprises.

The balance of this chapter presents the specific statistical characteristics of the sub-Saharan public enterprises for the 1980s. The analysis relies heavily on World Bank data. The World Bank's researchers must be commended in their efforts in bringing together disparate and incomplete official reports.

THE ANALYSIS

National government enterprise investment in Africa has been ubiquitous. Among some thirty sub-Saharan African states there are approximately 3000 public enterprises employing 1.5 million workers (Table 1.1, columns 1 and 2), constituting an average 25 percent of the formal sector work force. While the

Table 1.1
Africa's Public Enterprise (PE) Sector: Selected Characteristics

COUNTRY	# of PE's (Most recent) figure	# Employed in PR sector[1] (000)	PE Contribution to GNP (%)	PE Share of Domestic Investment[1] (%)	PE Share of Domestic Credit Outstanding (%)	PE Share External Debt Outstanding (%)
BENIN	57	28.0	–	–	45.3	35.4
BOTSWANA	9	–	–	–	–	14.0
BURUNDI	64	16.9	5.0	36.6	13.1	.7
CAMEROON	58	–	–	–	–	43.0
CAR	29	6.1	4.6	17.0	–	18.6
CONGO	94	32.3	10.0	39.8	–	20.6
COTED IVOIRE	150	–	–	17.9	–	9.3
ETHIOPIA	108	83.4	4.6	–	–	14.3
GAMBIA	19	9.4	–	–	–	1.2
GHANA	181	104.9	–	25.0	18.6	14.8
GUINEA	101	112.2	25.0	–	–	0.9
GUINEABIS	36	3.5	–	–	–	–
KENYA	175	93.4	–	20.7	3.5	0.1
LIBERIA	21	–	–	–	11.7	10.8
MADAGASCAR	184	30.9	2.3	–	14.5	29.3
MALAWI	13	41.2	7.8	14.2	7.8	12.9
MALI	51	12.2	12.1	8.1	–	2.6
MAURITANIA	112	11.0	25.0	–	–	16.7
MAURITIUS	23	20.2	7.2	–	–	4.8
NIGER	44	11.0	4.9	19.5	23.8	19.6
NIGERIA	110	417.0	13.8	20.0	–	11.9
RWANDA	40	–	–	–	5.3	0.5
SENEGAL	50	–	9.5	32.7	34.5	14.7
SIERRALEONE	22	12.2	–	1.2	–	34.6
SOMALIA	45	7.6	1.9	–	–	2.2
SUDAN	200	117.6	47.5	–	16.9	3.0
TANZANIA	420	–	13.0	25.5	20.6	18.2
TOGO	65	12.5	–	–	–	5.5
UGANDA	130	–	–	–	3.2	3.1
ZAIRE	129	150.0	22.8	–	0.6	35.3
ZAMBIA	123	130.8	31.8	54.1	14.6	38.5

[1]Average years 1980–1986

Source: Africa's Public Enterprise Sector: World Bank Technical Paper Number 95, World Bank, 1989.

numbers of firms and employees bear little relationship to the importance of public enterprise as a significant constructive or negative element to the economy, these numbers indicate the belief that there is a paucity of managerial resources. (The use of skilled managerial labor within the public enterprises drains the private sector of these very same skills. The argument that it was necessary to establish these public enterprises because of scarce labor resources has become a self-fulfilling prophecy in that the pre-empting of managerial talent assures that there are shortages for private enterprise. It may also be argued that the curtailment of private sector activities also led talented and educated managers to leave the country, creating the heralded "brain drain," with the Western free enterprise economies the beneficiaries.)

The importance of public enterprise to the economy is determined by its contribution to the national income, and, in part, the percentage of total domestic investment it represents (Table 1.1, columns 3 and 4).

As calculated from Table 1.1, the public enterprises' average amount of value added as a share of GDP approximates 15 percent, with the median at 12 percent. The range of contributions extends from 2 percent for Madagascar to 48 percent for the Sudan.

The enterprises' average share of domestic investment amounts to 24 percent, while the median is close to the average at 25 percent. The World Bank indicates that both the share of value added and the percent of domestic investment is higher for Africa than for Latin America or Asia. For Latin America the shares are 12 and 19 percent, while for Asia they are 3 and 17 percent. A similar pattern emerges with respect to investment shares, with Asia at 17 percent, and Latin America at 19 percent. While there may not be an appropriate average for either of the two indicators, the higher share of domestic investment by public enterprises in Africa does point to the higher probability of a "crowding-out" of private investment.

The last column in Table 1.1 relates the share of the public enterprises' foreign borrowing to the percent of total foreign debt outstanding. The majority of the debt is from foreign commercial banks, and is nonconcessional. In recent years the foreign borrowing percentages have been marginally decreasing due to internal financial restructuring, as well as to shifting to indirect loans from government intermediaries. The World Bank points out, however, that the major reasons for the decline are the caution exercised by the foreign lending agencies (given the credit-worthiness of the enterprises, as witnessed by declining export revenues) and the weakening of government guarantees.

Public enterprise loans amount to fourteen percent of the total value of all sub-Saharan African external borrowing. The median value is similiar. These averages tend to understate the true level of public enterprise borrowing as governments often borrow on behalf of the enterprise. The World Bank uses Togo as an example of this understatement. For Togo the reported public enterprises' share of external debt is indicated at 5 percent. However, the actual share, if government loans on behalf of the enterprises were included, would be closer to 50 percent.

The first column in Table 1.2 captures the operating profits less losses of the sub-Saharan African public enterprises. Of the twenty-two countries listed, only six show positive profits, contributions to GDP. In part, those nations that do show positive inflows of revenue stem primarily from the operations of mining enterprises. The fact that the majority of the African nations show negative net operating revenues does not necessarily indicate inefficiency at the enterprise level. A number of factors may account for their negative performance; a poor market enviornment is an example.

Table 1.2
Africa's Public Enterprise Sector: Selected Financial Characteristics

COUNTRY	Net Financial Results/GDP[1] (%)	PE Payments to Govt/Govt Revenue[1] (%)	Govt Payments to PE/Govt Expenditure[1] (%)	Subsidies as share of Govt Current Expenditure[1] (%)
BENIN	-1.5	7.4	6.3	-
BOTSWANA	-	-	-	.02
BURUNDI	0.4	4.3	4.8	-
CAMEROON	-1.9	0.5	13.1	7.3
CAR	-1.4	2.5	-	-
CONGO	-2.7	-	-	4.5
COTED IVOIRE	-3.9	-	13.1	2.2
ETHIOPIA	-	-	-	-
GAMBIA	-4.3	1.1	-	2.8
GHANA	-1.2	4.0	-	5.9
GUINEA	-	20.3	17.9	-
GUINEABIS	-	-	-	1.7
KENYA	0.3	-	2.8	0.8
LIBERIA	-	-	-	-
MADAGASCAR	-0.1	-	-	-
MALAWI	-0.4	-	10.6	0.2
MALI	-1.7	4.6	-	-
MAURITANIA	-0.6	-	5.5	-
MAURITIUS	-0.8	6.5	11.2	5.5
NIGER	-0.9	14.2	7.6	3.7
NIGERIA	1.3	69.4	14.5	-
RWANDA	0.3	-	-	0.4
SENEGAL	-0.4	-	-	3.0
SIERRALEONE	-0.2	1.7	6.7	2.2
SOMALIA	-0.04	8.4	-	-
SUDAN	-	-	-	-
TANZANIA	-	2.1	4.4	3.6
TOGO	-	6.9	-	-
UGANDA	-	-	-	-
ZAIRE	2.5	8.9	-	-
ZAMBIA	1.4	9.4	-	-

[1] Average years 1980–1986

Source: Africa's Public Enterprise Sector: World Bank Technical Paper Number 95, World
    Bank, 1989.

The financial results of the enterprises have far-reaching implications, affecting
government expenditures, domestic credit, and external debt. If losses are indicated, government expenditures will bear the burden of lower tax revenues
collected, as well as subsidies for capital expenditures and for operating expenses.
Domestic money markets will be strained by the lack of loan servicing, and
foreign exchange debt inflows will be diverted to cover operating losses.

Columns 2, 3, and 4 of Table 1.2 are subsets of column 1, and are self-
explanatory. What they indicate is the burden of the public enterprises on the

economy. However, in interpreting the economic meaning of the data, the reader should continually bear in mind the intent of the public enterprises. These firms were often established for noncommercial objectives; that is, they were organized for targeted social goals such as the provision of low-cost necessities, inherent externalities, and infrastructure development. To properly evaluate the financial operations of these firms, their social benefits should be costed either as revenues or deductions against expenditures. Only in this fashion can the true costs of the public enterprises to the national economy be calculated and evaluated.

The argument for privatization is based almost singularly on the improvement of the efficiency of enterprises. Critics of African public enterprise argue that the basic cause of public enterprise inefficiency stems from inappropriate investment decisions, an adverse operating environment witnessed by weak capital bases, price controls, poor accountability, and diffused decision-making. It is further stated that these firms receive unfavorable export prices, pay high import prices, and have limited access to foreign commodity and capital markets. Privatization is seen as a remedy to a number of public enterprise inefficiencies.

The rationale for privatization is that not only will it make more efficient use of a nation's resources, it will also increase the level of income as the nation responds to the competitive forces of the market. As public enterprise decision-making is constrained under political and equity motives, market competition will remove inherent economic inefficiencies. Enterprise suppliers will receive no more than competitive input prices, and workers no more than competitive wages. The consumer pays full value for the resources used, and premiums paid to political interests are minimized, benefitting the economy accordingly.

Additionally, with privatization the government budget will be relieved of the strain of subsidies, and federal revenues can be expected to increase. Expenditures will now be freed from the constraint of the subsidy and benefits can be redirected. The foreign debt burden may well be eased if, upon sale or liquidation, the purchasers are overseas buyers bringing in fresh capital (foreign exchange) for the firm's purchase and for firm expansion.

The pitfalls of privatization can be addressed as well. Many of the public enterpises operate as state monopolies. While state revenues can be maximized by selling the monopoly firm, all of the usual private monopoly costs will now be incurred by consumers and the nation. Government revenues may not be maximized, and economic resource use may become further distorted. Foreign purchasers will not necessarily bring in fresh foreign exchange as they will have advantages in domestic capital markets, through size and credit-worthiness. The balance of payments may acually worsen over time as repatriated profits flow to overseas investors. This foreign exchange drain would be amplified if the firm were not directly involved in the external markets.

The conversion of the African public enterprises is, however, taking place. Almost all of the sub-Saharan African nations are undertaking some kind of reform program, ranging from rehabilitation of plant and finances, to divestiture. The selling off of the public enterprises has taken two forms (Table 1.3), either

Table 1.3
Africa's Public Enterprise Reform (1983–1987)

COUNTRY	Privatization completed or underway # of Enterprises[1]	Enterprises Liquidated or Underway # of Enterprises[2]	# of PE's Studies for Divestiture
BENIN	–	–	11
BOTSWANA	–	–	–
BURUNDI	–	4	–
CAMEROON	1	5	1
CAR CONGO	–	4	2
COTED IVOIRE	14	24	–
ETHIOPIA	–	–	–
GAMBIA	4	1	3
GHANA	5	5	–
GUINEA	30	18	–
GUINEABIS	–	–	–
KENYA	1	–	–
LIBERIA	–	–	–
MADAGASCAR	–	5	35
MALAWI	1	–	5
MALI	2	7	–
MAURITANIA	4	5	30
MAURITIUS	–	–	–
NIGER	18	4	22
NIGERIA	8	–	–
RWANDA	1	4	–
SENEGAL	22	23	–
SIERRALEONE	1	5	10
SOMALIA	1	–	–
SUDAN	4	–	–
TANZANIA	3	–	–
TOGO	6	12	7
UGANDA	12	1	–
ZAIRE	1	–	–
ZAMBIA	1	–	–

[1] Sale of shares
[2] Sale of shares

Source: Africa's Public Enterprise Sector—World Bank Technical Paper Number 95, World Bank, 1989.

sale of the shares, that is, privatization, or sale of the assets, that is, liquidation. An example of a nation undertaking all styles of reform is Madagascar.

While a change to the market orientation for public enterprises has been slow, Madagascar now permits the manufacturing public enterprises to set their own prices, and wholesale and retail trade no longer have profit margins controlled by central authorities. Import restrictions have been relaxed and capital rehabilitation programs have begun. Liquidation orders were issued to fourteen public enterprises, and privatization procedures were begun for seven of the public enterprises, three of which were the largest users of bank credit.

African progress toward divestiture has been admittedly slow; some 140 enterprises were placed in the private sector between 1983 and 1987. An additional 133 firms were under serious study for further divestiture.

While the African experience with the public enterprise is undergoing significant change, what should be noted is that the initiative for change was external, not African. Whether this will have any bearing on the speed and magnitude of privatization will be determined in the 1990s.

PART I

PRIVATIZATION AND INVESTMENT INCENTIVES

Privatization in Africa: Domestic Origins, Current and Future Options

ERNEST J. WILSON III

Few phenomena in recent years have sparked as much fervent support and militant opposition as "privatization." Narrowly defined, privatization means selling state-owned assets to private buyers. Its proponents insist that privatization improves micro-economic efficiency and enhances macro-economic growth. Its opponents counter that privatization is a non-starter politically and impractical economically. One side tends to see privatization as a private sector panacea; the other as an imperialist curse.[1] Part of the difficulty in objectively evaluating either position is that the number of privatizations that have actually occurred around the world, and especially in Africa, is rather modest. The outcomes are also ambiguous for both the firms involved and the sector or the economy as a whole.[2] If African privatization has been modest in number and impact, then why is such passion involved pro and con?

"Privatization" touches deeply-held values and attitudes. People feel strongly about what they think is the most appropriate role for the state and market. In Asia, where liberal markets are more widely accepted than in Africa, the term has not generated the same degree of heat as it has among Africans and among those who study Africa. When applied to Africa, "privatization" collides with received notions of economic nationalism, redistributive politics, and high degrees of state intervention. Opposition arises because in part privatization's principal proponents are either conservative politicians or ideologues (e.g., Margaret Thatcher, the Adam Smith Institute) or international donors (the IMF and the World Bank). In addition to partisan beliefs, there is also the reality that privatization affects material interests and shifts power among local government officials, businessmen, and multinational corporations.

Unfortunately, the ideologically driven arguments of privatization's strongest supporters and its most vocal opponents do a double disservice to Africa and to scholars interested in the continent. On the one hand, dismissing privatization or treating it uncritically wastes an opportunity to seize one of the most important questions in social science—the relationship between the public and the private sectors. What social and political differences are there among countries with large, or small, public sectors? This central question lies at the core of the concerns of the classic texts of Marx and Weber, Polanyi and Gerschenkron.

On the other hand, privatization, in the broadest sense of deregulation and greater market competition, provides an important and useful policy tool that African governments can employ to re-start their stagnant economies. As in China, the USSR, and Britain, privatization can be one instrument among many to promote growth. It should be neither oversold nor undersold. Privatization in Africa is neither all curse nor perfect cure. All healthy political economies walk on two legs, a strong public sector and a strong private one.

This chapter focuses first on the domestic political conditions in Africa in the 1960s and 1970s that made economic reform and privatization inevitable in the 1980s and 1990s. Then it provides selected illustrations of current privatization practices. Finally, using three scenarios, it speculates on the future of privatization in Africa, concluding by indicating lines for future policy inquiry.

Two caveats: first, this chapter is a meditation on the origins and evolution of public-private sector relations as they are highlighted in the current privatization debate. It is not a detailed review of the African privatization experience to date. Second, while no one can deny the clear importance of the IMF, the World Bank, bilateral aid agencies, and other external actors in forcing privatization onto the policy agenda of many African states, we focus on the domestic economic and political origins of the reform movement in Africa. There is a tendency to ignore the domestic features prompting economic reform in favor of the more visible effects of the international capitalist system.

STATE AND MARKET IN AFRICAN STUDIES

Until recently the conventional wisdom in the Africanist development literature has been that given a choice between state and market, Africans should choose the state. It was the state that could control hostile multinationals and bend them to serve national purposes. It was the state that could replace rapacious middlemen and redistribute goods and services away from white expatriate interests toward the black poor.

There were persuasive practical and theoretical reasons for Africans to prefer state intervention to market laissez-faire. Mostly these reasons had to do with the foreign domination of the economy and the market failures associated with poor countries. One reason given for state intervention was the small size of the African commercial class, which left the state to undertake activities that in other regions the private entrepreneur would perform. The colonial legacy of an economy dominated by foreign firms meant that African elites were naturally hostile to what they saw as the continuation of an exploitative private sector presence. There was also the lack of the most basic public infrastructure, investments typically made by government. Intervention was helped, too, by an ideological mix in the terminal years of colonialism that combined anti-European and Pan Africanist nationalism, as well as anti-capitalism and a redistributionist philosophy, for which state control seemed a perfect tool. Finally, state expansion was fed by an ambitious search for power by the post-colonial politicians and civil servants that maximized their personal and collective power thorough the manipulation of markets and privilege by the state. Since many of the original economic and political conditions that gave rise to state ownership and control have still not been resolved, we can expect significant state ownership to be with us for a long while in Africa.

To understand why privatization has come to the fore (while discussions of further nationalization have slipped into the shadows) we consider the evolution of what we can call the political bargain of African economic policy.

THE POLITICAL ECONOMY BARGAIN

The call for privatization and economic reform should be seen against the background of an implied economic bargain struck by the first generation of post-colonial elites with their less-favored fellow citizens. In carrying out state action to overcome the constraints cited, the elite insisted on the authority necessary to maintain tight control over the commanding heights of the economy (initially, mainly foreign corporations). In return, the elites would use their control to provide greater distributional equity than would likely occur under entirely free market conditions. State control would enhance both equity and efficiency.

Later, as government-owned companies, or public enterprises, came to take more economic control and ownership, their performance proved disappointing.[3] The bargain was re-interpreted to accommodate experience. As the state-run enterprises did not work well, a slightly lower level of economic efficiency was conceded. It was argued that the elite would still capture greater equity benefits than would otherwise occur. The lower efficiency was admitted to come from slightly longer bureaucratic delays, slightly less efficient use of inputs like labor or capital. In the aggregate, however, the "logic" was that a unit of efficiency might be sacrificed to gain two units of equity. Efficiency losses were supposedly more than compensated by equity gains. Since a public enterprise "loser" was at minimum still assumed to generate net employment benefits, the public bargain was not questioned. The rising price for products that Africans sold on the international market helped support this perception. The bottom line was that the state, and not the market, would bring more efficient, equitable and (implied) more democratic outcomes.

By the early 1980s, however, international markets had collapsed and the picture had changed. It appeared that the political economy bargain had given Africa the worst of all worlds. High state intervention (and low government probity and efficiency) helped squander both efficient investment and equitable consumption. Even for countries like Tanzania, with demonstrable public commitments to greater egalitarianism, the poor aggregate production levels meant there was less and less surplus for distribution.

On the political side, the elites greatly narrowed the avenues of democratic participation in the years following independence, but without the deepening capital accumulation that has led elsewhere (some Latin American countries) to capitalist or socialist transformation. As the subsidies from the public enterprise system helped cushion the declining standard of living for the elites more than for the peasant producer of worker, there was little incentive for the state elites to reform the institutions they controlled and, often quite literally, consumed. Twenty years of political demobilization, on top of an essentially dispersed and agrarian population, made popular anti-state uprisings unlikely. Still, the combination of growing domestic discontent and external pressure has forced economic reform of African governments.

RE-INTERPRETATIONS

Seasoned writers on Africa have reviewed the cumulative evidence of twenty years of mismanagement and malfeasance and have rethought their earlier positions.[4] Analysts of Africa discovered instead of imperfect markets and perfect states, the imperfections of state economic control. It was the government's turn to be the target of criticism. Unchecked political authority over economic affairs could prove as reactionary, exploitative, and arbitrary as exploitation through purely commercial exchanges.

Two analyses stand out. Goran Hyden's work on the "economy of affection" indicated the severe limits on state economic action in countries at low levels of development. The state gets "captured" by a variety of external claimants and gutted from within by the self-interested re-direction of state officials manipulating "public resources of private uses."[5] He concludes that Africa could develop only through greater reliance on the market.

A December 1985 issue of the *Review of African Political Economy* (a journal that has championed the new political economy of Marxist interpretation) on the theme of "Market Forces" questions the reflexive support many Marxists and others render for states over markets. Concluding an article on Marketing Boards in Nigeria, Gavin Williams writes, "Against all the evidence [the need for the state to intervene to promote 'orderly markets'] maintains a strong appeal for bureaucrats, technocrats and, regrettably, many socialists. Socialists have no business defending or reforming such exploitative institutions. *De jure* state monopolies on the marketing of crops impose high costs on producers, on government budgets, and on consumers. They create *de facto* monopolies for favored and protected traders and the opportunities for profitable collusion between businessmen and officials, that is, civil, monopolistic arrangements. Socialists should support free trade." Williams calls on other socialists not to defend ossified dogma over popular interests, and insists that the market is not always bad, nor is the state always good.[6]

To illustrate the privatization process in Africa, we cite several cases studies where privatization and economic reform are occurring:

Nigeria

The Financial Times called the Nigerian experiment in economic reform the "most radical in Africa." It includes liberalizations (with the elimination of import licenses), a large currency devaluation, reductions in price-fixing by government, and a form of privatization of the country's marketing board system. All of the export boards—for commodities like cocoa, rubber and palm products—were liquidated. At the same time, the price was permitted to rise and private companies were encouraged to enter the market: producers and private middlemen gained and export volumes shot up. The down side of the reform was a decline in quality control as government ceded part of its regulatory functions to the market. The interesting political economy question is the following: why would the regime of General Babangida select this, the most radical option available to him, to reform the boards?[7]

Cote d'Ivoire

There has probably been relatively more privatization in this country than in any other in Africa except Nigeria, with twenty-eight companies already privatized and others on the way. Interesting is the modality used by government to privatize. Instead of identifying in advance the sectors, industries, and particular firms it was willing to privatize, as most African countries do, the Ivorian government announced that it was willing to consider bids from the private sector for state enterprises which private companies wanted to buy. Of the firms sold, most were in industry or agro-allied industries. Twenty-one were not profitable at the time of sale, but a number are now operating more efficiently than before. About half were sold to Ivorian nationals and half to foreigners, mostly French firms. The sales included management buy-outs by the Ivorian managers of 100 percent state-owned companies, privatizations through the stock exchange (a tobacco company), and a number of purchases of local companies by foreign firms that were their competitors (Unilever bought a local rival) or firms that held management contracts. This privatization exercise was closely controlled by President Houphouet-Boigny.[8]

Senegal and Ghana have both identified enterprises they will put up for sale, and have actually sold a handful. Kenya has announced sales, but the government is reluctant to proceed, in part due to the complicated ethnic and racial divisions in the country. The government of President Moi, himself a non-Kikuyu, doesn't want to sell to the people most likely to buy (Kikuyus and Indians). Significant liquidation sales or leases have also been registered in Togo (steel mill, dairy, oil storage tanks) and Guinea. Interesting political struggles over privatization have occurred in Mali, Tanzania (the city buses in Dar es Salaam), Nigeria, Zambia and Egypt.

THE FUTURE OF PRIVATIZATION IN AFRICA

Is what we have seen so far just a flash in the pan, or does it herald the beginning of a new era of African political economy? Is it the beginning of a sustained process that will develop domestic roots and nourishment or the end of a charade played for foreign donors? The answers to these questions are not insignificant for Africa's future development.

If we relate the likely incidence of privatization reforms to changes in the international economic environment, then we can construct three scenarios that yield different pictures of the future. The following three figures indicate privatization reform as the reduction in the scope of the public enterprise sector as enterprises are sold or liquidated. The three scenarios cover the main logical alternatives, as well as the current thinking that emerges in discussions with African government officials, with World Bank and IMF staff, with private businessmen, and with other scholars.

SCENARIO NUMBER ONE: REFORM IS HERE TO STAY

Some see privatization as the (belated) recognition on the part of Africans that state intervention has gone too far and has ruined national economy after national economy. Excessive intervention has brought severe budget deficits domestically and heavy loan obligations internationally. With world pressures for greater international competitiveness, and strong signals from the multilateral and private banks and investors, African governments have learned their lesson and will not try to artificially reflate their economies using public enterprises. The leadership is mending its spendthrift ways. Chastened by experience, the African leadership will stay the course. The downturn in the business cycle has entrenched reform. Privatization is here to stay (Figure 2.1).

SCENARIO NUMBER TWO: ECONOMIC REFORM IS CYCLICAL

In contrast to scenario number one, others argue that economic reform movements closely follow the ebb and flow of the business cycle. Government leaders respond to economic pressures and to the political heat they feel. Scenario number two agrees that government elites are now pressed by unfavorable circumstances to correct the errors of their past spendthrift ways; but they fundamentally disagree about the lasting impact of the lessons. The second hypothesis says belt-tightening and privatization occur when times are hard; but when the "vache grasse" (fatted cow) times return, privatization disappears. Renewed international demand for a country's commodities and the resultant higher government revenues will knock

Figure 2.1
Scenario #1: Reform Is Here To Stay

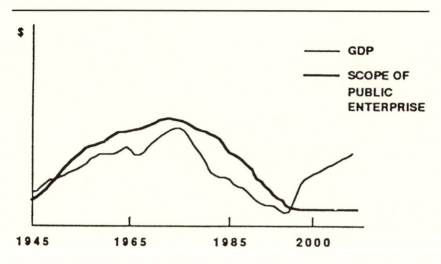

the bottom out of reform, since there will be less pressure once again to pay attention to bottom-line issues of enhanced efficiency.

These two stories paint different pictures of the future of privatization in Africa. A picture of the first scenario might be a downward-sloping curve of reduced state ownership and control. It would initially be associated with the economic downturn, but would gain an unstoppable upward momentum of its own, irrespective of future economic performance.

A picture of scenario two would show the curve of privatization perfectly matched to the up-and-down (but inverted) curve of the business cycle. When the economy is low, governments also reduce their public enterprises; when the economy is high, governments expand public enterprises and ignore reforms. We can chart the relationship between the ups and downs of the business cycle and the path of privatization and reform.

Scenario number one insists that a new political economic rationality of reform will overcome cyclical market swings. Number two argues that the market swings will swamp the new reformist rationality. A third position or hypothesis captures more of the political dynamics involved.

SCENARIO NUMBER THREE: STRUCTURE AND CYCLES

Number three assumes that the etatiste movement after World War Two had a distinct political imperative that was analytically separate from the economic

Figure 2.2
Scenario #2: Reform Is Cyclical

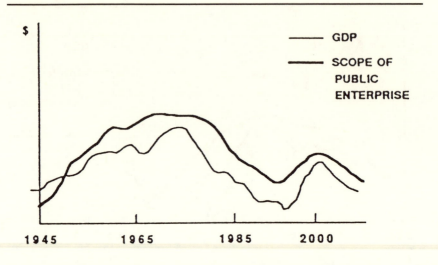

imperatives of the period. These political imperatives are derived from the degrading colonial status to which most African states were subjected until the middle of the twentieth century.

Nationalism's victory over formal colonialism was based in part on the postcolonial pact we described above—elite promises to the popular classes to redistribute goods and services via the state. It is important to note that the successful push for political independence occurred during an expansionary period of the world market. Economic surpluses were available to elites to re-distribute to popular classes and to cover the inefficiencies that often followed nationalization. Popular and elite demands were satisfied on a wave of widespread nationalization that lasted a generation. Nationalization on the upswing of business cycles was more a political than an economic strategy.

Between the early wave expansion and the current contractions we discover a kind of reversed symmetry of economic and political factors. Politics is the primary driving force on the upswing of this historical process. The expansionary phase of the African state was pushed mainly by nationalist political factors, especially the interaction of mass mobilization, welfare demands, and elite transformation in the immediate post-war period. The economy was merely the enabling factor.

In the current period economic factors appear to dominate the pressures to stop or reverse the growth of the state. Debt and budget deficits, not "pure" politics, bring privatization. Privatization is an opportunistic response to debt and budgetary pressures by an African elite for the most part unconvinced of

Figure 2.3
Scenario #3: Reform Is Cyclical/Structural

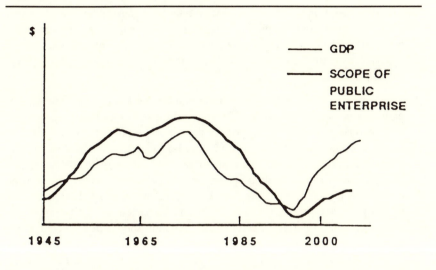

the superiority of market solutions to development problems. Political factors now are at best secondary: neutral constituencies in some countries, oppositional constituencies in others, with the main constant the pressures from the multinational agencies.

In the future, if scenario number three is correct, state elites will probably be less etatiste, having learned that state overextension on the upside of the business cycle can deepen the trough of stagnation on the downside. When growth resumes, we will see some increases in state expenditures (e.g., investments in infrastructure and productive capacity allowed to collapse during the recession), but not on the same munificent scale that we saw for much of the post-1945 period.

In the future, the prospects for sustained and continuing reform may go beyond short-term utilitarian responses. Continued privatization will then hinge on whether or not national leaders, pressed mainly by economic recession to privatize state assets, will be able to create a viable political constituency for economic reform.

NEW DIRECTIONS

Questions arise in privatization that guide future investigations. These questions can be answered only by studying actual privatization cases in African countries.

1. Why do some countries embrace privatization more quickly and thoroughly than others? Why do some countries resist? The evidence suggests that support for privatization in an African country requires a sizable indigenous business class, political leadership willing to take risks of alienating key constituencies opposed to economic reform, and ethnic and racial competition that is manageable. As these three factors diminish, the likelihood of successful privatization declines.

2. What impact, if any, has privatization had on the level of performance of particular privatized enterprises? What are the effects on industrial, sectoral, and national performance? Is privatization more important because the restructured firms are more efficient or because the budgetary burden on government is reduced? Are some sectors more likely to be privatized than others? Is privatization more effective in some sectors other than theirs? The sectoral evidence is not clear, and there have been successful and failed privatizations in many markets, though it appears that privatization in small-to-medium-sized firms may be most effective. This situation should be expected, since management skills are the scarcest factor of production in Africa. The more modest the market size and complexity, the easier it will be to find African buyers and managers to operate privatized firms successfully.

    But two other important conclusions emerge from the international experience. First, changing ownership is not the only key factor to improve the performance of a reformed enterprise. Ownership may take a back seat to the quality of management designated to run the newly privatized enterprise. Second, some de-control of the commercial environment is required. Privatization unaccompanied by a reduction in state controls over product or factor pricing, in import restrictions and in other burdensome government constraints, will not yield the desired efficiency benefits.

3. Do African governments have the administrative and political capabilities to develop a regulatory approach to the economy to complement or substitute for direct ownership and control? The unsatisfactory efforts at less intrusive arms-length regulation of the 1960s led to the nationalization experiments of 1970s. It is time to try regulation again; inefficient regulation may be better than inefficient nationalization. Clearly a better mix is required.

4. When privatization occurs, who have been the winners and losers? Does the business class gain power at the expense of workers? Do chambers of commerce become more vocal and influential? Are alliances between local and foreign business strengthened or strained? In the short term there are more losers—parastatal employers and managers, potentially their clients, and businessmen who sell parastatals goods and services at inflated prices. Proponents argue that over the medium-to-long-term all groups will benefit, as resources are shifted from unproductive uses into directly productive ones. Enhanced production will expand the supply of local goods, driving down prices. It

appears that local business organizations are gaining enhanced access to government circles.

5. Are there consistent cross-national relationships in Africa between privatization and economic reforms, on the one hand, and political reforms and democratization, on the other?

6. What is the actual development capacity of the private sector itself? How well have privately owned African firms held up under the recession of the past years? Do they perform as well as some suggest, far better than comparable public firms in the same markets?

7. Are domestic savings being mobilized for domestic development? Is there evidence of new exchanges between capital and management in the informal sector and new investments and entrepreneurship in the formal sector, now that external capital flows are drying up? Is there room for a greater role for the informal sector in the economic reforms now underway? African governments and the multilateral agencies must pay much more attention to directly developing the informal and the formal private sector in Africa.

NOTES

Reprinted with permission from *Issue: A Journal of Opinion*, 1988.

1. The World Bank and the IMF are among the strongest supporters of liberal reforms and privatization. The Lagos Plan of Action prepared by African heads of state is far more critical. The United States has the most visible bilateral privatization programs; as is often the case, the French seem to talk less but do more privatization deals than the Americans.

2. The small universe of actual privatization deals makes generalizations about their impact extremely tentative and modest. Much of the argumentation begins with appeals to neo-classical economic logic. It then demonstrates that the public enterprise sector is a major drain on development funds. Proponents then argue, logically, that reducing the size of the sector will reduce the drain on resources. In fact, liquidating firms or privatizing them has helped reduce some state expenditures. The evidence is far more mixed as to whether the privatized firms have significantly improved their own performance. There is even less evidence linking company improvements to enhanced national economic performance.

3. Information on public enterprise is available in John Nellis, "Public Enterprises in Sub-Saharan Africa," World Bank Discussion Paper No. 1, November 1986. For privatization generally see G. Yarrow, "Privatization in Theory and Practice," *Economy Policy*. Vol. 1, no. 1, 1986. For Africa, see Thomas Callaghy and Ernest Wilson, "Privatization in Africa," in *The Challenge of Privatization*, ed. Raymond Vernon, New York: Council on Foreign Relations, 1988.

4. Mary Shirley discusses the impacts of the poor public enterprise performance in *Managing State-Owned Enterprises*, Washington, D.C., World Bank, 1983.

5. Goran Hyden, *No Shortcuts to Progress* (Berkeley: University of California Press, 1983).

6. Gavin Williams, "Marketing Boards in Nigeria," *Review of African Political Economy* 34 (December 1985): 4–15.

7. Material on the cases is drawn from the author's field work in Nigeria, Cote d'Ivoire, Senegal, Zambia, and Tanzania. While in Nigeria, I concluded from my interviews that there was not a strong constituency for abolishing the Marketing Boards. At the same time, the old, powerful pro-Board constituency had withered away. Nonetheless, President Babangida took a great leap beyond the limits that his constituency would clearly support, and tried to bring them along with him. In other words, he exercised leadership. Big reforms, by their nature, are risky business.

8. See my *Privatization in Cote d'Ivoire: Three Case Studies*, Cambridge, Mass.: Harvard University, Kennedy School of Government, Center for Business and Government Working Paper, December 1987.

Foreign Private Investment, Capital Flows, and Property Rights in Africa

GANGA PERSAD RAMDAS

INTRODUCTION TO PROPERTY RIGHTS THEORY

A special class of rights which enable or "empower" the individual to make and implement decisions is described in the literature as *property rights*. Furubotn and Pejovich noted that the concept of property rights is defined "*with some precision . . .* property rights do not refer to relations between men and things but, rather, to the sanctioned behavioral relations among men that arise from the existence of things and pertain to their use. . . . The prevailing system of property rights in the community can be described, then, as the set of economic and social relations defining the position of each individual with respect to the utilization of scarce resources."[1] If we agree with the literature, rights over material things and "human" rights in society could be included in our definition.

The property rights approach to economic analysis expands the determinants of economic choices. It extends the traditional neoclassical economic theory, which uses market income and prices as its main variables in analysis. Property rights as an attribute of commodities and a source of utility may be used as part of the calculus of individual decision-making. Prices help the individual to weigh benefits and costs. Property rights allocation plus income determine the total constraint influencing choices. Like Becker's analysis of time in consumer decisions,[2] property rights may be used as an argument in the maximization of individual utility. Following Lipsey and Lancaster,[3] some combination of income, as a surrogate for economic rights, and a value of property rights, or a surrogate for institutional variables, may define a higher level of constraint, which can advance the maximum level of satisfaction an individual experiences from utility maximization. In cases where there is a partial denial of rights, a lower optimum may be experienced. With attenuated rights, the voluntary market exchange and distribution processes revert to a non-market mode, as in communist or socialist countries, under a lower total constraint. With property rights recognized as a source of utility and a determinant of individual choice, the traditional constructs in neoclassical theory—demand functions, production functions, and the behavior of costs—remain the same. However, the implications for distribution and exchange would change in an extended model. Income distribution theory, in a property rights model, concerns not only market wage-setting, it also includes the determination and composition of the total income of an individual. The system of property rights influences the character of prices, including factor income (wages). Such prices may emerge from free markets, or they may be administered by a monopolist or by the state. An individual's income is determined by the amounts of various classes of assets owned, and the rental wage rate that accrues to each class of asset. Property rights relations in the society thus become endogenous to a model of economic behavior, acting through the distribution of income and wealth. The economic policy implication under traditional theory of perfect competition emphasizes specialization in production and exchange as a means of increasing the level of national income. The opportunity for consumption, saving, and investment is also increased by this process. In a world of scarcity, the principle of comparative advantage in production, followed by free trade, is the main driving force that promotes economic growth. The benefits under this theory are permissible only if all goods and factor markets are competitive everywhere in the economy. An ownership structure that vests all ownership in the state is noncompetitive. A structure that is concentrated in the hands of monopolists is also noncompetitive, as is a combination of public and private ownership. In addition, full rights, as defined above, may not exist, or they may be partly vested in particular groups in society. To create the environment of competitive markets, the tendency should be towards creating more, not less, rights in society. The degree of attenuation of rights and its concentration in a ''free enterprise'' economy tend to weaken policies based on the traditional welfare maximization solution. An economy may be unable to induce the required pattern of growth and economic development under an attenuated rights structure—marking the absence of competitive markets.

Short-term demand management policies should therefore be tailored to complement policies aimed at improving and extending property rights. Such policies should aim at long-term solutions through the incentives implied by alternate property rights structures. A practical example is the International Monetary Fund's insistence on few or no restrictions on individual travel as a condition to use Fund resources. In a world of market imperfections and government-provided goods and services, it may not be necessary to focus policies towards a competitive economy[4]. It may be sufficient to reduce the distortions induced by a lack of property rights in order to increase social welfare. A comprehensive approach to property rights, spanning all factor owners, and all economic activities, may be superior to a partial approach that deals only with managing expenditure activities, under the assumption of perfect competition everywhere. In this chapter, I will follow the wider approach taken by Furubotn and Pejovich; I will propose a distinction between constitutional rights and economic rights. Constitutional rights alone, favoring individual liberty, are inadequate without considering the distribution of property rights. Property rights consist of both economic and ''human rights,''[5] and a comprehensive definition covers the various economic activities in an economy. Rights in consumption, production, exchange, investment, savings, distribution, and finance may be distinguished. In the private sector of a free enterprise society, we have subcategories of rights, which are associated with various contractual forms governing these activities. The right of ownership in an asset is comprised of three major elements: (a) *usus*, the right to the use of an asset, (b) *usus fructus*, the right to appropriate the returns from an asset, and (c) *abusus*, the right to change the asset's form and/or substance.[5] These rights are exclusive and are limited only by explicit provisions under the law. Where these rights are nonexistent, a degree of economic attenuation of rights has occurred.

The principles of legal rights operating under public policy programs, on the other hand, are somewhat attenuated. Laws that tax increasing incomes at progressively higher rates of taxation transfer rights from the taxpayer to the government. Society may be permissive about these changes, since they seek to promote some form of distributive justice via changes in the distribution of income or provision of benefits from public spending. A mitigation of attenuation occurs in the latter case. Similarly, the public sector may attempt to define rights of particular groups in the society based on an income criteria, or some alternate form of needs test. The assignment of rights to income and transfer payments out of government revenue helps to offset the degree of attenuation in the public sector.

It is apparent that a comprehensive definition of rights would be needed to assess the full power of property rights, if it is to be used as a tool of public policy and private sector incentives.

In recent times, statements made by public officials in the United States indicate some of the value inputs used to support public policy. One that supports an emphasis on property rights as a determinant of democratic institutions was made by the Honorable Richard Lugar, Chairman of the Senate Foreign Relations Committee.[6] The broadening of property ownership is seen as a tool of economic development:

The concept of economic justice, in America and the rest of the world, pivots around a central idea: *restoring and broadening private property ownership in the means of production as a fundamental human right*. Private property tools for economic development should continue to be refined in the United States and exported as government and *private sector* policy.

PROPERTY RIGHTS AS DETERMINANTS OF INVESTMENT BEHAVIOR

Institutions are to be seen as mechanisms to facilitate the implementation of rights. Endogenous institutions—cooperatives, the Ujaama (family-hood) in Tanzania, etc.—have been used to create new rights to use resources and to participate in the income redistribution process. Forms of social organization of production or business are separate from the institution of individual rights. The latter is, in turn, separate from common rights, or those reserved by the state. These distinctions are needed to implement programs and policies based on property rights.

Investment behavior under various forms of property rights regimes has been variously influenced by legal, economic, financial, demographic, political, social, and international factors. These include[7]:

Legal Factors

• Licenses, franchises, patents
• Repatriation rights
• Noncompeting rights
• Mining rights, sub-surface rights
• Land rights—surface rights, sub-surface, and airspace rights
• Water-use and waterway rights
• Pollution rights
• Legal forms of business organizations
• Guarantees under international laws and treaties
• Laws governing breach of contract
• Treaties and international laws honored

Economic Factors

• Product Life Cycle—determining investment or trade opportunities
• Surplus of exports over imports
• Type of investor
• Country endowments: Multinational and host
• Technology
• Raw materials supply
• Cost of living, low-wage rates, and cheap sources of raw materials, land, and other inputs
• Market size
• Distribution channels
• Emergence of unofficial or underground markets

- Trading and commercial associations
- Transportation systems
- Education systems
- Health facilities
- Social services
- The state of competitiveness in local markets
- The existing level of economic development and growth

Financial Factors

- Government deficits
- Subsidies
- Taxation of income, profits, imports, exports, etc.
- Money supply growth
- Interest rate differentials
- Exchange rate differences
- Government and national solvency
- Access to capital and money markets, borrowing privileges
- Availability of banking and other financial intermediaries
- Foreign exchange availability
- Domestic currency convertibility
- Domestic savings

Demographic Factors

- Population size, secular changes in growth rates
- Population composition—age, sex distribution
- Birth and death rates
- Migration patterns

Geographic Factors

- Proximity to resources or markets
- Climatic conditions and changes

Political Factors

- Threat of nationalization
- Form of government, political stability
- Unionization, degree of labor unrest
- Political control of resources within a hemisphere or region

Social Factors

- Cultural norms and taboos
- Religious tolerance

- Track record in dealing with multinationals
- Management philosophies and business ethics posture
- Forms of social security systems

International Factors

- Foreign laws and regulations
- Foreign economic incentives
- Foreign political influences
- Foreign aid disbursements
- Geo-political influences

These factors cover a broad spectrum of human and economic rights, defined here under the umbrella of property rights. Because markets are either nonexistent or the price system is imperfect, each factor has to be weighed both qualitatively and quantitatively in order to determine its role as a determinant of investment and capital flows in a country analysis. Factors that affect internal investment opportunities in a country become exogenous to a foreign country, and vice-versa. In reality, the increasing tendency of countries to establish economic, political, cultural, and other forms of international cooperation, and agreements, makes all the determinants endogenous to a world economy, and, in particular, to international capital flows and financial investments. The lack of competitive market structures in the world economy reinforces the need for a new approach to capital flows and investment. *Laissez-faire* cannot guarantee the amount or timeliness of real or financial capital flows to particular countries in the world, despite their commitment to democracy, and principles of law and order comparable to more wealthy countries. Deliberate focus on variables, linking one economy with another's capital markets, technology, entrepreneurial skills, and other resource bases, is needed to influence the movement of international financial capital and real investment goods.

APPLICATION IN AN AFRICAN CONTEXT

Some or all of the above theory and concepts may already be in place in countries at various levels of economic and political development. However, these trends may have emerged as a result of involuntary restraints or short-term financial and economic policies required under agreements with international lending agencies. The predicament of capital shortage that many African and other less developed countries find themselves in could have been reduced if such trends had been the result of long-range planning. Countries could have anticipated and planned how to attract more capital. The actual amounts of foreign capital flowing into African economies were more the result of bilateral agreements, rather than the workings of international competitive markets. In the case of official loan capital from overseas governments, the quantities and terms are negotiated at financial bargaining tables. The scope for planning exists. African countries can develop consistent plans within the framework of full property rights to all resource owners, over all activities.

The actual use of the capital tends to follow domestic priorities, which have been known to depart from the stated purposes of many a project loan. Here the establishment of property rights is essential. Can a government bureaucracy appropriate the consumption, production, exchange, and distribution rights of its citizens? Attenuation of rights in these areas can destroy the environment under which capital flows occur. The viability of capital to provide intended benefits becomes jeopardized. More rights for capital to flourish are needed. Private markets emerge, by definition, with the delineation of rights. More rights to use resources in the public sector will tend to weaken the workings of private markets and institutions. The unintended effects are economic decline and the loss of utility by individuals who survive life-threatening hardships.

Quite recently, countries that changed their form of economic organization from democratic government to socialism have experienced great difficulties in promoting economic growth and development. Some of these countries include Tanzania, Nigeria, Uganda, and Ghana. In these countries property rights structures changed moving away from private markets, in favor of their respective governments and their sponsoring political parties. The core rights of individuals, *usus, abusus, and fructus,* were reduced or eliminated across some or all economic activities.

A selection of four African countries that experienced major upheavals in political and economic changes, resulting in severe attenuation of both economic and human rights at times, are used to illustrate the effects of changes in rights structures and their influence on capital flows. In all cases analyzed capital flows from official development agencies increased simultaneously with privatization initiatives.[8]

Tanzania

Tanzania became the United Republic of Tanzania in 1964, after a merger with Tanganyika and Zanzibar, following the granting of an independent sultanate status to Zanzibar from the British a year earlier. Dr. Julius Nyerere was president and Rashidi Kawawa was vice president. In July 1965 Nyerere declared a one-party state government. The subsequent political changes, the assassination of the president of the ruling Revolutionary Council of Zanzibar (which kept a separate administration within the union) reflected the rivalry for political power and the control of economic and financial resources. Despite these setbacks, Tanzania emerged with a new constitution in 1985, which allowed more representative government and the right for defense lawyers to appeal court cases, a right that may go unnoticed in a modern democracy. By 1987 two ideological camps had emerged, the "conservative socialists" supported by Nyerere, and the "pragmatists" supported by Ali Hassan Minwyi, who was the president of Zanzibar and the vice president of Tanzania.

This political background was used to steer the country's economic development under a scheme described as Ujaama (family-hood), a communal agricultural scheme. In 1973 about 200 medium- and small-sized farms were nationalized as Ujaama advanced. This change reduced private property rights and was intended to increase the consumption rights of the rural population working at the communes. The Ujaama experiments may appear to favor an increase in economic rights in consumption. These gains are, however, at the expense of private ownership rights and the effects of the loss of power of such incentives to attract other resources in investment and production.

From 1981 to 1984, the government's top-down policies were reversed. Cooperatives were allowed to take over the distributing functions from state enterprises. This change signalled the government's recognition of the elemental nature of an economic right as a tool for designing incentives through public policy. This case should support property rights as an endogenous variable in economic and political analyses.

Other processes that increase rights may be internalized through the market mechanism or through transfers from the government. In 1985 and in 1986 higher prices were paid to producers, increasing between 40 to 57 percent. Output of food and export crops was increased. At times of critical shortages of foreign currency to buy imported goods, the government may have to trade consumption rights for the privilege of borrowing from other nations and international agencies—the International Monetary Fund and the World Bank, by devaluing the nation's currency. Devaluation reduces the purchasing power of the domestic currency to purchase imported goods for consumption and for investment. It also translates into higher prices for local goods, thereby lowering the value of the local currency even further than the initial devaluation. These actions are rationalized as attempts to "strengthen" the domestic currency.

The strengthening of a currency may come about if foreign investors recognize the improvement and invest in the production of goods and services. While the devaluation guarantees the decline in value, the behavior of investors may not be in the complementary direction. This lack of response may require even further trades of consumption rights through devaluation as a condition to borrow foreign capital. Tanzania devalued its shilling by 20 percent against the United States dollar in 1983, 26 percent in 1985, another 33 percent in 1986, plus additional weekly adjustments amounting to 51.8 percent between mid–1986 and the end of 1987. In 1988 there was yet another devaluation of 21 percent, a condition for using the I.M.F. and World Bank loan packages.

These changes suggest that Tanzania is prepared to trade consumption rights for the acquisition of production rights by acquiring financial capital. Financial capital is then used to acquire real investment goods and the labor services required to install them, or to acquire other kinds of consumer goods through imports. Payments for the latter are made through short-term settlement accounts at international banks, and the I.M.F.

Nigeria

Nigeria adopted a Federal system of government on October 1, 1960, under Sir Alhaji Abubaker Tafawa Balewa as head of state. The country became a Federal Republic under the leadership of Dr. Nnandi Azikiwe three years later on October 1. Between 1966 and 1985 there was intense rivalry and political instability, with eight changes in leadership, involving five military administrations, and one civilian government under democratic elections, which restored Alaji Shehu Shagari as executive president in 1979 and in 1983. On December 31, 1983, only two months after the elections, a military coup under Major General Muhammadu Buhari replaced president Shagari. In another military coup on October 27, 1985, Major General Ibrahim Babangida ruled as the unchallenged leader.

The frequent political changes dissipated the economic potential in the Nigerian economy, including oil revenues, which could not obviate the necessity to borrow large sums of money from international bankers. However, Nigeria avoided the high cost of currency devaluation by adopting import controls in 1982, and a 30 percent levy on imports in 1985. These measures were strengthened by wage reductions in the public sector, that is, selective attenuation of consumption rights, a reduction of public transfers in the form of subsidies to domestic fuel, producers' export rebates on non-oil products, importers' rebates on imports of raw materials and spare parts, and measures that would lead to the privatization of some state enterprises. In addition, Nigeria introduced a new foreign exchange management program under a "two-tier" exchange rate system in 1986. This was replaced by a single exchange rate determined at fortnightly "auctions."

Nigeria went a stage further following a lesson from Ghana. Privatization of ninety-six state enterprises was made legal by special decree in 1988, the same year that the Ghanaian head of state visited Nigeria. These enterprises were to be wholly or partly transferred to the private sector.

Uganda

Political independence was granted to Uganda on October 9, 1962, under the leadership of Prime Minister Dr. Milton Obote, who led a successful coup against the king of Buganda, Kabaka Matesa II in 1966. In 1967 a new constitution absorbed Buganda under a unitary republic with a central government. After an unsuccessful assassination attempt on President Obote, all opposition parties were banned. This attempt paved the way for his military successor, Major General Idi Amin Dada in 1971, to suspend all political activities and parts of the 1967 constitution. This suspension was followed by the many reported murders, and the confiscation of properties held by British Asians who were expelled en masse in 1972. In 1979 Tanzanian troops and exiled Ugandan soldiers, under the name of the Uganda National Liberation Army (ULNA), marched upon the city of Kampala and overran Amin's forces, overthrowing Amin's government. Amin fled to Libya, and later found asylum in Saudi Arabia. A provisional government was formed with Dr. Yusuf Lule, a former vice chancellor of Makerere University, as president. Two months later, in June, Dr. Lule was forced to resign after he was unable to secure the cooperation of the National Executive Council in a reshuffle of its members. Dr. Lule's successor, Godfrey Binaisa, was overthrown by the Military Commission of the Uganda National Liberation Front. National elections under the supervision of this commission returned Dr. Obote as President for the second time in 1983. After much anti-government guerilla activity, Obote was overthrown in 1985 by a military coup led by Brigadier Basillo Okello. Obote fled to Kenya and then to Zambia, where he was granted political asylum. Under the Okello government, ULNA continued as an auxiliary force to crush opposition elements. In August 1985 Yoweri Museveni led a successful campaign that led to the overthrow of Okello, who fled to Sudan. Museveni immediately dissolved the Military Council. All of the neighboring countries surrounding Uganda pledged support for Musevini. He formed resistance committees at the village, parish, county and district levels to maintain security and eliminate corruption. Despite these efforts to achieve stability, murder and strong opposition from rival political groups continued to challenge his administration. These problems were compounded by the return by Kenya of an estimated 350,000 Ugandan refugees who had fled during the civil war. The border problems remain unsettled.

The political climate fostered the attenuation of rights in the Ugandan economy. From 1971 to 1979, under Amin's rule, all foreign-owned land, sugar, tea, coffee, and cotton industries and estates were nationalized without compensation. In 1983 the restoration of property expropriated under Amin was made legal. In agriculture, tea output fell continually after the 1972 nationalization of the tea plantations. The coffee-marketing board came under investigation for misappropriation of funds in 1986. Coffee production was down, largely from lower prices and distribution problems.

In international finance, a short-lived two-tier exchange rate system was replaced by a fixed rate for the shilling, placed at 1,400 shillings per U.S. dollar. The government assumed control of importing and distributing essential commodities. Under these conditions the black market rate reached 8,000 shillings per U.S. dollar. Foreign capital inflows slowed down to about a third of customary levels, necessitating a rehabilitation development program in 1987. The shilling was devalued by 76.7 percent, and in 1988 plans to privatize one quarter of Uganda's state enterprises were introduced, while the World Bank loans, I.M.F. credits and aid-donors commitment increased considerably. These increases were negotiated and the effects of these changes on other autonomous private capital are likely to be felt in the future, after political stability and economic recovery begin to take shape.

Ghana

The famed Gold Coast and Togoland, a United Nations Trust Territory, were merged in 1956 to form the state of Ghana. Dr. Kwame Nkrumah, the Prime Minister elected in 1952, established an authoritarian regime under the banner of African socialism in the post-independence period on March 1957. He became a founding member of the Non-Aligned Movement, headquartered in Georgetown, Guyana. This connection linked President Tito of Yugoslavia, Nasser of Egypt, and Nehru of India, aligning them with widespread support from other newly independent states of the British Empire. A one-party state was installed, with the ruling Convention People's Party being the only legitimate political party. Despite his early successful leadership, Nkrumah was deposed by the army and police on February 24, 1966.

Since his reign, General Joseph Ankrah, and Brigadier Akwasi Afrifa have held positions as heads of state. In a 1969 general election, the Progressive Party, led by Dr. Kofi Busia, won a majority of the seats of government and Busia was appointed Prime Minister. In 1970 Edward Akufo-Addo was inaugurated as civilian president. Less than two years later the army seized power—in January 1972. The constitution was nullified and all political organizations were replaced by the National Redemption Council under the chairmanship of Lt. Col. Ignatius Acheampong. By early 1979 Acheampong favored a return to civilian rule without political parties, under a "union" government. Later the same year Acheampong was displaced from office by his deputy, Lt. Gen. Frederick Akuffo, in a bloodless coup.

By June 1979 another military coup was staged by Flight Lt. Jerry Rawlins, whose faction accused the military leaders of economic mismanagement and widespread corruption. At a "Revolutionary Court" Acheampong, Akuffo, Afrifa, and six other senior officers were found guilty of corruption and were summarily executed. The next elected president, Dr. Hilla Limann, took office on September 24, 1979. By 1981, further dissatisfaction led Flight Lt. Rawlins to seize power in a coup, installing himself as chairman of a governing Provisional National Defense Council (PNDC). Many arrests, detentions, and executions followed in the ensuing period, 1982–87. From 1987 on the country moved progressively toward a system of decentralized government in which district assemblies were to be the main political and administrative entities, holding deliberative, political, and executive power. This mobilization took place as Ghana introduced a major scheme to privatize the economy.

While the data is slowly emerging, the Ghanian experience offers a profile that shows improved economic performance as a result of restoring property rights structures in a comprehensive manner. The Ghanian success in using broad-based programs that increase rights may have implications for other democracies. Ghana has suffered economic decline for about twenty-six years under African socialism, since March 6, 1957.[9] In 1983, specific measures were introduced to support free enterprise and capitalism. The previous order of self-reliance, self-sufficiency, and government agricultural marketing boards was gradually dismantled. In response to the International Monetary Fund guidelines, massive currency devaluation of Ghana's Cedi, counted in hundreds of percentage points, occurred as a means of restoring "confidence" in the national currency and as a condition to raise the level of official capital flows. Private sector expenditure and employment contracted considerably. This followed a new era of privatization. A new stock exchange was inaugurated, and a greater reliance on private contracts and markets was used to allocate resources and to distribute goods and services.

In 1988, under the economic recovery programs, sixty percent higher producer prices were paid to cocoa farmers. Production bonuses were also used to strengthen economic incentives and to raise productivity. The improved economic changes in Ghana support the case for using property rights as a variable in public policy design.

Indirect evidence of economic attenuation of rights in the countries selected above may be observed somewhat by the allocation of huge amounts of domestic financial resources to the government sector of these countries. Since the equilibrium level of the ratio of government spending to the gross national product, g, varies from country to country, changes in the ratio may be used to indicate the effects of changes in policies occurring at or after the year policy was introduced. A relatively high ratio may suggest a strong government sector and a correspondingly greater degree of economic attenuation of rights in the private sector. A decrease in the ratio may indicate that the impact of the loss of rights through devaluation, together with an increase in official capital inflows, raised the level of the GNP by more than the increase in government sector expenditures, which itself may be the object of discretionary policy cuts. An increase in the ratio may signal a tendency for a deterioration of rights as the public sector siphons off a larger share of the GNP as wages and salaries for its civil servants. Changes in g may indicate a changed rights structure. Table 3.1 shows some of these trends.

In the four countries reviewed, large increases in the amounts of capital flows from the International Monetary Fund, the World Bank and the "Paris Club" (a consortium of creditors committed to helping the less developed countries with their debt rescheduling problems) occurred simultaneously with major shifts in processes and laws that supported an increase in property rights. The institutional changes prominent in these areas were the dismantling of the marketing board arrangement for purchasing domestic exportables from farmers and selling abroad. Low prices paid to farmers represented an expropriation of agricultural surpluses by the respective state agencies. These export earnings represented extra-budgetary sources of financing government expenditures, and a rich source

Table 3.1
Allocations to Government Ratio of Government Expenditure to Gross Domestic Product (GDP)

Year	Ghana	Tanzania	Nigeria	Uganda
1970	0.21	0.13	0.11	0.16
1971	0.21	0.14	0.09	0.20
1972	0.20	0.12	0.12	0.22
1973	0.17	0.15	0.10	0.16
1974	0.18	0.16	0.07	0.17
1975	0.23	0.11	0.10	0.15
1976	0.25	0.16	0.12	0.14
1977	0.24	0.15	0.14	0.10
1978	0.20	0.17	0.11	0.09
1979	0.17	0.16	0.10	
1980	0.13	0.13*	0.11*	
1981	0.13	0.12	0.10	0.09
1982	0.11*	0.12	0.10	0.11*
1983	0.10	0.12	0.10	0.12
1984	0.11	0.12	0.10	0.17

(1) An asterisk is used to indicate a year in which a major development program was launched and changes in privatization measures and official capital inflows occurred.
(2) Blanks indicate missing (unpublished data).

Source: International Financial Statisics annual publications by the International Monetary Fund, Washington, D.C.

of funds for political patronage. The widespread failure of major state enterprises were also the targets of privatization.

Attempts at social reorganizations in the countries selected are now under way, although with varying degrees of commitment to democratic institutions, free and fair national voter registration and electoral processes, and the establishment of property rights, including economic and human rights. The institutionalization of rights is a necessary, if not sufficient, condition to make all forms of social and economic planning work. A total rights structure, embracing all facets of economic, social, and political rights is more appropriate to increase the rate at which capital flows to these countries. A partial approach to property rights may provide weak incentives, not only for owners of capital, but owners of all other resources to engage in economic activities. International, as well as domestic, owners of resources evaluate various forms of risks under attenuated rights. It is the effects of the sum of these risks that determine whether or not capital moves.[10]

CONCLUSION

An attenuated property rights structure and a *laissez-faire* approach to public policy may be the strongest impediment to economic development and growth in African and other countries experiencing economic decline.[11] An institutional approach that sets the framework for private contracts and free-enterprise activities may be the focus of public policy. More recognition of the strength of property rights to induce investors to increase the flow of capital may be required. The Ghanaian success is a sterling example in this direction. In the design of public policy, the need for an economic definition of property rights is also recognized. An expanded definition that contains all of the essential concepts of a right, *usus, abusus, and fructus,* applicable to all economic and financial activities in the economy,[12] would be needed to implement a program of comprehensive property rights.

NOTES

The author wishes to thank the Lily Grant Foundation for providing a generous stipend during the Summer of 1990 to support this research.

1. Erik G. Furubotn and Pejovich Svetozar, "Property Rights and Economic Theory: A Survey of Recent Literature," *Journal of Economic Literature* Vol. 10 (1972): 1137–1162.

2. Gary S. Becker, "A Theory of the Allocation of Time," *Economic Journal,* Vol. 75 (September 1965): 493–517, and "Irrational Behavior and Economic Theory," *Journal of Political Economy,* Vol. 70 (February 1962): 1–13.

3. Kelvin Lancaster, "A New Approach to Consumer Theory," *Journal of Political Economy,* Vol. 74 (April 1966): 132–157.

4. R. G. Lipsey and K. J. Lancaster, "The General Theory of the Second Best," *Review of Economic Studies,* Vol. 24 (1956–7): 11–32.

5. Erik G. Furubotn and Pejovich Svetozar, eds., *The Economics of Property Rights* (Cambridge, Mass.: Ballinger Publishing Company, 1974). For an introduction to the provisions of human rights, see Levin Leah, *Human Rights* (Paris: United Nations, 1981), and *The United Nations and Human Rights* (New York: United Nations, 1984).

6. The concept of economic rights is also appropriate to the call for economic justice. For example, see the National Conference of Catholic Bishops, *Economic Justice for All,* Pastoral Letter on Catholic Social Teaching and the U.S. Economy (Washington, D.C., 1986), and Douglas Rasmussen and James Sterba, *The Catholic Bishops and Economy Debate* (New Brunswick: Transaction (Books) Inc., and Social Philosophy Policy Center, 1987). Part 2: Economic Rights Versus Human Dignity: The Flawed Moral Vision of the United States Catholic Bishops, p. 45.

7. These factors are being researched by the author for country-specific details in a forthcoming publication.

8. The data for individual countries was developed from the much-detailed and thorough accounts given in *The Europa World Yearbook,* Volume I (London: Europa Publications Ltd., 1989). Without these accounts, I would have had to use personal experiences and the oral tradition, so customary in the civic education of peoples in less developed countries.

9. See *The New York Times,* May 13, 1987.

10. In the literature, this is referred to as the management of exposure to political risk. Under the property rights approach, a wider set of risks is to be evaluated. These would

include risks associated with each economic, political, or social activity likely to induce a movement of capital.

11. Attenuated rights may tend to initiate the environment of poverty, directly or indirectly. See Bradley R. Schiller *The Economics of Poverty and Discrimination* (Englewood Cliffs, N.J.: Prentice Hall, 1989); Sheldon H. Danziger and Daniel H. Weinberg, eds., *Fighting Poverty, What Works and What Doesn't* (Cambridge Mass.: Harvard University Press, 1986). See Michael R. Sosin, "Legal Rights and Welfare Change," p. 260; and James O. Grunebaum, *Private Ownership* (London and New York: Routeledge & Kegan Paul, 1987). (See Chapter I, section D, "The impossibility of a society without ownership.")

12. See Ganga Persad Ramdas, "Utilitarian Ethics: A Basis For Joining Law and Economics," a paper presented to the Association of Behavioral Scientists, Tallahassee, Florida, March 1990.

4

Private Investment Incentives in Sub-Saharan Africa

REXFORD A. AHENE

INTRODUCTION

Many excellent, detailed studies diagnosing the demise of sub-Saharan development in the 1980s have been made by agencies of the World Bank, scholars, and other international research organizations. There is unanimous agreement that the economic decline in sub-Saharan Africa is the combined result of severe exogenous shocks, such as drought, prolonged global recessions, increasing international protectionism, and declining economic assistance in real terms. Government misallocation of investments (often with the contrived assistance of aid donors), and the mismanagement of domestic economies in the face of declining export demand, coupled with other long-term trends, such as rapid population growth, have compounded these problems. Since 1970, overall living standards have plunged 20 percent and urban unemployment has increased to 33 percent. By international standards, 70 percent of the rural populations in sub-Saharan Africa live in extreme poverty.

The cumulative result of continuing decline in economic and social welfare is reflected by the widening balance of payment deficits and the lack of self-sufficiency in food and agricultural production and industrial underdevelopment. Whatever the cause, stagnation in the 1970s and the declines in net international capital flows, in real terms, in the early 1980s resulted in the loss of creditworthiness and an increase in the importance of liquidity to sovereign borrowers in sub-Saharan Africa. The stifling effects of deficits in the financial claims between sub-Saharan Africa (already indebted to the extent of over $100 billion at the beginning of 1985) and the rest of the world encouraged most African governments to undertake economic and financial reforms.[1]

Under the auspices of the World Bank and the International Monetary Fund, the macroeconomic difficulties of the 1970s and 1980s brought the structural weaknesses in developing African economies into the open. Bleak prospects of restoring the collapsing international terms of trade for primary commodities, and for lowering international interest rates placed many countries in sub-Saharan Africa in serious jeopardy. Consequently, the need to reverse the decline in net capital flows to Africa by reforming investment policies became one of the critical starting points for economic adjustment.

First this chapter will examine some of the foreign investment decision considerations of entrepreneurs. Next, an overview of the principal objectives behind the common use of investment incentives as policy instruments for attracting private investments in sub-Saharan Africa will be presented. The final segments of the chapter will present a synopsis of the changes in the climate for private investment in Africa and a summary of the prevailing policy towards private direct investment.

INVESTMENT DECISION CONSIDERATIONS

In the evaluation of private investment decisions, three basic considerations have prominence: access to raw materials, acquiring manufactures at a lower cost, and expanding profitable local market penetration. For most multinational firms, the purpose of foreign investments is to locate lower cost supplies of inputs, that is, components or finished goods that complement the firm's operations. The establishment of a production assembly plant or marketing base inside a host country may therefore be part of an overall global strategy.

The investment options available to foreign direct investors and the potential return on investment depend on the environmental elements. However, the project's competitiveness is dependent ultimately on the investor's understanding of the main features of the host business environment and the opportunities for adapting investment and operating strategies. It is clear the constrained business environment of sub-Saharan Africa requires careful analysis. This theme will be amplified throughout this chapter.

Fundamentally, direct investment involves the establishment of an entire enterprise in a target location or host country. The logical advantages of direct investment include duty-free access to less expensive local inputs, a preferential market share (where import quotas are used), better control over quality, and better sensitivity to political and cultural risk through assimilation. Direct investment, however, also entails a higher level of managerial and capital commitment, and consequently, a higher level of risk exposure. This exposure may be evaluated, given a firm's specific advantages, by explicitly recognizing the firm's opportunity costs.

Given the history of development in Africa, markets have been distorted by nonmarket forces and various governmental policy instruments. In some instances, these distortions can be justified, given developmental priorities. However, "red tape" in the form of cumbersome legal and administrative requirements, and lengthy procedures for obtaining investment privileges have, until recently, imposed a sufficiently high cost to reduce or even eliminate the expected flow of private investments.[2] In Cameroon, for example, manufacturing firms must apply individually for an authorized price for each product, and a slight change in the product design requires a new official price. The same is true of an increase in the price of raw materials or any other input. In practice, delays of six months or longer can occur. Such an environment could prove very intimidating for a firm, and could even preclude any actual investment.

Reforms reflecting these factors were initiated in the 1980s and have begun to offer the kind of incentives and business environment that will make investing in the sub-Saharan Africa attractive. In most cases this attraction is expected to be achieved by means of investment incentives and by offering guarantees of a protected market environment.

INVESTMENT INCENTIVES: OBJECTIVES AND EXPECTATIONS

In the interest of encouraging comprehensive development, most nations specify their investment goals by the criteria for admission and by incentives that direct resources into certain priority areas. However, some countries provide incentives designed to enhance the general level of investment in all sectors. While these may be aimed at increasing the levels of domestic savings and investment, the broader objective includes the attraction of domestic as well as foreign investors. The explicit objectives may include a desire to encourage management and technology transfer, to increase domestic value added and employment, to indigenize selected sectors, to provide local equity participation, and to improve the balance of payments.

While private investors are concerned primarily with the economic aspects of their investments, a sovereign host country has to address a myriad of other issues related to private investment. The host government is concerned not only with the economic gains that investment produces, but also with the externalities that profit-motivated private investment produces. For example, while it is advantageous to allow an investment that expands a nation's technological frontier, foreign investors or multinationals must not be allowed to use obsolete and inefficient methods of production. While foreign investors could increase local employment, the host government must attempt to minimize adverse effects upon the population such as occupational health hazards and distortions in consumption patterns. Furthermore, the politically fragile governments in Africa are extremely sensitive to the threat to their power by the intrusions of large, economically strong entities over whom they do not posses any direct jurisdiction. Recent economic reforms have implicitly demonstrated the desire to increase the size and contribution of the private sector in sub-Saharan Africa; however, the incompatibility in goals with regard to expected private and public benefits of private investment more often than not lead to conflict and mutual distrust.

Perception of Risk

The preferred approach to offset this perception of risk is to enhance the investment climate. Although each sub-Saharan country is socially, culturally, and economically discrete, the legal framework and policies of governments concerning private sector investments are set out by their national investment codes. According to Helmboldt (1986:338) investor confidence in the rule of law is perhaps the most important single determinant in any investment decision. Perceptions of high risk act as an obstacle to new investment. Both domestic and foreign investors find arbitrary regulations a major obstacle. The investment code should, therefore, clearly specify the laws with which the investor must comply and should provide the legal protection that ensures fair and equitable treatment to all investors. It is in the interest of sub-Saharan African governments to provide all the information the investor needs to lower the opportunity cost of investment if they wish to compete successfully.

Studies by Baker (1983) and Galenson (1984) concluded that the reluctance of major American banks to lend and the skepticism of multinational corporations to invest in Africa are due partially to uncertain institutional perceptions. After peaking in 1982 at $9.4 billion, long-term lending from external creditors declined to $2.1 billion in 1985 before increasing to $5.2 billion in 1987.[3] During the same period, net foreign direct investment continued to reflect investor uncertainty, decreasing from $1.2 billion in 1982 to $498 million in 1987 (UNDP, 1989:43).

For their part, Africans no longer have high expectations of foreign investment. Foreign contractors have delivered shoddy products, including entire turnkey projects, and corrupt and conceited African policymakers have milked investors or thwarted programs. According to Helmboldt (1986:337) both sides have been hurt by antecedent abuses of trust. It is generally understood, therefore, that investors who have been burned once will not rush to return at the first sign of reform.

The attitude of private investors towards Africa is also shaped by other operating problems. Baker's 1983 survey of potential foreign investors found six recurring obstacles to business activities in sub-Saharan Africa: (1) markets were too small, (2) government officials were too slow or too complicated in their responses to business questions, (3) ideological leanings of some governments were hostile to private investment, (4) prospects for political instability were deemed high, (5) creditworthiness was lacking because of mounting debt and exchange controls, and (6) public intervention was deemed excessive. Hence, a crucial step toward improving the investment decision process lies in streamlining government procedures when they impact on routine business operations.

Finally, economies of scale and the need for a significant learning period in the uncertain investment climate in sub-Saharan Africa create the case for incentives in infant industries that become profitable only in the long run. In the interim, such investments will not be undertaken if distortions in the capital market preclude an interim financing solution. The use of incentives may impose both financial and administrative burdens on the government. In the case of investment that is economically profitable for the country as a whole, however, appropriately designed incentives and implementation schedules can narrow the gap between public and private returns and induce the investor to undertake the investment.[4]

There is no question that investors will compensate for uncertainty by increasing the acceptable rate of return on investment necessary to encourage investment. Exploitative short-term, high-return investments may be conducive to private investors in an uncertain environment, but may not serve the long-term interest of the host nation. Thus, for private investors, clearly specified investment objectives, consistent interpretation of investment laws, and agreed-upon processes ("the rules of the game") are the *sine qua non* of their involvement.

Previous Investment Environment

A recent report in the *Economist* concluded that "looking around the world in the 1980s, Adam Smith would find more to dismay him in Africa than in any other region." Opting for socialism and casting off the "invisible hand," most African countries "have seen decades of not merely stagnation but regression."[5] A typical example of the sub-Saharan economic decadence is illustrated by the post-independence economic history of Ghana.

In 1957 Ghana stood poised on the threshold of development. It was the richest country in sub-Saharan Africa. It had the most educated population, it was the world's leading exporter of cocoa, it produced 10 percent of the world's gold, and it had a flourishing export trade in tropical hardwoods. Its income per head was almost equal to South Korea's: $490 as opposed to $491. By the early 1980s, Ghana's income per head had actually fallen by 20 percent, to $400. As economic problems mounted, the government compounded its difficulties by nationalizing industries. Capital as well as skilled labor, escaped abroad. By 1980, Ghana was to Africa what Peru and Argentina were to Latin America: a distillation of everything that had gone wrong with the continent's investment climate. Only the Ivory Coast and Cameroon were labelled "moderately outwardly oriented" in their government policies during the period from 1963 to 1973.[6] From 1973 to 1985, they had been labelled as "moderately inwardly oriented."[7]

The environment of excessive state intervention in domestic economies, foreign exchange restrictions, and state monopolies in crucial sectors of the economy were hardly harbingers of an inviting investment environment. Most independent African governments undertook industrialization with a sociopolitical agenda first, and economic ends second. The location of key investment projects in particular regions, for example, demonstrated the government's commitment to create employment and develop a skilled labor force, to improve the status of an ethnic group or to improve regional income distribution. Although the spillover benefits of the objective cited above have merit, they did not always appeal to private investors, nor did they justify the use of special incentives. Instead, they promoted a preponderance of inefficient public enterprises.

The advantages of a free-functioning market, where prices play a key role in allocating investment capital and other resources efficiently, were for ideological and other reasons considered undesirable or given scant support in the long-term development plans in most of post-colonial Africa. The ensuing structure of production, in such cases as Tanzania, Nigeria, and Ghana, became distorted, inconsistent with the resources available, and consequently unattractive to private investors.

Profitable investments are undertaken in an efficient market without further incentives. However, in the sub-Saharan world of administered prices, minimum wages, and protective tariffs, it is naive, in the short run, to expect compensating measures in the form of investment incentives to completely eliminate market distortions that have long constrained the investment environment.

The Changing Investment Environment

The investment climate in sub-Saharan Africa has improved considerably during the past several years, mostly as a result of successful initiatives by pragmatic governments and through support for IMF-sponsored reform programs. Governments that have gradually realized the limits of public sector intervention are opening the economy to more private sector participation. One by one, the nations of sub-Saharan Africa are rolling up their old collectivist economies and putting a new emphasis on market forces.[8] Tanzania illustrates this change. For six years, the government of Tanzania refused to follow IMF advice to reform a stagnant economy. Under a rampant black market, consumer essentials were either unavailable or very expensive. Since 1985, a new administration has cut taxes, devalued the currency, and agreed to denationalize some key agricultural plantations. In Guinea, the government's denationalization of banks, devaluation, and reduction of government controls in favor of a free market in 1985 caused commodity prices to rise from 20 percent to 80 percent of world market prices, and export commodity output to increase by more than a third in 1986–87. A report by the U.S. Agency for International Development (AID) found that eleven African states are reforming or denationalizing inefficient public sector businesses, ten are trying to cut government spending, and fourteen have raised prices paid to farmers. Other states are cutting government subsidies for consumer goods and energy. Still others are freeing officially overvalued currencies to stimulate trade.[9]

In a recent analysis by *Newsweek,* foreign investment in sub-Saharan Africa in 1987 stood at a little over $400 million in U.S. dollars, down from almost $1.2 billion in 1982.[10] But the continent does show some promise for a recovery. According to the development, about seventeen countries from East and Central Africa have made a concerted effort to create a free trade area. In addition, the successes of the EEC have strengthened efforts at integrating the economies of West Africa. This step is essential, as no single country has resources or markets to offer an efficient number of economically viable investment alternatives. Another step that needs to be taken is to lower investor perception of political risk through political stability. Unless a steady and predictable political and economic climate is available to investors, they will be unwilling to enter the market.

Public agencies in Kenya, Malawi, Ghana, Zambia and Zaire are now seeking foreign investors after years of ambivalence about the merits of encouraging private foreign investors. The Kenya Investment Promotion Center, for example, is a state-run agency that offers customized incentives to facilitate foreign investment. Similar agencies in a host of other countries provide an overview of the principal types of incentives and describe the government policy towards private direct investment (specifically official screening and approval procedures), investment incentives and performance requirements, profit repatriation and restrictions, investment agreements, and anticipated changes in investment policy.

TYPES OF INVESTMENT INCENTIVES

A wide choice of instruments becomes available once the decision to use incentives is made. The more direct instruments include import tariffs to encourage local production, tariff exemptions to encourage capital-intensive activities or to promote import-substituting investments, and direct production subsidies. A broader range of interventions such as the provision of capital, infrastructure, training, and employment also affects investment decisions. The most important incentive, however, is the guarantee and assurance of reducing the political and economic risk faced by investors.

Investment Codes

Investment codes are designed to articulate the government's desire to provide a stable environment for investment and to spell out the obligations of the government and the investors. A common feature of sub-Saharan African incentive systems is the provision of concessions and fiscal relief to firms and investors that meet specific desirable criteria. Changes in investment code privileges relating to foreign investors had occurred in thirty-three African countries by the end of 1988.[11] For example, Ghana's investment code, signed on July 13, 1985, allows foreign ownership of enterprises that earn foreign exchange, and it also guarantees against nationalization. Under the investment code adopted by Zaire in 1986, the country reversed its "Zaireanization" program, under which numerous enterprises were nationalized. The new investment code allows various tax and duty exemptions linked to industry, employment, export orientation, and value to be added to local resources. Because Malawi's economy is dominated by agriculture, it offers incentives that focus heavily on food processing and agro-industrial ventures. In exceptional cases, investors may even be granted exclusive production rights and tariff protection.

Taxes, Concessions, and Exemptions

As an integral part of the incentive packages offered, tariff concessions, such as duty exemptions for material and equipment imports, and export incentives are frequently specified in investment codes to attract priority industries. The specific instruments frequently used to promote exports include export tax exemptions, export subsidies, free trade and export processing zones, tax credit for duties paid on imported inputs, and export insurance. Generally classified as tax holidays, they are designed to offer full or partial exemption from income and other taxes for a specified period. In some instances, the duration of exemption varies with the magnitude of the investment. These instruments may last as long as five to ten years, although periods as long as fifteen to twenty-five years for major projects are not uncommon in Togo, Niger, and Guinea.

Most governments favor the use of tax concessions as a policy instrument for creating a desirable climate for investment. An analysis of the impact of lower tax rates and special tax concessions on multinational investment and revenues revealed that investors prefer moderate taxes with equitable enforcement to high concessional rates administered in a discriminatory or arbitrary manner.[12] As an incentive, tax holidays are intended to provide additional liquidity to firms in their earlier years of operation and to accelerate capital recovery. As a policy instrument, they are designed to reduce the perceived risk of operating in an unfavorable environment.

There is, however, evidence that such exemptions for capital-intensive industries tend, at the margin, to increase the capital intensity of production processes beyond the levels expected under the labor market conditions in sub-Saharan Africa today.

Furthermore, exemption from duty increases the effective rate of protection for inefficient firms. It also discourages competition from local producers of the exempted goods and may in the long run increase the nation's import dependence. Most infant industries earn little profit in their early years of operation. In most cases, such firms find a tax exemption during the period when they incur no tax liability worthless. Nigeria and Malawi solve this problem by allowing losses incurred during the period of exemption to be written off against profits earned later.

Despite these shortcomings, the benefits offered and the profits expected in the early years of an investment, according to Dan Usher (1977:130), provide the greatest impetus to investors. It is also pertinent to recognize that the more protracted the period of exemption, the greater the cost to the government relative to the value to the firm.[13] The potential revenue losses can be very costly to the treasury, although one can argue that without the tax incentive, investors would not have considered the project feasible. One way to limit the revenue losses to the treasury is to set a ceiling or to allow a tax credit up to a specified amount. Senegal has a ceiling equal to 100 percent of the original investment. Other countries suspend the exemption if annual earnings exceed a specified percentage of the invested capital. For most governments, however, poor accounting practices make such rules difficult to enforce.

Capital Cost and Overhead Allowance

Other tax-related incentives include accelerated depreciation, which allows quicker capital recovery, and reinvestment allowance, which exempts reinvested earnings from corporate income tax. Multinational firms are also able to further minimize the impact of cross-country differences in tax regimes by transfer pricing, by using their bargaining power to wring one-sided concessions from host governments, or by short-term accelerated exploitation during the concessionary period. These practices invoke an important moral proposition. Incentives to promote investment in exhaustible resources must weigh the lower current price against a higher future price in determining an optimal rate of exploitation.

Public Infrastructure

It is common practice in Africa for governments to offer incentives to firms that will consider locations outside the principal centers of development. The goal is to facilitate a more equitable development by providing an infrastructure to encourage the establishment of new firms in rural and more remote areas. Until recently, however, the practice of channelling public funds into public enterprises without making adequate provisions for maintaining infrastructural support services resulted in the deterioration of public utilities, including communication and transportation services, in most sub-Saharan African countries.

With the trend towards the privatization of public enterprises, public funds have been channeled increasingly into direct investment in modern telecommunications systems, building and maintaining roads, rural electrification and sanitation, and the establishment of industrial estate and export-processing zones. For example, most countries in Africa have invested in real-time, international, long-distance telecommunication by satellite. In 1988 Kenya set aside 7,000 acres of land for new industries and export-processing zones. Seven months after the government streamlined its investment and foreign exchange procedures, thirty one projects, mostly joint ventures in textiles, pharmaceutical, agribusiness and food processing worth approximately $75 million, were approved.[14]

Noneconomic goals aside, building international highways to link neighboring countries, extending well-maintained local roads into resource rich regions, and improving communication and distribution access increase locational advantages and could remove much of the disincentive associated with investments in remote regions. However, the costs should be recognized explicitly, and the social opportunity cost of such indirect subsidies emphasized as savings to investors.

Employment Incentives

Finally, several arguments might be offered for providing incentives to promote employment in the labor-surplus economies of sub-Saharan Africa. Although not always explicitly stated, Frank (1980:87) observed that the presence of labor market distortions—frequently caused by minimum wage legislation that fix the cost of labor above its opportunity cost, guaranteed employment or restrictions on retrenching workers and high severance pay policies—encourages firms to employ more capital intensive methods of production than they would otherwise use.[15]

The removal of these distortions should be considered an efficient solution; however, this is not always politically palatable. Instead, some countries provide a wage subsidy or incentives related to labor use as a compromise. In the Senegal, for example, enterprises that create at least 100 jobs for local labor qualify for investment code benefits. Niger allows the creation of 500 jobs to substitute for performance requirements related to size of investment and value added. Payroll taxes and the cost of apprenticeship account for a significant share of the operating expenses of firms. According to Lent (1967) the effects of these factors on the allocation of capital and labor is a function of their incidence. Incentives designed to shift the tax to the employee affect both the supply of labor and the distribution of income.[16] A subsidy to reduce the level of payroll taxes or credit based on wages or training costs is an alternative used by some governments. The argument for this form of incentive is based on the presence of externalities. For example, if poorly-trained workers contribute to the existence of high wages, rather than minimum wages, in a particular industry, the opportunity for on-the-job training by employment in the industry could benefit the economy as a whole and should be promoted. If employment mobility is not restricted, then firms cannot internalize all the benefits, and training subsidies would be appropriate in the long run.

Financial Incentives

The financial situation of most of sub-Saharan Africa deteriorated markedly throughout the 1980s. The annual rate of economic growth was 1.3 percent in 1981–83. Prior to this period, the combined external current account deficit had risen sharply from $4.5 billion, or 10 percent of export goods and services, in 1973 to $14.1 billion in 1981.[17] A number of adverse external factors contributed to the deterioration in the financial situation in most countries; a severe global recession in 1981–84 resulted in a marked softening of demand for African exports. Meanwhile, an unprecedented rise in international interest rates impacted heavily on the debt service obligation on non-oil-producing countries. Total debt service a percentage of exports rose from 10.9 in 1980 to 22.1 in 1989.[18]

Additionally, inadequate domestic monetary and fiscal policies contributed to the worsening balance-of-payments position and the rise in inflationary pressure. According to Ouattara (1986:71) budget deficits were frequently financed by external borrowing, large recourse to domestic credit, and in some instances, by the accumulation of domestic and external arrears.[19]

This misallocation of credit occurred at the expense of the private productive sector and was compounded by rigid credit and interest regulation, which often resulted in negative real interest rates. There was also a tendency to allow exchange rates to appreciate in real terms, resulting in lower profits in the export and import substituting sectors, an erosion of competitiveness, and market distortions that hampered the mobilization of savings and investments. Furthermore, the distortion in the financial market was often aggravated by administrative and price controls leading to thriving parallel markets for goods and foreign exchange.

A wide variety of actions aimed at strengthening financial intermediation and enhancing structural reforms of the financial sector have been included in recent policies. In some cases, overvalued currencies have been devalued to enhance the competitiveness of local investments. To improve resource allocation and the mobilization of savings, Somalia, Ghana and Kenya, for example, revised interest rates upwards and adopted flexible exchange rate policies. These reforms were frequently accompanied by the adoption of appropriate pricing and marketing policies to promote domestic production.

The adoption of an appropriate investment environment as a key element in recent reforms also involved limiting public investments and reallocating investment in favor of the directly productive sectors. Other qualitative performance guarantees, such as agreement not to introduce or intensify restrictions on payments and transfers for current and international transactions, have created a more conducive environment for investment and the repatriation of funds by foreign investors. For example, Kenya no longer require "blocked" funds to be invested for five years in low-interest treasury bonds. Instead, the funds now earn market rates of interest, and investors are permitted to remit 20 percent of blocked funds plus interest annually for five years.[20] The government of Zambia took a major step toward the correction of prices by the creation of a free market and a two-tiered exchange rate mechanism that offers unrestricted access to foreign exchange to exporters. The government has also rewritten its investment code to include exemptions on dividends for five years.

An important service frequently provided by specialized government agencies is assistance in securing funds to finance investments. In the absence of developed financial markets in sub-Saharan Africa, assistance in identifying investment opportunities, financing, and managing investment projects is available in a number of countries. Publicly-funded agencies such as the Chamber of Commerce in Malawi, the Office for Overseas Private Investment Corporation (OPIC) and the U.S. AID Office for Private Investment, both funded by the U.S. Government, and the Investment Promotion Board in Ghana are examples of agencies that publish lists of investment opportunities, and also assist with funding for feasibility studies, the identification of interested investors, and donors.

The incentives described above have been of varying value to investors, but taken together, and combined with the economic and structural reforms currently sweeping across sub-Saharan Africa, they have undoubtedly improved the environment for investment. In many respects, the regulatory environment closely follows the patterns found in other market-oriented economies. Although the laws and remaining regulations pertaining to foreign investment are similar to controls used in other developing countries, the substance of these laws has not discouraged recent investor interest.

A Concluding Framework

Investment decision considerations include preconceived notions of regional and country risk levels that lead investors and feasibility analysts to consider a particular country for investment. Taking national priorities as given, the goal of this chapter was to examine the role of investment incentives in redefining the environment for private investments in sub-Saharan Africa.

The main influences on the decision to invest are economic considerations as defined by markets and the policies of host nations. Faced with severe foreign capital shortages and limited capital for domestic investment because of recessions and structural adjustments, a number of African countries have introduced new rules or revised existing laws to encourage private direct investment. In fact, most countries package their incentives in investment codes or laws that specify the nature of the benefits and the obligations of the beneficiaries. Other, sometimes more powerful, incentives arise from policies in the area of trade and tariffs, credit allocation and interest rates, price, wage, and labor regulations, and government investment in infrastructure or productive projects. Their basic objective is to reduce the risk and to enhance the expected return on investment.

The foregoing survey suggests two primary observations. First, although the effectiveness of investment incentives as an instrument to increase direct investment is still being debated, recent changes in national investment incentive systems have begun to attract investments from both foreign and domestic sources. Second, the profit expectations of investors cannot be changed without a clear understanding of the negotiating process required to isolate those aspects of the environment that seem to facilitate investment from those that appear to be detrimental to it.

Choice of Strategy

In making economic policy, sub-Saharan African governments are constantly faced with basic choices of strategy that must be kept in harmony with political ideas. The reference to strategy draws attention to the broader, guiding choices required for organizing and directing the economic resources at their disposal. Given the fragility of governments in Africa, a significant amount of time and resources is wasted in maintaining stability and continuity in policy focus.

Investment incentives and procedures, as policy instruments, are limited to definite spheres of activity and are subject to frequent debate and re-definition. Should privatization and unrestricted markets be encouraged as the principal ideology for resource allocation and wealth distribution? To what extent should the exploitation of domestic resources be based on internationally-oriented markets and rates of extraction? According to Jose de la Torre (1988:184), the politics of governing development strategy and policy decisions remain convoluted and subject to interest group pressures, accommodation, and compromises. They are, however, rooted in antecedent experiences and social reality.

Commitment to Reform

The investment environment in sub-Saharan Africa seems to indicate that from the economic reforms of the 1980s will emerge the basic evidence as to whether the expanded role of the private sector and cooperation with foreign investors is an acceptable compromise for development. It is easy to find fault with the failed policies that emphasized the inward-looking, import-substituting development strategies of the recent past. In most instances, local investors, foreign firms, and public enterprises were engaged in similar industries and enjoyed similar levels of subsidy with equally devastating effects on economic performance. The fault lies with the government and the mismanagement it sustained.

The renewed interest in the ability of private sector investments to sustain economic development goals is in the recognition of the role of self-interest and market incentives in promoting a more efficient allocation of resources in sub-Saharan Africa. Private investment is not a zero sum game, according to Jose de la Torre (1988:185). As long as the environment is deemed conducive to high yields from investment, real benefits will accrue to both the investor and the host environment.[21]

Efficiency, Sovereignty, and Equity

A careful analysis of the changes promoted to date and the incentives systems currently in place suggests three evaluative measures: efficiency, sovereign rights, and equity. The efficiency and sovereignty issues are simple and straightforward. There is an obvious desire on the part of governments to promote investments that contribute to domestic value added and foreign exchange. The criteria for efficiency on the part of governments in Africa is to internalize the benefits generated and to minimize the extent that any benefits accrue to third parties beyond the investor and the host country. Sovereignty as measured by the government's ability to set its own agenda was, until recently, illustrated by

Tanzanian economic nationalism and social goals that added to national utility, but discouraged private investment by increasing the perception of political risk among potential investors. The problem of equity is considerably more complex. Sorting out internal conflicts among a large number of ethnic groups, establishing procedures for equitable regional development, and distributing income and political favor to special interest groups frequently result in difficulty in separating social objectives from private investment objectives, and tangible rewards from intangible rewards.

Sub-Saharan African policymakers concede that the elements that represent the highest potential private benefit can also act to enhance social returns without having to forego private sector investments altogether. The severity of conditions, regulations, and performance requirements that apply to private investors, either on entry or during their period of operation in the country, affects the investor's economic and social performance. Most recognize that certain restrictions on the freedom of action by private investors increase "net returns" to the host country, but not for an indefinite period. As a consequence, investment reforms now regard the need for regulation, controls, and limitations on profit repatriation, for example, as part of an investment incentive package that includes offsetting tax concessions and unrestricted interest earnings when an investor decides to reinvest retained earnings. Additionally, there is evidence to indicate that over-zealous application of controls and regulations can, in a competitive global market for investments, also reduce an investor's commitment to capital expansion, to further investments in technology, and to export markets.[22]

Looking Beyond the Short Run

Most policymakers now consider various levels of benefit and the timing of the incidence of such benefits to the host nation when evaluating investment proposals. The provision of investment code privileges and the extent to which the level of controls is to be relaxed are also tailored to encourage desirable corporate practices and to minimize traumatic experiences to the firm. In fact, by relaxing profit transfer limitations, despite worsening balance-of-payments positions, African governments have attempted since 1985 to encourage investors to expand their commitment. Finally, although investment incentives might reduce net contributions to the host government, more countries in Africa have moved towards the creation of more liberal environments for private investment as further evidence of their commitment to privatization. By encouraging an open-door policy and by setting competitive levels of entry and performance regulations, sub-Saharan Africa hopes to account for a steady response of private direct investments as its economies move to embrace the global market in the ensuing years.

NOTES

1. Financial claims are defined by changes in foreign assets and liabilities that are due to international transactions and transfer payments.

2. In the Cameroon, for example, as many as sixty copies of an application for investment code privileges are required, and four ministries are involved in the decision. Heavy verification and contradictory signals in Nigeria add to the application burden. They can introduce uncertainty, possibly discourage potential investors, and even reduce competitiveness.

3. UNDP and World Bank, *African Economic and Financial Data* (New York and Washington, D.C., 1989, Table 2.9).

4. Alice Galenson (1986), p. 5.

5. C. Crook, "Third World Survey." *The Economist*, Vol. 312 (Sept. 23, 1989): 35.

6. Incentives favor production for domestic rather than export markets. But the average rate of effective protection for the home markets is relatively low and the range of effective protection rates relatively narrow. The use of direct control and licensing arrangements is limited. The effective exchange rate is higher for imports than for exports, but only slightly.

7. Incentives clearly favor production for the domestic market. The average rate of effective protection for home markets is fairly high and the range of effective protection rates relatively wide. Direct import controls are extensive. The exchange rate is somewhat overvalued.

8. Duffy, Collins, Shapiro, and Knight, "Black Africa: A Taste of Capitalism," *U.S. News & World Report*, Vol. 101 (Sept. 1, 1986): 24.

9. Duffy et al., *U.S. News & World Report*, pp. 24–25.

10. Masland, Wilkinson, Barry, Whitmore, and Marshall, "A Longing for Liberty," *Newsweek*, July 23, 1990, p. 27.

11. United Nations, Center on Transnational Corporation (CTC), *Transnational Corporations in World Development: Trends and Prospects* (New York: United Nations, 1988.)

12. U.S. Department of Commerce, *Survey of Current Business*, May–June 1987.

13. Dan Usher, "The Economics of Tax Incentives to Encourage Investment in Less Developed Countries." *Journal of Development Economics*, Vol. 4, No. 2 (June 1977): 119–140.

14. *Journal of Commerce*, February 27, 1989, p. 4a.

15. Isaiah Frank, *Foreign Enterprise in Developing Countries* (Baltimore: Johns Hopkins Press, 1980).

16. George E. Lent, "Tax Incentives for Investment in Developing Countries." *IMF Staff Papers*, Vol. 14 (July 1967): 249–321.

17. World Bank, IMF Occasional Paper No. 27, 1984.

18. World Bank, *World Development Report 1991*, Table No. 24, pp. 250–251.

19. Alassanne Ouattara, "Adequacy of Fund Programs," in *Africa and the International Monetary Fund*, ed. G.K. Helleiner (Nairobi, Kenya, 1986).

20. Statements attributed to John Kimeria, managing director of the State Investment Promotion Center, published in the *Journal of Commerce*, February 27, 1989, p. 4a.

21. Jose de la Torre, "Foreign Investment and Economic Development," in *International Business Classics*, ed. James C. Baker et. al. (Lexington Books, 1988: 179–203).

22. de la Torre, "Foreign Investment," p. 186.

5

Patterns of Foreign Investment in Africa, 1970–1988

MULATU WUBNEH

INTRODUCTION

Foreign direct investment (FDI) plays an important role in sustaining the economies of less-developed countries (LDCs) by providing badly needed capital. Direct investment by transnational corporations (TNCs) can also assist in transferring new technology and management, developing local resources, and providing access to external markets and credits.

Historically, FDI in Africa has been intimately linked to colonial ties. In the early 1980s, British and French TNCs accounted for 40 and 18 percent, respectively, of all foreign-owned corporations operating in Africa, as opposed to 22 and 5 percent, respectively, for all developing countries. All foreign affiliates of Portuguese corporations were located in Africa (UNCTC 1985, 27; Tiewul 1986, 43; Green 1981, 343). By contrast, only 16 percent of foreign-owned enterprises in Africa were affiliates of U.S.-based TNCs, compared to 31 percent for all developing countries (UNCTC 1985, 29). In the last two decades, African governments have taken the initiative to diversify their sources of foreign investment by concluding bilateral and multilateral investment promotion treaties that provide a wide range of incentives and investment guarantees. In contrast to the 1970s and early 1980s when FDI was viewed as a form of neocolonialism, today FDI is welcome by many African countries. Since 1988, a number of African countries have signed an international agreement to be members of the UN-sponsored Multilateral Investment Guarantee Agency (MIGA), and more than one-third of them have modified their investment codes or guidelines in order to attract foreign investors.

Despite these efforts, FDI inflow to Africa has remained erratic in the last decade. During the period 1981–88, Africa attracted only 11.7 percent of the $15 billion average annual FDI inflows to developing countries, compared to 44.2 percent for Latin America and the Caribbean, and 40.9 percent for South and Southeast Asia (UNCTC 1990, 29). About 79 percent of the FDI inflow to Africa during this same period went to the three major oil-producing countries: Egypt, Nigeria and Tunisia. (Although Libya has been the largest producer of oil, there has been disinvestment from Libya because of its political problems with the West.) This situation leaves less than $300 million a year for the non-oil-exporting, sub-Saharan countries. Even for middle-income countries such as Cote d'Ivoire (Ivory Coast), Morocco, Namibia, and Zimbabwe, the volume of foreign investment inflows rarely exceeded $50 million and frequently was well below $25 million per year. For a majority of the low-income African countries, FDI inflow ranged from a negative balance to a few million dollars per year. In comparative terms, in 1988 the whole of Africa received 76 percent of the FDI inflow to Singapore. Consequently, FDI accounts for a very small proportion of the gross domestic investment of African countries.

Some important questions arising from this low level of FDI inflow need to be raised. Why has Africa remained unsuccessful in attracting large amounts of FDI? To what extent are internal and external economic and political factors responsible in influencing FDI inflow into the region? The purpose of this chapter is to seek answers to some of these questions by: (1) examining trends in FDI inflow during the period 1970–88; (2) identifying factors that have influenced these trends; (3) examining relationships between FDI and some of the economic and political factors influencing foreign investment; and (4) suggesting policy options that could contribute to an improvement of Africa's share of foreign investment.

FDI IN AFRICA, 1970–88

Anyone attempting to examine trends in FDI inflow in Africa is quickly faced with the simple fact that there are inadequate national statistics. The different estimates published by international agencies have limitations related to inconsistency, fluctuating exchange rates, and lack of clear definition of control of assets. Despite these limitations, data published by the Organization for Economic Cooperation and Development (OECD) and the United Nations (based on IMF data) seem to indicate some firm trends. According to the IMF, total world inflow of FDI has more than tripled between the period 1980–88, attaining a record high of $152 million in 1988 (see Table 5.1). Despite this change, there were three major developments that changed the global pattern of FDI, particularly since the worldwide economic crisis of 1981–83.

First, after experiencing an average annual increase of 15.9 percent for the period 1970 to 1980, overall global FDI inflow fell by more than 13 percent between 1981 and 1985, and then jumped by an average increase of 86 percent between 1986 and 1988 (UNCTC 1985, 208; 1990, 29). Second, despite these changes, developing countries fared relatively worse than developed countries; developing countries' share of FDI dropped from 32 percent in 1975 to 18 percent in 1988 (see Table 5.1). Third, some developed countries, such as the U.S.,

Table 5.1
Inflow of Foreign Direct Investment, 1970–1988 (in millions of dollars)

REGION	1970 $	1970 %	1975 $	1975 %	1980 $	1980 %	1985 $	1985 %	1988 $	1988 %
DEVELOPED COUNTRIES	9122.4	81.3	14910.0	68.4	41280.3	79.2	35604.7	72.8	123875	81.5
DEVELOPING COUNTRIES	2102.5	18.7	6877.6	31.6	10856.3	20.8	13286.5	27.2	2802.5	18.4
AFRICA	320.4	2.9	477.0	2.2	316.3	0.6	2587.3	5.3	2118.8	1.4
LATIN AMERICA AND THE CARIBBEAN	1167.2	10.4	4041.3	18.5	7114.0	13.6	5567.9	11.4	11305.3	7.4
SOUTH & EAST ASIA	596.4	5.3	1648.9	7.6	3211.2	6.2	4584.5	9.4	13864.4	9.1
OTHER	-0.7	0.0	661.3	3.0	47.6	0.0	402.5	0.8	329.7	0.2
WORLD	11224.9	100.0	21787.9	100.0	52147.6	100.0	48906.2	100.0	151916.3	100.0

Source: UNCTC. Based on IMF, Balance of Payments data tape as of November 20, 1990.

Figure 5.1
Foreign Direct Investment in Africa, 1970–1988 (as percentage of Total FDI to LDCs)

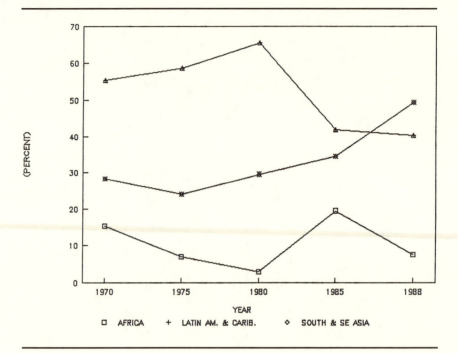

became major host countries rather than investors. The American share of FDI inflow increased from 13 percent in 1970 to 41 percent in 1988 (UNCTC 1990, 29). The U.S., which was the leading investor accounting for over half of the total capital investment abroad until the mid–70s, became a major recipient of FDI. By 1985, the U.S.'s share of the world-wide FDI was only 22 percent, while Western Europe took over the role as the dominant supplier of FDI. One of the major reasons for the continued expansion of FDI in the U.S. is the rising power of the dollar. Between 1981 and 1984, the dollar appreciated by 44 percent relative to other major currencies (OECD 1987, 19).

Among the developing countries, there have been significant changes in trends as well. Latin America had been a major recipient of FDI until the mid–70s, but lost its lead as South and Southeast Asian countries became the major desirable targets of FDI in the 1980s. In the case of Africa, both in absolute values and percentage shares, FDI stagnated, with the exception of 1985 when the figures began to show an increasing trend and then declined again in 1988 (see Figure 5.1). Even then, it must be noted that about 79 percent of the FDI during the decade 1975–88 went only to the oil-exporting countries of Egypt, Nigeria, and Tunisia. A majority of the non-oil-exporting African countries received a few million dollars or, in some cases, had a negative balance. Con-

Figure 5.2
FDI Capital Stock

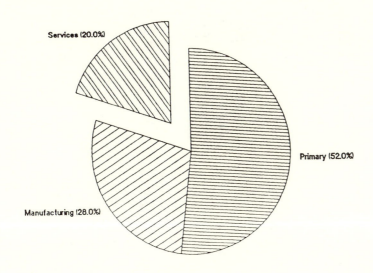

Services (20.0%)

Primary (52.0%)

Manufacturing (28.0%)

sequently, FDI accounts for a very small proportion of the total flow of resources to Africa. FDI inflow for the period 1981–89 accounted for less than 5 percent of total net resource flows to Africa (OECD 1990, 39). Overall, average annual flow of FDI to Africa between 1981 and 1987 was 12 percent of the flow to LDCs, or 3 percent of the worldwide flow (UN 1990, 4).

Sectorally, investment is dominated by the primary sector, particularly petroleum and mining (see Figure 5.2). Investment in manufacturing and services has remained around 30 and 20 percent, respectively, since the mid-1960s (UN 1988, 5; Green 1981, 338–339).

An analysis of the stock of capital in Africa shows a similar trend to that of flow of capital. Africa's share of stock of FDI declined from about 6.6 percent in 1960 to 2.8 percent in 1980, with a slight increase to 3.5 percent in 1985 (see Table 5.2). A number of factors helps to explain why African countries fared poorly in FDI in the last decade. For the purpose of analysis, these factors will be grouped into internal and external factors.

INTERNAL FACTORS

Poor Economic Performance

The economies of many African countries performed poorly in the last decade with many slipping to negative growth rates. The average annual growth of GDP

Table 5.2.
Stock of Direct Investment from Abroad by Major Recipient Region, 1960–1985 (in billions of dollars)

Region	1960 $	1960 %	1971 $	1971 %	1978 $	1978 %	1980 $	1980 %	1985 $	1985 %
Developed Countries	36.7	67.3	108.4	65.2	251.8	69.6	313.7	71.1	478.2	75.0
Developing Countries	17.6	32.3	51.4	30.9	100.4	27.8	117.4	26.6	159.0	25.0
Latin America/1	8.5	15.6	29.6	17.8	52.5	14.5	62.3	14.9	80.5	12.6
Africa	3.0	5.5	8.8	5.3	11.1	3.1	12.4	2.8	22.3	3.5
Asia	4.1	7.5	7.8	4.7	25.2	7.0	30.3	6.9	49.6	7.8
Southern Europe	0.5	0.9	1.7	1.0	3.4	0.9	4.1	0.9	-	-
Middle East	1.5	2.8	3.5	2.1	8.2	2.3	8.3	1.9	-	-
Other Unalloctaed/2	-	-	6.5	3.9	9.5	2.6	9.8	2.2	6.6	1.0
TOTAL	54.5	100.0	166.3	100.0	361.7	100.0	440.9	100.0	637.2	100.0

[1] 1985 figure includes the Caribbean.
[2] 1985 figure includes Fiji, Papua New Guinea, Saudi Arabia, Turkey and Yugoslavia.
—data not available.

Sources: J. M. Stopford and J. H. Dunning, *Multinationals, Company Performance and Global Trends* (London: Macmillan, 1983). Data for 1985 are from UNCTC, "The Process of Transnationalization in the 1980s," *The CTC Reporter*, Vol. 26 (Autumn 1986): 8.

among sub-Saharan African countries for the periods 1973–80 and 1980–87 was 2.5 and 0.5 percent, respectively, compared to 5.9 for the period 1965–73 (World Bank 1989, 222). To give a comparative picture, the GDP growth for all low-income economies (those with GNP of $400 or less) for 1973–80 and 1980–87 were 4.6 and 6.0 percent, respectively. These poor performances could be partially explained by the fact that African economies are based on the export of one or two primary commodities whose terms of trade have deteriorated significantly in the last decade, drought that has gripped the continent since the mid–1970s, the global economic crises of the early 1980s, armed conflict with neighboring countries (as well as internal conflicts), and a whole range of institutional and infrastructural constraints (for more on this topic, see World Bank 1989, 166–233).

Undeveloped Natural Resources and Lack of Infrastructure

Many of the African countries have few developed natural resources. They also lack a pool of low-cost, skilled labor to attract TNCs to invest. While African countries may be potentially rich in mineral and other natural resources, most of them have not surveyed their resources adequately to establish the feasibility of their commercial exploitation. This problem is compounded by a weak infrastructure—lack of roads, railway lines, and shipment facilities—all important in exporting commodities. The interest of TNCs is often contingent upon the existence of proven, viable deposits (e.g., mineral resources) and the availability of a technology and infrastructure to exploit commercially these resources. In the case of landlocked countries, the problem is much more serious because they would have to depend on their neighbors' infrastructure. Thirteen of Africa's independent countries are landlocked, with severe problems of access for export opportunities.

A Small and Fragmented Market

Another major economic problem affecting investment in Africa is the lack of a large market. Many African countries do not have a very large internal or regional market. For instance, with a combined population of about 7 million, Burkina Faso, Malawi, and Mali have a GNP of about $1 billion, or one-tenth of the GNP of Guatemala, a middle-income country with a comparable population (UN 1988, 14). The investment opportunities in markets that are so small and fragmented are clearly very limited. Access to markets is one of the major reasons that TNCs invest abroad, as illustrated in a survey conducted by the Group of Thirty (an independent international research organization headquartered in New York) to determine the reasons for investment in LDCs. Over 80 percent of the respondents ranked access to host country's market among the top three factors (see Table 5.3).

Table 5.3

Main Influences on Foreign Direct Investment Decisions[1]

	Reasons for Investment in:			
	Industrial Countries		Less Developed Countries	
Percent of Respondents Mentioning a Factor in their "top Three"				
	1970	1983	1970	1983
Access to host country's market	89	67	82	87
Access to markets in host country's region	41	37	29	34
Avoidance of existing or anticipated tariff barriers	24	16	51	43
Avoidance of existing or anticipated nontariff barrier	13	8	29	28
Integration with your company's existing investment	26	37	4	17
Change in your industry's structure	20	22	11	9
Slower growth of home market	17	18	11	11
Access to raw materials	13	10	13	11
Inducements offered by host country	11	12	16	13
Integration with other companys' investment	4	8	4	4
Comparative labor cost advantages	4	6	11	13
Comparative material cost advantages	4	6	2	4
Shifts of political and social stability	2	8	9	8
Tax advantages	6	4	7	0
Market Presence	6	5	3	0
Distribution of risk	0	5	0	3
Return on Investment in R & D	3	3	3	3
Development of local market	3	3	3	0
Aquisition opportunities	3	3	0	0
Exchange rate movements on siting (not financing) investment	0	2	0	0

[1]The information requested was the following: "You will find listed possible influences on foreign direct investment. Please rank the six most important to your company's new foreign direct investment in industrial countries and in less developed countries, in both 1970 and in 1983, by writing the number "1" for the most important factor, "2" for the second most important factor, and so on."

Source: Group of Thirty, Foreign Direct Investment, 1973–87. Cited in OECD, International Investment and Multinational Enterprises (Paris, OECD, 1987), p. 206.

The Debt Burden

Sharp increases in national debts have significantly limited the flow of capital to many LDCs. In contrast to the 1970s, when international banks were willing to extend credits to countries considered credit-worthy, in recent years banks have become increasingly reluctant to give out loans in view of the debt crisis that has impacted many developing countries. A 1984 estimate showed that loans U.S. banks were making abroad dropped by $13 billion during 1984 (*The Economist*, 1985, 84). Banks in the U.S. have found that lending within the U.S. is much more profitable than it has been for some time because of a larger than usual differential between the prime rate and the cost of funds (Helmboldt 1988, 336).

The accumulation of debt among African countries has become a critical problem in the last decade. During 1987, total debt in sub-Saharan African countries increased by 18 percent, jumping to $129 billion; the figure for 1980 was $56 billion. It is projected that the total will rise to $138 billion by 1988 (World Bank 1988). Total debt as a percent of exports and of GNP in 1987 was 362.3 percent and 100.1 percent in contrast to the 1970 figures of 97.5 and 28.2 percent, respectively (World Bank 1988, 9). The net effect of such a heavy burden has been to force African countries to turn to FDI as a major source of capital. FDI helps to redress the imbalances between debt and foreign equity, eases balance-of-payments constraint, and serves as a major source of development finance. The sharp increase in debt has also led to increases in the debt service. The debt service ratio for Africa (debt service payments as a percentage of annual export earnings) jumped from 15 percent in 1980 to over 50 percent in 1987, with 62 percent for Ghana, 67 percent for Zambia, 84 percent for Equatorial Guinea, and 205 percent for Mozambique. Africa's debt has been growing at the alarming rate of 23 percent per annum (Onimode 1989, 1).

EXTERNAL FACTORS

Decline in Price of Primary Commodities and Problems of Resource Development

Most of sub-Saharan African countries depend on a few primary commodities for export, such as cocoa, coffee, palm oils, cotton, and bananas, which have experienced poor commodity prices and whose prospects for recovery seem poor. The value of African exports has declined at an annual rate of 7 percent during the period 1980 to 1987, whereas those from Western Europe have increased at an annual rate of 5 percent, those from the U.S.A. at 3 percent, and those from Asia at 8.5 percent (GATT 1988, 19). Because the production of primary commodities for export is often one of the major reasons that TNCs invest, African countries became less desirable for FDI as primary commodities prices continue to decline. Moreover, much of sub-Saharan Africa is located in an area that has been affected by unpredictable climatic conditions and persistent drought since the early 1970s, which has made agricultural production problematic. Since favorable climatic conditions are often a prerequisite in guaranteeing reasonable returns in agricultural investment, investors avoid taking risks in areas where natural conditions are unpredictable.

Unfavorable Political Climate

One of the most important external factors influencing FDI flow is the perception of investors regarding the overall political climate of the host country.

As a result of the political crises that engulfed Africa in the 1970s and early 1980s, stemming largely from internal strife or border conflict, many investors have developed a perception that investing in Africa is "unsafe." Various studies have documented that the unsafe political climate and the unpredictability of government policy had a major influence in limiting foreign investment in Africa. In a survey of several major multinational corporations, the Group of Thirty found that the deterioration of the economic and political climate and the lack of stability were the two major reasons that investors did not find Africa a good area for investment (Group of Thirty 1984). Referring to the investment climate, Helmboldt et al. (1988, 327) note that "[investors] perceive Africa not only as a place where business costs are high, but also as a relatively unpredictable environment."

Foreign companies are reluctant to invest in countries where there is no stability or clarity in the rules concerning foreign investment. Frequent and arbitrary changes of economic and legal policies affecting profit remittance, foreign exchange allocation, and tax policy discourage investment. Investors expect fair treatment by host governments and explicitly stated legal protection for their investment. In a survey of U.S. investors, Baker (1983) found that the hostile attitude of host governments toward private investment and the prospects for political instability were two of the six major factors that influenced U.S. investors not to invest in Africa. The other factors are related to the slow response of host governments or the complicated requirements, the absence of large markets, the lack of credit-worthiness (as indicated through mounting debt, a shortage of foreign exchange, and sudden import bans) and excessive government control of the economy (Baker 1983, cited in Helmboldt et al. 1988, 377–78). Baker also noted that "inefficiency, capriciousness, and/or corruption of bureaucratic processes and government decision-making were some of the major complaints voiced by firms already operating in Africa" (Helmboldt et al. 1988, 338; Baker 1983, 50). It is interesting to note that nationalization and expropriation, two major problems that affected many TNCs in Africa in the 1970s, are no longer a major concern because many African countries are moving in the direction of privatization of their firms. Moreover, where state ownership is the desire, the objective is often achieved through negotiation rather than sweeping nationalization. Although many African countries have modified their codes and policies to attract investors, the perception that the investment climate is "unsafe" (one of the most powerful disincentives to any kind of foreign or domestic investment) often lingers. It takes years for a country or a region to re-establish its image as a safe place for foreign investment, even after the political disturbances have ceased.

While both internal and external factors may account for Africa's poor performance in attracting FDI, the efforts of many African countries to entice investors are worth noting. An analysis of the national policies in the last decade can shed light on the changing attitude of African governments toward FDI.

FDI and African National Policies

Historically, the policies of African countries towards TNCs were quite diverse and depended on a number of factors such as political and economic ideology, history, and size of the respective country. Foreign investors were often viewed as extensions of colonialism in the early years following independence. Nationalization of foreign-owned companies was extensive, and where there was no outright expropriation, foreign investors were required to accept minority state participation (UN 1990, 12).

Since the mid-1970s, many African countries have either enacted new investment legislation or have modified the old laws with the objective of attracting more foreign investment. Between 1982 and 1987, more than one-third of the African countries have either introduced new codes or have made adjustments to their investment codes or guidelines (UN 1988). The major elements of the legislation are often related to the development objectives of the country. The objectives are then followed by specific provisions governing the establishment, ownership, and operating environment of FDI. Some of the specific provisions concern authorization and registration, taxes, remittances of profits and capital, and employment and training of local personnel. Recent legislative developments include the establishment of special agencies with overall responsibility in investment matters (e.g., Ghana's Investment Center), the development of export zones (e.g., Ghana, Togo, Kenya), and the privatization of state and parastatal enterprises (e.g., Nigeria, Guinea, Niger, Togo).[1] Although it is difficult to develop a typology of FDI legislation in Africa because of its diversity and complexity, Islam and Majmudar (1990) maintain that three clusters of countries could be identified based on the direction of change of their codes. The three clusters include:

1. Countries that had pursued restrictive policies towards FDI in the 1960s and 1970s, but have adopted major liberalization measures since the 1980s. In this group could be included countries such as Ghana, Senegal, and Somalia.

2. Countries that were pursuing liberal policies in the 1960s and 1970s, and generally have continued to do the same in the 1980s. However, they have introduced certain changes to liberalize some aspects of FDI policies and have tightened the restrictions in others. A majority of the African countries probably fall in this category. Some examples include Burkina Faso, Central African Republic, and Niger, to mention a few.

3. Countries that have maintained a restrictive stance even though they have amended some sections of their FDI laws during the 1980s. Benin, Ethiopia, Guinea, and Tanzania fall into this group. Most of these countries followed, or at some time in their history adopted, socialist ideology to guide their economic policy. The major problem facing many of these countries is that the policy changes they have introduced have not been perceived as credible

and permanent, factors that are important in winning the confidence of investors.

Many of the African countries have incorporated new measures beyond the traditional incentives, such as the liberalization of tax regimes, the elimination of provisions on the exclusion of certain sectors and the requirement of local participation in the ownership of foreign-controlled enterprises, the simplification of administrative procedures, and the streamlining of regulatory frameworks. Unfortunately, since many of these liberal measures were introduced in the last decade, their impact has not been adequately assessed. Furthermore, FDI is influenced by a range of economic, political, and institutional factors, and the introduction of liberal legislation is only a necessary but not a sufficient condition for attracting sufficient amount of FDI. To have any success, the new liberal FDI promotion measures should be supplemented with other fundamental political and economic changes that would create an environment conducive to foreign investment.

EMPIRICAL ANALYSIS

Corporate decisions to invest are influenced by a number of internal and external factors related to the desire to (a) secure access to resources found in the host country, (b) take advantage of local markets by replacing imports from abroad, and (c) rationalize investment by integrating operations so that a firm can establish a division of labor among the parent company and its subsidiaries, locating the latter according to the comparative advantages of host countries (Dunning 1988, chapter 2). Other factors are related to (consistent) government policy, political climate, and the economic climate of host countries (OECD 1987, Goldsbrough 1985, Cable and Mukherjee 1986, Vukmanic 1983, Helmboldt 1988, Root and Ahmed 1989, Frank 1980, Galenson 1984). In general, economic opportunities that investors hope to seize, good economic conditions, and current government policies are three major factors important to FDI (UN 1988, 9). Balance-of-payments problems and debt burdens concern investors because such problems might hinder the repatriation of earnings as the host country faces foreign exchange difficulties. Many countries have introduced restrictive measures with a view to servicing debt payments; hence, an improvement in the debt burden could help eliminate some of the restrictive measures. Similarly, the lack of credible and permanent government policies keep out investors, who fear losing their investment.

To test the relationship between FDI inflow and the economic and political factors affecting investment, a series of regression equations was run by, including some of the economic and political variables as explanatory variables. The hypothesized relationships were expressed as follows:

$$FDI = f(\overset{+}{POP}, \overset{+}{GNP}, \overset{-}{TT}, \overset{-}{CACTB}, \overset{-}{DEBT}, \overset{-}{DGRO}, \overset{-}{DSERV},$$

$$\overset{-}{POL1}, \overset{-}{POL2}, \overset{-}{POL3}) \tag{1}$$

where the variables are defined as indicated in Table 5.3. The signs above the various independent variables ($+$ or $-$) indicate the expected direction of influence on FDI.

Selection of the variables is influenced by empirical studies suggested in the literature and by availability of data. The dependent variable, average annual FDI inflow for the periods 1980–85 (FDI), was derived from an IMF data tape made available through UNCTC. The independent variables included population (POP) (used as a surrogate for market size) and a range of economic variables— average annual growth of GNP (GNP), terms of trade (TT), and current account balance (CACTB)—included to indicate the performance of the economy. Previous studies have suggested that there is a strong correlation between economic growth in LDCs and their success in attracting FDI (OECD 1987, 86). The debt burden was measured by including total debt (DEBT), annual growth of debt (DGRO), and debt services (DSERV). The data on political climate (POL1, POL2, POL3) indicate political developments between 1970 and 1977. Although the data on political variables do not reflect recent developments, they were included because perceptions of the political climate often linger and take years for their influence to diminish. The political variables were grouped into three categories to identify the separate effects of each variable.

Three sets of equation (1) for thirty-six countries and for only thirty non-oil-exporting countries were used to test the hypotheses. The three sets represented FDI for the periods 1970–85, 1981–85, and 1970–85. In the first set, all variables in the first equation were included. The result indicates, however, that debt is the only significant explanatory variable that could enter into the equation estimated by using the stepwise regression method. Debt explained 58 percent (R^2 = .5847) of the relationship between FDI and the economic and political variables, but it has the opposite sign from the hypothesized relationship and also has problems of multicolinearity.[2] Therefore, in order to examine the effect of the remaining variables, debt was removed from the equations in the second set. In the third set only those variables that had significant correlation coefficients at the 95 percent or above level in the bivariate relationships were included.

The results indicate that the R^2 are high (ranging between .7600 and .8250) and the F-values are significant, suggesting that the model gives a "good" fit in explaining the relationship between FDI inflow and some of the economic and political variables (see Tables 5.4 and 5.5). Market (POP), current account balance (CACTB), and political environment (POL1) have the expected signs and are statistically significant at the 1 percent level. Hence, the hypothesized relationship between FDI and some of the political and economic variables affecting the investment climate are valid. The lack of statistical significance of the debt burden variables (DGRO—annual growth of debt—and DSERV—debt service) and the positive relationship between debt and FDI raise some major

Table 5.4
Variables Used in the Regression Analysis

Variable	Measure	Source
FDI	Average Annual Foreign Direct Investment Inflow, 1980-85	UNCTC, 1988a IMF, 1988
POP	Total Population, 1985 (surrogate for Market)	World Bank, 1989
GNP	Average Annual Growth Rate of GNP, 1965-85 (%)	World Bank, 1989
TT	Terms of Trade, 1985	World Bank, 198
CACTB	Current Account Balance, 1985	World Bank, 1989
DEBT	Total External Debt, 1985	World Bank, 1989
DGRO	Annual Growth Rate of Debt, 198-84 (%)	World Bank, 1986
DSERV	Debt Service as % of Exports, 1985	World Bank, 1989
POL1	Total Number of Reported Protest Demonstrations, Riots and Strikes, 1970-77	Taylor and Jodice, 1983
POL2	Total Number of Reported Armed Attacks, 1970-77	Taylor and Jodice, 1983
POL3	Total Number of Reported Successful and Unsuccesful Government Changes (Coups and Attempted Coups) 1970-77	Taylor and Jodice, 1983

*All coefficients are significant at the 95% or above level.

questions. Although the literature suggests that the debt burden has affected the credit-worthiness of many of the developing countries, the issue might be more relevant to Latin American and Asian countries, where the debt burden is relatively higher, than to African countries. The data for Africa show that those countries that have relatively heavy debt burdens (such as Nigeria and Egypt) are among the countries that have been successful in attracting a significant amount of FDI. These countries are also rich in oil resources. Thus it is plausible to argue that when profits are sufficiently high, as in the case of oil, the attraction outweighs worries about a country's debt problem.

CONCLUSION

This chapter had three major objectives: (1) to examine trends in FDI in Africa during the period 1970–88; (2) to identify factors that influenced these trends; and (3) to suggest policy options that could help improve Africa's share of FDI. Analysis of the trends reveals that Africa is the least-preferred continent by

Table 5.5
Results of Regression Analysis*

Variables	All Countries		Non-Oil Exp. Countries	
	(1)	(2)	(3)	(4)
POP (total population)	8.6665	8.4148	4.4085	4.5884
	(7.42510)	(7.410)	(7.892)	(7.921)
GNP (gross national product)				3.5876
				(2.449)
CACTB (current account balance)	-0.1835	-0.1784		
	(6.46223)	(-6.423)		
POL1 (protest demonstrations, riots and strikes)	-5.2482	-5.1297	-2.8902	-3.0398
	(-2.139)	(-3.216)	(-6.495)	(-6.646)
Constant	-37.3964	-28.9767	-6.3148	-8.3191
R^2	0.8250	0.8079	0.7723	0.7603
F-Value	33.0072	33.6633	31.4006	21.1151
df	21	24	18	20

*All coefficients are significant at the 95% or above level.

investors. In the eyes of TNCs, Africa is a region dominated by drought and famine, debt burden, unstable political climate, and governments unfavorable to FDI. The major problem stems from the perception and stereotyping that TNCs developed toward Africa during the 1960s and 1970s. Consequently, investors have shied away from investing in Africa, even though it is a resource-rich region. The empirical evidence reveals that FDI inflow has been on the decline in the last decade, and according to some estimates, FDI in Africa is likely to decline further in the 1990s.

Developments in the last few years, however, including the revision of investment codes and regulations, the signing of multilateral and bilateral investment-guaranteeing arrangements by many countries, privatization, the removal of administrative and institutional impediments, and the establishment of export zones could improve Africa's chances to attract foreign investment. African governments are making attempts to entice investors by improving the investment climate, restructuring policies and guidelines to accommodate investors, and appreciating the importance of TNCs in transferring technology, providing the necessary capital for investment, alleviating the debt and balance-of-payments crisis by augmenting the flow of capital, and engaging in the production and marketing of export products.

Among TNCs with a long history of involvement in Africa, there is an interest in expanding investment. In Nigeria, for instance, UACN, John Holt, and Dunlop are among half a dozen TNCs that are either expanding their operations or moving into new areas of activity. In Kenya, the Del Monte subsidiary, Kenya Canners Ltd., is involved in a $25 million investment and expansion program. In Zimbabwe, various TNCs' subsidiaries have reinvested between $10 to $150 million during the period 1980–86 (UN 1988, 8). But the increasing interest by TNCs with a long history of investment in Africa should not negate the fact that a large number of British, French, U.S., and Japanese firms are pulling out of Africa. The continuing decline in rate of return and the chronic shortage of foreign exchange in many African countries are believed to be two of the major factors responsible for the large disinvestment by TNCs in Africa.

African governments are taking the initiative to reverse the disinvestment process by enacting legislation that would entice potential investors. While the efforts of African governments are critical in improving investment climates, they cannot have significant impact unless the efforts are orchestrated (coordinated) with the objective of changing the perception of TNCs toward Africa. Therefore, the goal of improving FDI inflow to Africa should include some of the following measures.[3]

- African countries should develop legislation that is consistent, credible and permanent. One of the most frequent complaints of investors in Africa is that government policies tend to be transitory and, in some cases, capricious. TNCs consider long-term prospects seriously and, therefore, countries that have a history of altering legislation frequently are likely to be avoided from consideration for investment. When legislative changes are made, retroactive application of the new law to already established firms should be avoided. Since predictability is an important factor in investment decision, government policies should be clear and consistent.

- Investors often find the administrative bureaucracy of governments intimidating and irritating. Delay often occurs because of technicalities in requirements, indecisiveness in decision-making and, in some cases, because of corruption. African governments must restructure their bureaucracy to provide prompt response to investors and also must establish ''one-stop'' offices with the responsibility of facilitating investment procedures and requirements. The operation of such an office could be expedited if staffed by knowledgeable personnel and if licensing procedures were streamlined.

- Clear guidelines and requirements should be developed to make investment benefits automatic, provided that the investor meets the requirements. Requirements are often not clear even to agencies or ministries in the country, much less to investors. Legislation that clearly spells out conditions for investment provides investors with the confidence and the options to make quick decisions.

- An information campaign that explains the attitude of host governments is essential. The negative view of Africa that is now prevalent can only be eliminated by developing an information campaign that explains the opportunities available and the attitude of host governments. International forums and arms of international organizations such as the UNCTC could be used to help in stamping out the negative image of Africa.

- Many of the legislative codes governing investment tend to be ambiguous, which makes it difficult for an investor to factor the cost of compliance. In some cases the codes are inconsistent with the attitude of host governments. Many African nations have not resolved the issue of the role of foreign investment in national development. The debate on the merits and demerits of foreign investment tends to be murky as governments continue to send conflicting signals on whether to welcome or avoid foreign investment. Although many countries recognize the importance of FDI, their actions toward TNCs seem to conflict with their policies; TNCs are often viewed as being exploiters rather than partners that can help in developing resources and providing services for mutual benefit. It is, therefore, essential to (1) define the national objectives and the role that TNCs can play in meeting the objectives, (2) spell out clearly the requirements and circumstances for investment, and (3) with commitment and clear purpose, seek out foreign investors in sectors where foreign investment is considered beneficial. Whether the national goal is open access or restricted access to certain economies, African governments must be sensitive to the concerns of investors. Explicit legal guarantees may be needed to assure investors that they will be treated fairly and equitably and that their right to repatriate investment capital and dividends will be protected.

- African nations should seek regional cooperation to establish large markets and thereby leverage their collective market shares behind the particular investment opportunities of each country.

- The assistance of home countries should be sought to institute programs of encourage-ment targeted to Africa and to encourage their TNCs to invest in Africa. For instance, Sweden encourages its firms to internationalize by providing information on possible projects in host countries, by mediating contract arrangements, and by providing fi-nancial support such as loans and guarantees.

- An African Investment Promotion Center (AIPC) should be established to assist in facilitating investment decisions by providing information, technical assistance, and administrative linking. The Center can also serve as a clearing house to help identify projects in host countries as well as TNCs that are seeking investment opportunities. If the Center does not have the expertise or manpower to handle projects, it could enlist the support of outside experts or international organizations such as the UN Center for Transnational Corporations.

- Local entrepreneurs should be encouraged to undertake joint venture investment with TNCs entering as equity shareholders and providers of financial, technological, and managerial skills.

- Government programs should give priority to the development of an infrastructure base, such as roads and railway lines (which have become bottlenecks in exploiting resources). A partnership must be worked out in which the government would be willing to eliminate long-term structural obstacles to FDI by utilizing public funds or official development assistance to provide infrastructure, train labor, and help in developing resources—in return for expanding or undertaking new investments by TNCs. Here bilateral and multilateral assistance could play a major role in supplementing funds to finance some of the projects.

- Finally, international assistance to alleviate Africa's major economic problems—such as the debt burden, the balance-of-payments problems, and declining terms of trade—could help increase FDI in Africa. Innovative ideas, such as equity swaps, write-down of loans, comprehensive restructuring, and a Marshall Plan for Africa, have been suggested. Whether or not these measures and plans would work depends on the willingness and the good will of the international community to appreciate the nature of Africa's current economic problems. Meanwhile, creating a friendly climate for FDI while at the same time protecting their national interests remains the responsibility of African governments.

NOTES

1. The rapid evolution of laws, regulations, and bilateral arrangements makes it difficult to review fully policy changes among African countries. The categorization should, therefore, be viewed as an attempt to present a brief overview of the policies based on recent changes. For a detailed summary of the policies, see Appendix B.

2. The estimated equation was:

$$-19.8201 + 0.0178 \text{ DEBT} \qquad R^2 = .5846$$
$$(5.690) \qquad\qquad df = 23$$
$$F = 32.3783$$

The remaining variables in equation (1) had very low F-values to enter into the regression equation estimated by using the stepwise method.

3. A detailed discussion of some of these measures can be found in UN (1988), Ndegwa (1989), and Helmboldt et al. (1988).

6

Debt, Structural Adjustment, and Private Investment in Africa

JON KRAUS

At the end of the 1970s African economies were regarded as having experienced a dramatic slowdown in economic growth and development, having grown on average by 1.3% in GNP per capita in 1960–70 and by only 0.8% during 1970–79; when the Nigerian economy was excluded, the other African countries had negative per capita GNP growth during 1970–79. African economies were growing so slowly or stagnating, the World Bank and others argued, because, essentially, the governments were ignoring the development of exports, pursuing inefficient, highly protectionist, import-substitution policies, led by over-staffed, under-performing state industries. Price signals and thus incentives for efficient production and distribution, it was argued, were blunted by state price-setting for export and food crops, state interventions in production and distribution, and highly over-valued exchange rates, which discriminated against rural agricultural producers (and exports) in favor of urban consumers.[1] As a consequence primarily of these policies (not the incredibly disruptive world economy of the 1970s, it was argued), exports were down, and African countries experienced severe balance-of-payments crises, requiring increased borrowing and the build-up of external debt, while imports were choked off, slowing growth further.

As a consequence of African balance of payments and debt crises, the world-wide recession of the early 1980s, and the collapse of African export prices and volume, many African governments, regardless of their political orientation, were compelled to go to the International Monetary Fund (IMF) and accept its set of conditions for the temporary IMF balance of payments loans. As is well known, without successful negotiations with the IMF and a government's acceptance of and close compliance with policy conditions and performance targets, the World Bank (WB), other multilateral lending institutions, governments providing official development aid, and commercial banks would not renew their loans or reschedule the repayment of existing debt.[2] Thus, for much of the 1980s many African governments were compelled to adopt IMF stabilization policies and IMF and World Bank structural adjustment programs (SAPs). Stabilization has involved efforts to reduce balance of payments deficits by increasing exports and restraining demand for imports. These goals are sought by changing relative prices of foreign exchange, through major devaluations (making imports more expensive, exports more profitable), and of domestic prices, by ending price controls and subsidies and reducing overall demand (i.e., inducing recessions) by sharply cutting real government expenditures. The structural adjustment programs (SAPs) pursue similar goals in various sectors, trying to rebuild productive and infrastructural capacities by increasing price incentives for producers. This major effort to reestablish the salience of market signals involves reducing direct and indirect government interventions in the economy, i.e., letting economic forces apart from the government play major roles. A major part of this strategy has been to demand liberalization of the economies through *the encouragement of domestic and foreign capital*. Thus, the extreme economic difficulties experienced by African economies have been largely blamed by the IMF and WB, as well as by Western governments, on the pursuit of poor economic policies, carried out by poorly and inefficiently-managed state institutions.

The magnitude of Africa's debt crises in the 1980s gave to the IMF and WB and the Western aid donors a political leverage they have not possessed since perhaps the early 1960s. This political leverage has been used throughout the 1980s to make the IMF, WB, and Western governments into the major architects of new economic policies in many African states. In some cases, these Western institutions have had willing local allies in government leaders or, more frequently, technocrats and economists in economic and finance ministries. However, regardless of the nature of this international-national political alliance, the policy changes made have required major changes in the beneficiaries of policies and, thus, in political alliances and coalitions of regime support in Africa. Policies such as cuts in government spending and subsidies, large-scale layoffs of state workers, curtailment in educational and health expenditures, and reduced real wages have tended to generate recessions and thus undermine a government's political support, leading to widespread protests, demonstrations, and strikes. This situation has occurred in Algeria, Ghana, Nigeria, the Ivory Coast, and other countries in recent years. On some occasions the stabilization and SAPs have not generated recessions, but a renewal of economic growth and restoration of productive capacities where an economy had been deeply depressed and economic aid had been substantial, as in Ghana in the 1984–90 period. However, even in these economies the shifts in relative prices that are fundamental to stabilization and SAPs have generated austerity conditions for wage workers and the urban poor, while shifting incomes to rural producers and owners of capital.

The IMF, WB, and Western governments have argued that a restoration of economic growth and development would only be achieved through reliance upon capitalist incentives and markets and reintegration with the world economy. The leverage of Western institutions has, therefore, provided a major opportunity for domestic and foreign capital to play major roles in African political economies.

This chapter will examine the interrelationship between slow growth and debt, the imposition of structural adjustment, the renewal of opportunities for domestic and private capital, and the political and economic consequences of the policy changes made. Many economists and political economists, as well as African governments, have found the diagnoses of the problems unpersuasive in part and the policies insisted upon by Western institutions unhelpful and positively damaging to the ability of African societies to make the structural adjustments necessary. There is a significant ongoing debate on these questions, and we can look at the performance of African economies during the 1980s as one indicator of the worth of the diagnosis of the problems, as well as the worth of the policy remedies. In this chapter we will examine three things: first, the problems of economic growth and development experienced by African economies in the 1970s and 1980s, and the diagnoses of the problems articulated by observers; second, what progress has been made by African economies under the many SAPs implemented by African states in the 1980s; and third, what major efforts have been made to create a new or greater role for domestic and foreign private capital, and how successful have such efforts been. Are private markets replacing state controls? Are domestic and foreign private capital acquiring new roles and is state capital being diminished or privitized? While we raise these questions about African economies in general, we will examine in particular what has occurred in six widely different African countries with diverse economies and experiences: Nigeria, Ghana, and the Cote d'Ivoire in West Africa, Algeria, Kenya, and Zimbabwe. These questions are incredibly important because African countries at the end of the 1980s were experiencing even more severe economic crises than they faced at the end of the 1970s, with economic growth even lower and debt and debt service payments higher.

LOW GROWTH AND THE NATURE AND EXTENT OF THE DEBT CRISIS

The slow economic growth or stagnation of the 1970s, depending on the country involved, could be explained by a variety of factors. External problems were frequently noted: the oil price hikes of 1973–74 and 1979, which put enormous stress on African import capacities; the subsequent worldwide inflation, which compounded rising import costs; the sharp Western country recessions, which reduced demand for and (sometimes) prices of African exports; and a rise in Western protectionism. Internal factors were also cited: major, multi-year droughts in West and East Africa; sustained deficit-spending by government, increasing inflationary impulses, and import demand; over-valued exchange rates; and a combination of economic nationalism and state activism, which led to the widespread development of state corporations in many areas of production and distribution, in both statist "socialist" regimes and in capitalist ones, such as

Cote d'Ivoire (formerly Ivory Coast), Nigeria, Cameroon, and Kenya. Some economic nationalism was antagonistic to capitalist accumulation strategies, while in other African countries economic nationalism cultivated capital but insisted on a stronger role for indigenous capital. Thus, nationalizations occurred in some regimes which were strongly opposed to capitalism, foreign or domestic—as in Tanzania, Mozambique, Angola, Algeria, and Ethiopia after 1975. Elsewhere limited nationalization or state equity purchases occurred to give the state a stake in a major extractive industry—for example, Zambia in copper, Nigeria in the oil industry, Ghana in gold, bauxite, and banking. In some African countries certain sectors were reserved for either the state or local entrepreneurs, or foreign capital was required to offer a certain portion of equity for sale to local investors, a process of indigenization of capital that was widespread.[3] The net effect was to make more legitimate capitalist development strategies in Africa, even if the means strongly impinged upon the capital and profitability of foreign capital.

The second oil price explosion of 1979–80, occurring in the context of already declining export commodity prices, unleashed a more severe crisis than that of the 1970s. Huge new balance of payments deficits were experienced by most African states, as they were confronted with highly priced oil imports that often consumed 30 to 40 percent of total imports and inflation in other imports. In 1981–84 a major recession occurred in the OECD countries, creating huge declines in export volumes and in commodity prices to levels not seen since the depression of the 1930s. In addition, there were massive increases in real interest rates on existing debt as the U.S. and other industrial countries used monetarist means to choke off inflation.

In this environment, African countries in general were plunged into recession. Confronted with huge balance-of-payments deficits and declines in real aid levels and a sharp slowdown in commercial bank lending (to those few African countries that were credit-worthy), many African countries were compelled to approach the IMF for loans to cover the deficits and to maintain moderate levels of economic activity. During 1980–84, the gross domestic product (GDP) of sub-Saharan African countries declined by 1.1–1.4 percent, per year, per capita GDP by about 4.4 percent, export volume by 7.4 percent annually, and import volume by 5.9 percent annually, with the latter strongly undercutting growth.[4] Africa's oil exporters fared better initially, but ultimately did less well (with average GDP's of −2.8 percent per year, 1980–84), as the world recession led to sharp falls in oil consumption and, thereafter, in prices. The plunge in the terms of trade for the exports of the poorest African countries from 1970 on continued in the 1980s, making continued loans imperative in order to finance minimal import levels (the poorest are those eligible for International Development Association soft loans).

Sub-Saharan African countries increased their international borrowing from roughly $16–20 billion in 1975 to $56 billion by 1980, a three-fold increase in five years, on which interest rates turned from negative to positive. These much higher interest and principal repayments made it difficult or impossible for many African states to maintain their annual debt service payments (annual interest and principal payments) in the face of contracting export revenues. Overall, African debt continued to climb sharply in the 1980s as a result of new loans and rescheduling of old loans. Sub-Saharan African debt climbed from about $56 billion in 1980 to $79 billion in 1983, $82.7 billion in 1984, $95.98 billion in 1985, $112.6 billion in 1986, $137.7 billion in 1987, and $139 billion in 1988.[5] However, *net transfers* (loan disbursements minus repayments of interest and principal) did not grow in a like manner. Net transfers varied (including IMF loans): $1.76 billion in 1984, − $825 million in 1985 (− $1.59 billion excluding IMF), $2.07 b. in 1986, $3.34 b. in 1987, and $1.34 b. in 1988.[6] A very substantial part of all new lending, by governments and multilateral agencies, was to repay old debt or pay off commercial arrears. In 1987, moreover 54 percent of the sub-Saharan debt was owed by the poorest (IDA) countries (see Table 6.1), 32 percent by the region's middle-income oil exporters, and 14 percent by the middle-income oil importers. In 1988, the poorest owed 57 percent of the larger debt (Table 6.1). The poorest countries are more deeply indebted, in terms of their debt service ratio (debt service as a percentage of exports) or as a percentage of GDP. But their debt structure is somewhat more concessional, with a larger amount (57 percent) owed at nonmarket, low-interest rates.

However, the real measure of Africa's debt burden is not total size but ability to service the debt. Debt service obligations in the 1980s have been impossible for many African countries to meet. From January 1980 to September 1989, twenty-seven of the forty-four sub-Saharan African countries have had to have their debts rescheduled a total of 121 times, with some countries having to reschedule debt payments four, six, and eight times (Table 6.1). The average debt service ratio (payments as a percent of exports) for sub-Saharan African countries rose from 7 percent in 1975 to 11 percent in 1980, 23 percent in 1983, and 30 percent in 1985, with debt service *obligations* (vs. payments made) actually higher. Debt service obligations in 1986 were 45 percent of export revenues, falling to 36 percent in 1987, and to 49 percent for the poorest countries. As Table 6.1 notes, the IDA countries paid $2.69 billion in 1988 and were scheduled to pay $7.3 billion in 1989, or 43 percent of export earnings, while other sub-Saharan countries paid $4.7 billion in 1988 and were scheduled to pay $11.1 billion in 1989, or 51 percent of their exports. The inability of African countries to service these debts in the 1980s has not been unrelated to the major declines in export commodity prices (e.g., oil, cocoa, coffee, and copper) and have been reflected in the multiple debt reschedulings and in the large number of African countries that have fallen in arrears on interest payments. Sub-Saharan country arrears totalled $5 billion in 1987, or over 50 percent of the actual payments made.[7]

In this environment of economic stagnation and balance-of-payments crises in 1980 and 1981, orthodox neo-classical economists unleashed their counterattack against the strongly statist development models which predominated in

Table 6.1
Debt, Debt Service, and Debt Reschedulings of African Countries

	GNP per capita 1988 US$	Total debt per capita 1988 US$	Total debt, 1988 All creditors (US$ millions)	Total debt, 1988 Official creditors (%)	Use of IMF credit (US$ millions)	Long-term debt service Actual, 1988 (US$ millions)	Long-term debt service Scheduled, 1989 (US$ millions)	'89 scheduled/ 1988 exports (%)	Multilateral rescheduling Jan. 1980 to Sept. 1989
IDA-only Sub-Saharan Africa									
Benin, People's Republic	390	237	1055	71	4	17	88	26	1
Burkina Faso	230	101	866	93	3	36	57	17	0
Burundi	230	154	793	96	33	35	44	30	0
Cape Verde	910	378	133	95	0	7	11	31	0
Central African Republic	390	241	673	94	50	11	34	15	4
Chad	160	64	345	91	17	6	9	4	0
Comoros	440b	450	199	94	0	0	10	48	0
Djibouti	1010b	480	183	85	0	13	14	9	2
Equatorial Guinea	340	504	200	95	14	8	13	29	0
Ethiopia	120	65	2978	89	55	238	316	43	0
Gambia, The	220	298	327	88	35	13	19	14	2
Ghana	400	221	3099	95	762	204	242	25	0
Guinea	350b	386	2563	90	61	143	269	35	3
Guinea-Bissau	160b	450	423	92	3	7	27	91	1
Kenya	360	256	5888	78	455	475	667	32	0
Lesotho	410b	168	281	98	5	22	27	7	0
Liberia	450b	680	1632	75	309	14	158	30	6
Madagascar	180	320	3602	93	190	161	405	89	8
Malawi	160	165	1349	93	106	63	67	18	5
Mali	220	259	2067	96	74	47	46	18	1
Mauritania	480	1089	2076	91	71	111	185	34	4
Mozambique	100	294	4405	79	41	27	489	0	3
Niger	310	249	1742	79	95	131	181	47	8
Rwanda	310b	95	632	93	4	17	24	11	0
Sao Tome and Principe	280b	839	99	92	0	2	11	92	0
Senegal	630	506	3617	89	318	249	380	27	9

Sierra Leone	240	185	727	83	109	8	37	34	4
Somalia	160	346	2035	94	165	4	118	112	2
Sudan	340	499	11853	63	905	63	858	68	7
Tanzania	150	191	4729	86	69	88	464	86	2
Togo	370	360	1210	91	78	91	63	13	9
Uganda	280	119	1925	86	252	43	169	56	4
Zaire	170	252	8474	85	786	165	1272	53	13
Zambia	300	868	6498	78	940	176	481	48	4
Total IDA-only	280	256	78682	83	6007	2695	7259	43	102
Other Sub-Saharan Africa									
Botswana	1270[b]	429	499	99	0	74	78	5	0
Cameroon	1010	377	4229	70	100	569	621	33	1
Congo, People's Republic	930	2268	4763	53	15	261	904	82	2
Cote d'Ivoire	740	1219	14125	38	509	1085	2455	74	7
Gabon	2970	2473	2663	55	133	88	450	28	4
Mauritius	1810	822	861	84	103	147	100	6	0
Nigeria	290	279	30718	72	0	1984	6082	78	5
Seychelles	3800	2338	159	61	0	13	19	9	0
Swaziland	790	360	265	97	2	35	32	5	0
Zimbabwe	660	287	2659	79	70	474	408	22	0
Total other	450	411	60941	63	932	4730	11149	51	19

Source: World Bank, World Debt Tables, 1989–90, Supplemental Report (1990).

Africa, whether in substantially capitalist or state "socialist" regimes (strongly statist means here that the government's macro-economic policy had a broad influence, that it taxed agricultural exports for investment elsewhere, and had launched numerous state enterprises in various sectors). The attack was articulated in the World Bank's Accelerated Development in Sub-Saharan Africa: An Agenda for Action in 1981 and in many other analyses. The predominant development policies were strongly criticized for ignoring the African comparative advantage in agricultural and other exports, pushing inefficient state import substitution industrialization, regulating markets and trade in ways that were inefficient, ineffective, and that obstructed price signals. Thus the policies led to inefficient allocations of scarce capital and a stifling of entrepreneurial initiative by following damaging macro-economic policies. These policies were cited as high-deficit spending, over-valued exchange rates, and excessive tariffs and quotas that curtailed exports and growth while fueling inflation and excessive demand, especially for imports. The powerful positions of the U.S. and the United Kingdom in the World Bank and other international lending institutions were used to stiffen economic orthodoxy in analysis and the conditions under which loans would be extended. Moreover, the U.S. under Ronald Reagan, strongly blunted attempts to increase foreign aid by governments and to increase lending by the IMF and World Bank by curtailing efforts to expand the capital base (a policy later reluctantly abandoned). Developing countries, it was argued, should look to "the magic of the market" and foreign capital if they wanted economic growth.

The debate between orthodox and nonorthodox or leftist developmental strategies ranged around several major issues. The first, which persists, has been over whether external factors—such as world demand, terms of trade, dependency relations, and multinational corporate behavior—or internal factors—such as state macro-economic policies and management performance—were decisive in economic growth and development performance. The second issue involved market vs. statist orientations to development. The World Bank launched a sustained, fairly sophisticated, and often empirically-supported attack upon the waste and inefficiencies involved in the performance of many state enterprises and regulatory mechanisms, seeking a restoration of market means in state management, greater economic rationality, and a strong reduction in state economic roles.[8] The World Bank launched a series of studies on state enterprises in Africa and elsewhere, gathering some systematic data.[9] There was ample evidence in Africa that many state enterprises (but by no means all) are very high cost producers, with massive protection, highly dependent on imports for inputs of all kinds, highly favored in access to markets and foreign exchange, and often poorly managed and a major source of corruption. A third major debate occurred between advocates of import-substitution industrialization (ISI) and export-led development. The World Bank and neoclassical analysts pointed with joy to the four Asian tigers (South Korea, Taiwan, Singapore, Hong Kong) and their exceptional rates of export and economic growth; they sought to demonstrate empirically that the more outwardly oriented a country's macro-economic policies were, the higher its rates of growth, savings and investment, manufacturing value added, and employment (though the data did not really show this).[10] ISI advocates in Africa, who did not believe that their countries could successfully penetrate sophisticated, competitive Western markets, nonetheless wanted to diversify their countries' productive base, create backward and forward linkages in the economy, spur employment, and reduce the great dependence upon foreign markets for imports as well as exports. A fourth debate (which neoclassical economists generally ignore) has involved whether a development strategy should be one which was generally egalitarian or inegalitarian in its distribution of benefits. Few analysts any longer simply argue the probability of trickle-down and ignore the great increases in inequality under rapid capitalist development. (The World Bank itself during the 1970s embraced the concept of providing some basic needs to the poorest 40 percent of the population in various loans but abandoned this idea entirely in the more conservative 1980s.)

Ultimately, the World Bank and neoclassical economists were arguing the virtues of the capitalist marketplace, reliance upon foreign and domestic capital to stimulate growth in key sectors, comparative advantage exports as engines of development, and closer integration of African economies into the world capitalist political economy. Many readings of African economic history in the twentieth century do not stimulate confidence in these options.

The debate over strategies and policies for responding to Africa's development malaise has been intense and has involved the World Bank in major disputes with economists, governments, and international institutions, such as the Economic Commission for Africa. Something of a consensus has developed around the idea of "adjustment with growth," but this requires levels of external finance and international demand for Africa's exports that were not present in the 1980s.

Many of the elements of the critical diagnosis of Africa's problems applied well to some countries but little to others which had, indeed, pursued the highly-favored strategies but nonetheless were experiencing severe economic crises in the late 1970s and early 1980s. Table 6.2 provides some indication of the performance of the Cote d'Ivoire and Kenya, which have long pursued the recommended World Bank policies (favoring agriculture, exports, and foreign capital) in the 1960s to the 1980s, and Nigeria, Zimbabwe, Algeria, and Ghana. Nigeria and Algeria, which are major gas and oil producers, as well as Cote d'Ivoire and Kenya, tended to have relatively high growth rates during 1965–80, ranging from 6.4 percent to 8.0 percent per annum, although in all cases they had lower growth rates during the latter part of the 1970s and early 1980s, especially Nigeria (see GDP, 1973–84, Table 6.2). Ghana committed most of the policy errors criticized by the World Bank, while also suffering a severe decline in terms of trade. Its economy performed very poorly during the 1965–80 period and experienced negative growth during 1973–84.[11] When one takes into account the high rates of population growth of these countries (Table 6.2), virtually all have negative per capita GDP growth rates during 1973–84, except

Table 6.2
Population, Income, and Economic Growth in Some African Countries

	Popu-lation mid/1987 M.	Popu. Growth Rate % 1980/87	GNP per capita $ 1982	GNP per capita $ 1984	GNP per capita $ 1987	GDP[a] 1965/80	GDP[a] 1973/84	GDP[a] 1980/87	Agriculture 1965/80	Agriculture 80/87	Industry 1965/80	Industry 80/87	Manufacturing[b] 1965/80	Manufacturing[b] 80/87
								Average Annual Growth Rate %						
Algeria	23.1	3.1	2350	2410	2680	7.5	6.4	3.8	5.6	6.0	8.1	4.3	9.5	8.5
Cote d'Ivoire	11.1	4.2	950	610	740	6.8	3.7	2.2 (-0.3)	3.3	1.6	10.4	-2.4	9.1	8.2
Ghana	13.6	3.4	360	350	390	1.4	-0.9	1.4+ (-0.7)	1.6	0.0[f]	1.4	0.1	2.5	1.3
Kenya	22.1	4.1	390	310	330	6.4	4.4	3.8	4.9	3.4	9.8	3.0	10.5	4.3
Nigeria	107	3.4	860	730	370	8.0	0.7	-1.7	1.7	0.6	13.4[c]	-4.4[c]	14.6	-2.1
Zimbabwe	9.0	3.7	850	760	580	4.4	1.7	2.4	1.7	2.3	[e]	1.4	[e]	1.8

[a] Changing the cluster of years for these data can alter greatly the average figures, somewhat surprisingly. Note that the Ivory Coast average GDP % growth is 2.2% for 1980–87 but was − 0.3% for 1980–86. There are also big changes for Ghana and Nigeria when one compares the 1980–86 (in parentheses) to 1980–87.

[b] Manufacturing is included within the category of industry.

[c] Data for Nigeria under industry (but not manufacturing) reflect large positive and negative changes in oil production levels and prices.

[d] The large declines in many instances reflect not only economic problems but large devaluation of the local currencies against the dollar.

[e] Zimbabwe had relatively high growth in industry and manufacturing during 1965–80 under the white minority regime that faced economic sanctions.

[f] Ghana's GDP and agricultural growth were high during 1984–88; GDP rose over 5% per year.

Sources: World Bank, World Development Report(s), 1986, 1987, 1989, Statistical Tables.

Algeria. In contrast to Cote d'Ivoire and Kenya, Ghana and Nigeria neglected export crops and, to a lesser degree, food crops, and had low agricultural growth in the 1970s and the 1980s (except for Ghana, after 1983). Algeria and Nigeria both financed substantial industrial and manufacturing growth from oil export proceeds. Cote d'Ivoire and Kenya, in contrast, financed much of their economic and industrial growth from agricultural exports, which were diversified over this period, by attracting foreign capital and encouraging local capital.[12] Zimbabwe experienced fairly rapid development under an ISI program under white minority rule until international sanctions and guerrilla warfare weakened the regime, but, despite its small size, it has the most diversified economy and export base of any of the countries (suggesting ISI policies can be effective even in a small economy). In general, Cote d'Ivoire, Kenya, and, to a lesser degree, Nigeria have welcomed foreign private capital and fairly strongly encouraged local capital.[13]

Some of the strongest and most export-diversified economies in the 1960–80 period, Cote d'Ivoire and Kenya, experienced severe crises in the late 1970s and 1980s despite the pursuit of fairly orthodox economic policies. Two points follow. First, the World Bank's and orthodox critiques of Africa's development strategies failed to address the range of African experience and ignored the efforts made with orthodox policies. Second, the crises confronted by Cote d'Ivoire and Kenya have in significant measure been a function of uncontrollable external factors: weakening external demand, elimination of commercial lending to Africa, drastic declines in terms of trade, and high international interest rates.

THE IMPACT OF STRUCTURAL ADJUSTMENT POLICIES

There has been considerable resistance to the World Bank's structural adjustment policies and, particularly, to the severe range of conditions attached to program or sector loans. These conditions appear to have become more intensive and extensive, as they have been applied to everything from budget deficits as a percentage of GDP to abolition of utility subsidies, liquidation or privatization of certain state enterprises by certain dates, liberalization of import barriers (with their harsh impacts upon local producers), and reforms of road repairs, health services, and the financing and structure of education.

The World Bank made a major effort to justify its policy preferences and impositions in a 1989 study that argued that African countries with strong World Bank SAPs, especially those unaffected by strong "shocks," had much higher performance in 1985–87 than in 1980–84 and than countries with weak or no SAPs in such areas as GDP growth, agricultural production, export growth, import growth, real domestic investment, and per capita consumption.[14] The Economic Commission for Africa (ECA) quickly mounted an important critique of World Bank arguments and data. It criticized strongly its analytical efforts to isolate SAP reform from other major factors and assessed severely its methods and uses of data: categories and classifications were called inconsistent and ill-defined (e.g., what is a strong "shock"?); the crucial criteria for the crucial distinction between countries with strong and weak SAPs were not provided; the selection of base and reference periods was not uniform; and the ECA argued that the World Bank seriously misrepresented data on the terms of trade (with the ECA arguing that it was lower in 1987 than in 1970 and the World Bank arguing that it was still 15 percent higher). By reworking the World Bank's own performance data with different base assumptions, the ECA was able to argue that the countries with strong SAPs had a negative (− .53) growth rate, countries with weak SAPs a GDP increase of 2 percent, and those with no SAP a growth rate of 3.5 percent.[15] The ECA also argued, properly, that it was entirely possible that it was the shift in official development assistance (ODA) in the mid-1980s to countries with SAPs that permitted higher performance (if there was such a thing), since foreign exchange and import scarcities were among the most crucial constraints on economic performance.

Despite the important ECA criticisms, the very wretchedness of economic conditions in Africa in the 1980s makes it important to consider if the structural adjustment reforms had a discernible positive impact. Indeed, part of the World Bank's manipulation of its data was to attempt to isolate other factors: there was particular concern to control for the sharp decline in oil prices in 1986, since the five sub-Saharan oil exporters account for roughly 60 percent of sub-Saharan Africa's GDP. It is clear that certain reforms have had a positive impact. There was a fairly sharp decline in real effective exchange rates among African countries (a consequence of IMF stabilization policies as well) and a decline in the black market or parallel exchange rate as a percentage of the official rates. For the principal agricultural export commodities in thirty of Africa's forty-five countries, the average taxation declined significantly over the 1980s, which meant higher shares of the market price to producers. Indeed, agriculture (in Africa generally) experienced higher average growth in 1985–88 than in the last fifteen years, but then weather and rains in most parts of Africa were much better than in the 1970s. And in the area of state enterprises, World Bank policies had started a lengthy effort to make state enterprises more accountable and efficient by a variety of means: adoption of accounting and auditing systems, price setting, greater autonomy, greater managerial control, performance contracts, management contracts, and programs of rehabilitation. In addition, in thirteen countries there was agreement to liquidate some seventy-eight enterprises, while in another nineteen countries there was a program to privatize some eighty enterprises[16]. Countries with strong SAPs experienced much lower changes in export unit prices than countries with weak or no SAPs (− 8.2 percent during 1985–87 vs 6.7 percent), significantly higher export earnings if oil exporters are excluded from the strong SAP country category but a greater loss in terms of trade (excluding oil exporters, − 4.7 percent vs 1.4 percent). Countries with strong SAPs during 1985–87 had lower inflation rates than those with no or weak SAPs and substantially higher real export crop and local food crop prices. And, as noted, countries with strong SAPs not affected by strong shocks (excludes oil exporters) had substantially higher GDP growth rates, according to the World Bank, than those with weak or no SAPs (3.8 percent vs 1.5 percent) and significantly higher performance in other categories.

The World Bank did not report whether layoffs were higher in countries with stronger SAPs, or whether health and educational expenses for use of these facilities were higher, or real wages lower—all matters that profoundly affect how people live.

Of the six countries whose economic performance is noted in Tables 6.2 and 6.3, four are regarded as having strong SAPs (Cote d'Ivore, Ghana, Kenya, Nigeria), Zimbabwe's is weak, and Algeria's would have been regarded as strong had it been included. The performance data are not arranged for periods before and after SAPs were adopted. But the impact of SAPs can be briefly assessed using these data and other assessments. Structural adjustment efforts started in Algeria in 1979 when Benjedid Chadli became president, but liberalization has been slow, with resistance posed by party leaders in the previously single-party Front de Liberation Nationale (FLN). As oil and gas prices collapsed in the mid-1980s, the impact of this collapse swamped the reforms made. Oil and gas exports provide 98 percent of Algeria's export earnings. Although Algeria's GDP growth in the 1980–86 period was better than any of the other five countries except Kenya's (3.8 percent), production fell in industry and manufacturing; imports were sharply down throughout the 1980s. To ensure autonomy in economic policymaking, Algeria's leaders resisted seeking IMF funds or rescheduling an increasingly large debt service; in 1986 the debt service ratio rose to 57 percent. Although foreign borrowing has been curtailed and there has been a major decentralization and rationalization of the large state industrial and enterprise sector, growth has continued to decline. Austerity has been continuous and unemployment has increased sharply, with layoffs at state enterprises. Social protests against austerity, rising prices, and unemployment have broken out and shaken the regime, leading Chadli to end the FLN's political monopoly and permit other parties to contest elections.[17] The economy has been gradually opened to local capital; after much delay a major new investment code promulgated in 1990 opened most sectors apart from oil exploration to foreign capital.

In some senses Kenya has pursued structural adjustment policies since the 1960s.[18] But the SAPs adopted in the 1980s have had significant impacts in creating positive real interest rates, a market exchange rate, and lowering wages; it has contributed to the regime being able to offer high price incentives to agricultural producers.[19] Lower growth and high levels of corruption have made it more difficult to attract foreign capital.

While Nigeria has adopted, since 1984, a very strong SAP, the effects of its reforms have been swamped by the collapse of oil prices and export volumes, leading to a prolonged recession throughout the 1980s. Like Algeria, another oil producer, and the Ivory Coast, Nigeria borrowed heavily from commercial bankers during the glory days of high commodity prices. All three have extremely heavy debt service ratios, which severely impede their growth. In 1989 Nigeria owed over $6 billion in debt service on its almost $31 billion debt, or 78 percent of its export earnings (this amount was rescheduled to less; see Table 6.1). Nigeria's growth has remained anemic, despite very strong efforts to cut government employees, to rationalize and privatize the state sector, and to increase taxes and user fees for various public services. Regular government efforts to increase gasoline prices and university costs have led to nation-wide outbreaks of strikes and protests by union members and students, with continuous closings of Nigeria's universities and arrests of union leaders.

The Ivorian "economic miracle" of the 1970s is a miracle no longer, though it continues to produce gargantuan cocoa crops (with smaller crops of coffee, palm oil, and bananas), which drive down world prices. The Cote d'Ivoire has been less able or willing to implement all phases of its structural adjustment policies. But it is the devastating collapse of cocoa prices which has made it recurringly impossible to pay its debts. President Houphouet Boigny stopped making interest payments in 1988. He resisted strongly a reduction in prices to coffee and cocoa producers, the fundamental condition for a renewal of IMF and World Bank lending, a decision finally made in mid-1989. But the economy has been devastated for some years, and French capital is fleeing.

The economic disaster of the 1970s, Ghana, is the World Bank's success of the 1980s, with an average GDP growth of 6 percent for six straight years, from 1984–89. It has adopted SAPs in many sectors to rehabilitate a devastated infrastructure and productive capacity. Despite a renewal of investment in the gold mines, rehabilitated roads, transportation, and railways, an elimination of budget deficits, an end to price controls, higher prices to cocoa producers (which has led to a revival in cocoa production and exports), and a very substantial expansion in food output, life remains miserable for most Ghanians. Urban real wages have risen somewhat but remain at roughly 20–30 percent of their level in the early 1970s. Inflation remains high, as devaluations continue in order to be able to pay the cocoa producers high prices. There has been a very sharp shift in incomes from the already depressed urban workers to the rural producers. Previously unattainable goods are now widely available but beyond the means of virtually all Ghanaians. All income groups spend 70 percent of their income on food alone. As in Cote d'Ivoire and Nigeria, stabilization and structural adjustment are accursed words, though the reforms were imperative in Ghana.[20]

THE RENEWAL OF OPPORTUNITIES FOR DOMESTIC AND FOREIGN CAPITAL

The debt crises, slow growth, and structural adjustment programs have all animated a push for a reduction in state roles in the economy and a stimulation of the private sector, as a less costly, potentially more efficient engine of economic growth. Here we will look at three aspects of this renewal of opportunity for a strategy of capitalist accumulation: first, new efforts to create an environment conducive to capitalist investment and production; second, the current evidence that private investment activity, foreign or domestic, has been increasing in the 1980s under SAPs; and, third, to what extent the privatization process has led to increased private capitalist activity.

In some senses, it has been exceptionally difficult to create a positive capitalist investment environment in Africa in the 1980s. The very economic stagnation and debt crises that have created SAPs and the pressure for a renewal of capitalist activity have created major disincentives. Many of the economies have been in recession, with demand for much production low. Many existing industries are operating at exceptionally low levels of capacity utilization. Government expenditures which have been a major source of domestic demand have been cut in real terms in many countries; and government ministries are in arrears in paying for goods and services. The stabilization and SAPs imposed by the IMF and World Bank have required sharp reductions in money supply and bank liquidity, making it increasingly difficult in many countries to obtain bank credit for buying out existing businesses or starting up new ones. Protests of inadequate credit have been made by businessmen in Ghana, Cote d'Ivoire, and Nigeria, among other countries. Moreover, it has been a major part of IMF and World Bank strategy to increase local savings, which has meant that they have insisted that the government raise interest rates to the point where they exceeded inflation, which is often 25–35 percent. So credit, if available, has become extremely expensive.

Moreover, past histories of hostility to foreign or local capital, failure to pay debts and difficulties in repatriating profits fail to make Africa a friendly investment environment, in contrast to many other regions and countries. Economic nationalism has been extremely strong in many African countries; even economic nationalists, as distinct from radicals, are unenthusiastic about the new entry of foreign capital, which they may associate with colonialism (especially if the firm is from the ex-metropole).

In addition, some major characteristics of many African economies makes them unattractive to foreign investors. In general, most African countries have very small markets. Relative to other areas, such as East Asia and Latin America, African economies are high-wage and have low productivity.

Nonetheless, many governments with SAPs have been willing or have been repeatedly urged to create an investment environment more conductive to domestic and foreign private capital. In many African countries, often after considerable delay and intra-party or intra-governmental infighting, new investment codes have been announced and, after more delays, promulgated. In mid-1989, the long-time Zimbabwe Finance Minister, Bernard Chidzero, announced a new investment code that relaxes controls on profits and profit repatriation. Chidzero announced that this step was the beginning of the liberalization of Zimbabwe's highly regulated economy. The announcement coincided with the signing of investment agreements with the World Bank and most Western industrial countries as well as the creation of a one-stop invest-ment center, where all permissions could be obtained and decisions made within ninety days.[21] In early 1990 Algeria's FLN government reversed three decades of socialism and economic nationalism to announce an investment de-cree that permitted foreign capital into most sectors as well as foreign banks. Under the prior investment decree, foreign capital could be invested only in joint ventures, in which 51 percent control remained with the state. After sev-eral years of discussion and delays, in early 1990 Nigeria also reversed almost two decades of economic nationalism to open up prior sectors reserved for Ni-gerian capital and to permit 100 percent ownership in a wide range of economic activities; this action reversed provisions of the Nigerian Enterprises Promotion Decrees of 1972 and 1977. However, despite much lobbying by existing firms, they cannot increase their share holding if it is registered under the older de-crees. One hundred percent of foreign control is permitted when at least $2.6 million has been invested.[22] Many other African countries have also promul-gated similar investment codes. Others are moving to make the process of for-eign investment a much simpler and less interminable business; hence governments are encouraged to establish a single office where all those minis-tries involved in such decisions can be consulted.

In addition to the investment codes, African governments are engaged in many other aspects of economic liberalization that will make their environments more attractive to businesses. However, trade liberalization has, in a number of coun-tries, occurred under circumstances of great difficulty for domestic firms, driving some out of business, as in the case of some textile firms in Ghana.

The efforts of individual governments are encouraged and coordinated by many international institutions, including the World Bank, the International Fi-nance Corporation (which has assisted lending for capitalist firms since the mid-1950s); and a range of official and unofficial African institutions, e.g., the African Development Bank and the African Business Roundtable, established by thirty successful African entrepreneurs; both the ADB and the African Business Roundtable have been holding conferences to promote more communication between and interest among entrepreneurs.

What evidence is there that private investment activity, foreign or domestic, has been increasing in Africa? There have been high levels of investment in only one of the countries, Nigeria, in its oil industry. The one year in which Algeria received a high level of foreign direct investment, 1986, it was also for the oil industry. There is little data on Cote d'Ivoire, which in years past received significant French private investment, but other evidence indicates a sharp re-duction of this French investment in the 1980s. Kenya has also been a major recipient of foreign direct investment, which in 1982, 1984, and 1985 was higher than in 1970. Ghana and Zimbabwe have received miniscule levels of investment. The investments that were made in Ghana in the 1984–89 period in gold mining took the form of foreign loans borrowed by the local company as a means of protecting its capital.

Most foreign direct investment in developing countries has tended to be highly concentrated in a few countries. In 1986, of forty-one low income countries reported in the World Bank's *World Development Report*, net foreign investment is reported for nineteen, for $1.9 billion, of which three Asian countries received $1.79 billion or 93.6 percent. Of low middle-income countries, data for thirty of the thirty-five countries indicate net foreign investment of $3.99 billion, of which nine countries received $3.27 billion, or 82 percent. Of the upper middle-income developing countries, data was reported for nineteen of the twenty-four; twelve of these nineteen received $4.797 billion or 101.6 percent of the total (some of the others had net capital outflows). Hence, of sixty-eight developing countries for which data was reported, twenty-four of the countries received 92.8 percent of the net foreign investment. In sub-Saharan Africa, data was reported for twenty of the forty-four countries in 1986 (excluding South Africa); most of the countries for which data was not reported received little if any foreign investment. Of the 20 who received $579 million (or 5.45 percent of total net foreign investment in 1986 in developing countries), seven of the twenty received 91.7 percent. What is significant is that this large-scale investment all went to five oil-exporting countries, primarily for oil investment, and two major mineral producers (Botswana and Chad).[23] In 1987 net foreign direct investment in sub-Saharan Africa was reported for twenty-one of the forty-four countries. Of the seven who received more than $20 million, they received $745 million, or 110 percent, of the total (since there were large net outflows of foreign investment in three countries). Oil or mineral extraction investments were involved in six of these seven countries.[24] Therefore, unless an African country offers opportunities for investments in oil or large-scale mineral extraction, it has little opportunity for attracting significant foreign direct investment unless the country has a very large population and market, as Nigeria has.

There is other fragmentary evidence. The International Finance Corporation in its most recent annual report indicated the difficulties of inducing foreign capital to invest in Africa. And French and European investors in Francophone Africa have become extremely negative about business prospects in recent years, leading to capital flight from the French African currency, the CFA, into the French franc (they fear a devaluation of the CFA) and a drying up of investment. In 1987 French credit and foreign investment in Africa fell more sharply than at any time since independence of these countries in 1960. In the early 1980s, credits and investments were averaging 12 billion French francs, while in 1987 they were a negative 3.3 billion. French official flows tripled from 1981 to 1987, but the reform program clearly was not attracting French capital.[25] In the three year period 1985–87, there was a 25 percent fall in investment commitments of 1500 firms long established in French-speaking Africa. African subsidiaries of French banks which were controlled by Africans were failing in the late 1980s, and the French government-owned parent, the Paris National Bank, wanted to withdraw completely from its African commitments but was not permitted to do so by the French government.[26] In the decade 1979–89, no less than twenty-three British companies with industrial investments in Africa withdrew from Nigeria, an enormous blow to Nigeria's investment and industrial efforts. Even greater withdrawals were reported from Zimbabwe.[27]

It is in the area of privatization that significant progress has been made both in reducing and rationalizing the state investment role and in stimulating an increased role for domestic and foreign private capital. Privatization has been a slow progress for many countries, for example, Ghana. It has involved major efforts to assess the worth of existing companies and the devising of a strategy regarding what to keep, liquidate, or sell in whole or in part. This process is also very political, involving some advocates within state agencies, some local business investors interested in the investment potential, and strategic groups within society which have argued against selling out the state or people's property. In Kenya, where capitalism is well-established and a strong local capitalist class exists, privatization has actually been slow. In part, selling off state companies means selling them from an African government to an Asian business group or to African entrepreneurs who are from an ethnic group considered the competitors of those in power. In Nigeria the process of privatization is well under way, but many companies get sold not to the private sector but to other state agencies. Northern elites are uninterested in seeing southern businessmen acquire state property. Nonetheless, large numbers of state corporations are being sold, in whole or part (equity investments, shares sold on the stock exchange). In the Ivory Coast, more quietly, a large number of state corporations, since 1979, have been either liquidated or sold to Ivoirian or private investors.[28]

CONCLUSION

The economic stagnation and debt crises in Africa in the late 1970s and early 1980s opened the door to Western countries and international banks to reassert an influence over African economic policies. Animated essentially by a neoclassical economic vision of appropriate economic policies, Western countries have required African countries to accept economic reforms that emphasize market mechanisms and market forces. It is unclear thus far what the impact of these reforms will be. But they have already created the opportunity for the ideas of capitalism to be reintroduced in a powerful fashion in African economies. There is little evidence that foreign capital will demonstrate a strong interest in direct investment in African countries, except where there exist opportunities for mineral or oil investments. Foreign capital actually appears to be fleeing African economies, given the extremely poor economic conditions. However, in a number of countries one can now expect domestic capitalists to emerge as a much more important economic, social, and political force than they have previously. Elsewhere, in the absence of foreign or domestic capital, states will continue to play a dominant role in economic life.

NOTES

1. See World Bank, *Accelerated Development in Sub-Saharan Africa* (1981), especially chapters 3–5.

2. See Robert Wood, *From Marshall Plan to Debt Crisis* (Berkeley: University of California Press, 1986); Sidney Dell, "Stabilization: the Political Economy of Overkill," in *The Political Economy of Development and Underdevelopment*, 3rd. ed., ed. Charles Wilber (New York: Random House, 1984), 146–168; Tony Killick, et.al., *The IMF and Stabilization* (London: Heinemann, 1984).

3. See Adebayo Adedeji, ed., *Indigenizarion of African Economies* (New York: Africana Publishing Company, 1981) for chapters on Egypt, Zambia, Ghana, Nigeria, Kenya, Tanzania, Ethiopia, and Senegal. See also Thomas Biersteker, *Multinationals, the State, and Control of the Nigerian Economy* (Princeton: Princeton University Press, 1987), which examines indigenization as the outcome of a continuing political process in which state nationalists sought to reduce Nigeria's dependence, local capital developed some powerful stakes, and multinational capital eventually found some important ways to protect its interests.

4. World Bank, *Africa's Adjustment and Growth in the 1980s* (1989), p. 6; Thomas Callaghy, "Debt and Structural Adjustment in Africa: Realities and Possibilities," *Issue*, XVI, 2 (1988), p. 11.

5. World Bank, *World Debt Tables*, 1989–90, 1st Supplement (1990), p. 6.

6. Ibid., p. 6.

7. World Bank, *Africa's Adjustment and Growth in the 1980s*, p. 17.

8. World Bank, *World Development Report*, 1983, chapters 4–11.

9. John Nellis, "Public Enterprises in Sub-Saharan Africa," Discussion Paper No. 1 (Washington, D.C.: World Bank).

10. World Bank, *World Development Report*, 1987, chapters 4–9, especially pp.78–94.

11. See Richard Feinberg and Edmar Bacha, "When Supply and Demand Don't Intersect: Latin America and the Bretton Woods Institutions in the 1980s," *Development and Change*, 19, 3 (July, 1988), 371–400; "External Finance and Policy Adjustment in Africa," special issue of *Development and Change*, 17, 3 (July, 1986), with general assessments and case studies of Zaire, Sudan, Malawi, Mozambique, and Kenya; Laurence Harris, "Conceptions of the IMF's Role in Africa," and John Loxley, "The IMF and World Bank Conditionality and Sub-Saharan Africa," both in *World Recession and the Food Crisis in Africa*, ed. Peter Laurence (London and Boulder: James Currey and Westview Press, 1986), pp. 83–95 and 96–103; Gerald Helleiner, "The Question of Conditionality," in *African Debt and Financing*, eds. Carol Lancaster and John Williams (Washington, D.C.: Institute of International Economics, 1986), 63–91; and Paul Mosley, "Agricultural Performance in Kenya Since 1970: Has the World Bank Got it Right?" *Development and Change*, 17, 3 (July, 1986), 513–530; ODI, "Commodity Prices: Investing in Decline?" Briefing Paper (London: Overseas Development Institute, March, 1988), which severely critiques the World Bank emphasis on continued investment by developing countries in primary commodities where there are already many producers.

12. John Ravenhill, "Adjustment with Growth: A Fragile Consensus," *Journal of Modern African Studies*, 26, 2 (July, 1988), 179–210.

13. See A. Adedeji, ed., *Indigenization of African Economies*; Sayre Schatz, *Nigerian Capitalism* (Berkeley: University of California Press, 1977); Biersteker, *Multinationals, the State, and Control of the Nigerian Economy*; Paul Kennedy, *African Capitalism* (New York: Cambridge University Press, 1988); Paul Lubeck, ed., *The African Bourgeoisie: Capitalist Development in Nigeria, Kenya, and the Ivory Coast* (Boulder: Lynne Rienner, Publishers, 1987), with historical and contemporary chapters on capitalist development in each country; Nicole Swainson, *The Development of Corporate Capitalism in Kenya* (Berkeley: University of California Press, 1980); R. Kaplinsky, "Capitalist Accumulation in the Periphery—the Kenyan Case Re-Examined," *Review of African Political Economy*, No. 17 (1980).

14. World Bank, *Africa's Adjustment and Growth in the 1980s*, pp. 29–30.

15. *West Africa*, May 15, 1989, p. 791.

16. World Bank, *Africa's Adjustment and Growth*, pp. 20–26.

17. Rhys Payne, "Economic Crisis and Policy Reform in the 1980s: North African Development Strategies in Transition," in *Polity and Society in Contemporary North Africa*, ed. M. Habeeb and I. W. Zartman (Boulder: Westview, 1990).

18. Michael Lofchie, "Structural Adjustment in Kenya and Tanzania," presented to African Studies Association meeting, November, 1989.

19. Martin Godfrey, "Stabilization and Structural Adjustment of the Kenyan Economy, 1975–85: An Assessment of Performance," *Development and Change*, 18, 4 (October, 1987), 595–624.

20. Jon Kraus, "The Political Economy of Structural Adjustment in Ghana," in *Ghana: The Political Economy of Recovery*, ed. Donald Rothchild (Boulder: Lynne Rienner, 1991), pp. 119–155.

21. *New York Times*, May 15, 1989, D8.

22. *African Research Bulletin/Economic*, April 30, 1989, p. 9914; March 30, 1989, p. 9980.

23. World Bank, *World Development Report*, 1986, pp. 250–251.

24. World Bank, *World Development Report*, 1987, pp. 198–199.

25. *West Africa*, March 27, 1989.

26. *African Research Bulletin/Economic*, March 30, 1990, pp. 9878–9879.

27. *West Africa*, July 16, 1990, p. 2118.

28. Thomas Callaghy and Ernest Wilson, III, "Africa: Policy, Reality, or Ritual?" in *The Promise of Privatization*, ed. Raymond Vernon (New York: Council on Foreign Relations, 1988), 179–230.

PART II

STRATEGIES, STRUCTURE, AND PRACTICES

7

The Paradox of Protection and Monopoly in Sub-Saharan Africa

CATHERINE BOONE

In efforts to promote light industrialization, most sub-Saharan African governments use administrative controls over trade to "capture" markets for local
import-substitution industry. Most discussions of import-substitution industrialization in post-colonial Africa focus on the extent to which such policies contribute to long-term development. There has been less analysis of the internal
political forces that determine how trade controls designed to favor import-
substitution industry are forged and implemented in practice. These political
forces, however, may prove to be decisive in determining how official industrialization strategies are translated into concrete government actions that affect
the fortunes of light industry. In sub-Saharan Africa, as elsewhere, the continual
making and re-making of trade policy reflects on-going struggles over terms of
market competition and access. These struggles involve competition between
commercial and industrial interests, local and foreign interests, and consumers
and producers. Because the role of the state in structuring markets in sub-Saharan
Africa is central, competition for markets is played out, in large part, in the
political arena.

This chapter focuses on patterns of economic and political competition which
shape trade policy. The analysis is predicated on the assumption that restrictions
on domestic market competition designed to foster import-substitution industrialization (ISI) generate both "rents" and costs. Rents are distributed by governments to competing claimants in the industrial and commercial sectors. Costs
are imposed on, and felt in most immediate ways, by consumers of locally-
produced and imported manufactured goods. By focusing on struggles over the
allocation of rents and costs associated with ISI, the chapter locates the ISI
process squarely within the context of broader struggles over how state power
is used to distribute the economic burdens and benefits of economic change.

The analysis is concerned primarily with the political dynamics of industrial policy formation and implementation. Industrialists, importers, and those in control of state power (government agents) play the central roles. I focus on the case of textile manufacturing in Senegal, an ex-colony of French West Africa. The particular interest of this case is threefold. First, textile manufacturing was long thought of as "the classic import-substitution industry," and most African countries prioritized the development of local textile sectors in the 1960s and early 1970s. The strains and tensions that have affected the development of textile manufacturing in Senegal are not unique. Second, a basic textile manufacturing industry was established in Senegal before the end of the colonial period. This aspect of the case places ISI as a strategy for African industrialization in proper historical and international context, and thus draws attention to role of colonialism and neo-colonialism in defining many of the political, economic, and social parameters of Africa's contemporary policy dilemmas. Third, trade and monetary regimes governing import flows to Senegal and the rest of ex-French West Africa were and are, in general, even more restrictive and protectionist than those regulating trade elsewhere on the continent. The political dynamics that shape policy formation and implementation are conspicuous in this setting.

Part I of this chapter is an overview of the patterns of political and economic competition that gave rise to import-substitution industrialization in colonial French West Africa. Part II places the analysis market controls designed to promote ISI in the context of Ann Kreuger's and Robert Bates' studies of "non-competitive and administratively-generated rents."[1] This part of the chapter uses the notion of "rent-seeking" to focus attention on the direct relationship between the use of state power and the immediate economic interests of particular manufacturers and importers. Part III illustrates how the on-going struggle over the allocation of rents and costs shaped the development of the textile industry in Dakar, Senegal.[2] Part IV presents conclusions.

Unlike much of the work on industrialization in Africa, this chapter does not explore how ISI affects the structural features and development potential of African economies.[3] And unlike much of the current work on industry in Africa, it is not written from the managerial perspective that prevails.[4] My primary interest is in showing how political forces can shape the adoption and implementation of specific policies that have an immediate and critical impact on the viability of local import-substitution industry. The centrality of the state in the process of development and change is viewed as a necessary and immutable fact of economics in Africa. What is at stake, then, is not the extent to which states intervene in economies, but rather the balance of political forces that determine how state power is used.

PART I: ISI IN HISTORICAL CONTEXT

In sub-Saharan Africa, newly-independent governments adopted ISI as an official development strategy in the 1960s. Development economists provided a theoretical rationale for light industrialization via the "infant industry" approach and argued that injections of private foreign capital into nascent industrial sectors would contribute to the "take-off to self-sustained growth."[5] The World Bank and European development funds pushed the strategy of ISI with enthusiasm and provided African governments with loans to lay an infrastructure that paved the way for foreign investment in import-substitution industry.[6] By the mid-1970s, ISI began to fall from favor in international development ciricles. Export-led growth, not local production for local markets, became the new orthodoxy. In the early 1980s, African governments began to feel the full impact of this change in lenders' (and investors') thinking about manufacturing in the Third World.[7] Yet in spite of the shifting current of development theory and foreign lenders' advice, ISI remains the centerpiece of most African countries' indus-trialization strategies, and import substitution industries remain the bedrock of most countries' manufacturing sectors.[8]

Multilateral lenders' current critique of ISI faults post-colonial African gov-ernments for choosing an industrialization strategy that is high-cost and ineffi-cient. This line of argument frames the discussion in terms of technical and managerial options, and thus directs attention away from the historical origins and political bases of ISI in sub-Saharan Africa. In doing so, it obscures the political and economic forces that not only militate against "restructuring" of existing industry, but also have shaped the actual contours—and inefficiencies—of import-substitution industry in much of Africa.

In Francophone Africa, as in Nigeria and the settler colonies of East Africa, the origins of ISI lie in the last decades of direct colonial rule.[9] In Dakar, the administrative center of the French West African Federation (the AOF), the process was well underway by 1960, when an African government assumed power. The decolonization arrangements that gave birth to most of the new regimes of the former French West African Federation committed them to pushing full speed ahead with ISI. These arrangements protected and promoted the in-terests of established investors in light industry.[10] The strategy of ISI, and vir-tually all the legal and regulatory powers and mechanisms designed to promote it, was inherited from the colonial period.

In the late 1940s and 1950s, trade and investment policies hammered out in the parliament and boardrooms of France promoted ISI in Dakar in its colonial, rather than "developmentalist," incarnation. ISI emerged in the years after World War II to modify, not transform, the basic structures of the colonial import-export economy. This colonial economy was based on the principle of "non-competitive" economic relations between France and its African colonies. It was institutionalized in the increasingly protectionist regime of imperial pref-erence which France imposed on its West Africa colonies in the wake of World War I, the Great Depression, and World War II. A well-stocked arsenal of trade restrictions and controls eliminated foreign competition from France's trading zone in Africa and forced the colonies into their assigned role in the imperial economy. The cohesion of the Franco-colonial trading system was based on administrative control of markets *via* an elaborate system of tariff barriers, quantitative import restrictions, exclusive purchaser arrangements, and price and currency controls.

This trade regime guaranteed metropolitan control over African exports of agricultural commodities. At the same time, it provided markets insulated from the currents of international competition for some of the most uncompetitive branches of French industry.[11] Through customs duties, the protectionist regime also financed the costs of colonial administration. In the pre-World War II period, French exporters of manufactured goods, the trading conglomerates that dominated West African trade, and French industries processing colonial commodities benefited enormously from these arrangements. To protect these lucrative ties, they lined up firmly behind the policy of "no industrialization" in the West African colonies.[12] The colonial administration used its control over trade flows and investment to accommodate this demand.

Under these arrangements, the AOF developed as a high-cost trading zone. In the late 1940s, the f.o.b. prices of French manufactured goods and foodstuffs sold in the AOF ran 30–70 percent, sometimes more, above world market prices.[13] AOF import taxes of 15–25 percent on these same goods compounded the cost problem.[14] The oligopolistic structure of control over the colonial import trade also inflated costs within the AOF. Through collusion and price fixing, the trading conglomerates that dominated AOF trade were able to extract rents from African consumers. For textiles, the single most important category of French manufactures consumed in the AOF, commercial margins at the importation-wholesale stage of distribution made up about 50 percent of final retail prices.[15]

The political and economic upheavals of World War II set in motion the process that ulimately led to industrial investment in the AOF and to decolonization. During the war, a few industrial firms were established in Dakar to provide goods that could not be imported under war-time conditions. After the war, France reimposed tight control over AOF trade in an effort to speed the reconstruction of its war-torn economy. In the late 1940s, metropolitan exporters and the colonial trading conglomerates waged price wars against many of the AOF industries that were set up during or immediately after the war. The postwar revival of the imperial trade regime led to the closure of many fledgling AOF manufacturing firms.[16]

Just when France felt that it needed colonies more than ever before, it was beseiged by pressures to liberalize colonial trade. The United States and colonized peoples of Africa pressed for structural changes in colonial economies and, ultimately, for the dismantling of the imperial system. In the 1950s, these new commercial and political pressures led colonial economic planners and some French industrialists to consider investment in import-substitution industry— "the controlled transfer of manufacturing capacity from the metropole to the colonies"—as a way of ensuring access to established West African markets in the long run.[17] In their view, "complete symbiosis of metropolitan and local industry'' would protect the interests of French manufacturers and shore up the Franco-African economic ties for generations to come.[18]

These considerations led to a wave of French investment in Dakar industry in the 1950s. Investment was driven by commercial strategies aimed at securing privileged access to French West African markets in the medium-to-long run. In the textile sector, French manufacturers with interests in West African markets dating back to the 1930s created factories in Dakar in 1949, 1950, and 1951. These investors calculated that restrictions on the importation of non-French goods and taxes on French imports provided enough protection to ensure the viability of these investments, in spite of the high costs of local production.[19] In 1953, the colonial administration threw its weight behind these initiatives, promulgating an investment code and rewriting tax and tariff laws. The new investment code allowed the colonial administration to grant production monopolies to large-scale investors, thereby giving first entrants a formidable advantage.

By the mid-1950s, the colonial trading conglomerates saw the writing on the wall: their future lay in establishing control over local manufacturing operations, rather than in trying to hold the line against local industry.[20] A round of price wars broke the independence of the established Dakar textile manufacturers and cleared the way for a new form of tight integration between French manufacturers and the colonial trading conglomerates. Détente between Dakar industries and the trading conglomerates gave rise to an integrated and coordinated system of control over the importation, local manufacture, and distribution of basic textile goods on the AOF market. Market-sharing and price-fixing agreements, undergirded by the colonial administration's tight restrictions on imports, created the oligopolistic structure of control over local trade and manufacturing that guaranteed the viability of the Dakar textile industry in the late 1950s and beyond.

By the end of the colonial period, about thirty-six firms employing more than 200 workers each were established in Dakar.[21] Most produced basic consumer goods from imported inputs (textiles, processed foods and beverages, cigarettes, matches, cosmetics, basic building materials, etc.). For most of these firms, decolonization did not come when the future viability of their investments could be assured by the free play of market forces. The profitability of import-substitution industries remained dependent on colonial patterns of control over local markets. The government of Senegal, like nearly all the regimes that emerged from the peaceful transfers of power in the 1960s, was committed to propelling the ISI process forward. This required adoption, and elaboration, of the kinds of trade controls that induced direct foreign investment in ISI in the 1940s and 1950s.

In the 1960s, most newly-independent regimes echoed the development orthodoxy of the times in arguing that ISI represented a means of diversifying and modernizing economies, providing much-needed urban employment, and enhancing overall productive capacity. As African governments across the continent

began to erect more formidable restrictions on the importation of finished consumer goods in the attempt to promote ISI, the commercial incentives that led
metropolitan firms to begin manufacturing in Africa in the 1950s became even
more salient. Governments encouraged foreign firms to invest by delivering
captive markets. By constraining local market competition, regimes could promise high rates of return to investors. The regime that came to power in post-
colonial Senegal was no exception. In pursuit of ISI, it fortified administrative
restrictions on foreign and local competition that were established during the
colonial period. Enhancing the "security and profitability" of direct foreign
investment in light industry was the objective.[22] These arrangements, backed
by the World Bank and French bilateral lending institutions, led to the growth
and diversification of Dakar's light industrial sector in the 1960s and early
1970s.

For Senegal and other African countries with light industrial sectors at the
time of independence, continuity and acceleration of investment trends set in
motion in the 1950s were watchwords of the day. Political independence, however, introduced new factors into the equation. The new regimes of post-colonial
Africa were subject to domestic pressures and demands that the colonial administrations had ignored or suppressed. As these pressures became more acute over
time, industrial policy came to depart more and more markedly from the policies
of the colonial period. Demands for (partial) indigenization of control over local
industry led some African governments to adopt measures in the 1970s that
permitted Africans to acquire financial shares in import-substitution industries
created by foreigners. In some African countries, government loans helped nationals create new firms themselves. These initiatives are much discussed in the
literature on tensions and collaboration between local and foreign interests in
African industrial sectors.[23] Less discussed are the struggles over rents generated
by import restrictions, which may be equally, if not more, decisive in shaping
patterns of ISI and the fortunes of investors in local industry.

PART II: RENTS

Industrialization *via* "import-substitution" involves the local production of
previously-imported finished goods. The strategy is by no means autarchic. It
requires a change in the *composition* of imports (away from finished goods and
toward producer and intermediate goods) and not necessarily a reduction in the
overall import bill.[24] Governments use control over trade policy to bring about
this change. Tariffs, bans on the imports of certain goods, import licensing, and
foreign exchange rationing restrict the inflow of certain imports, thereby driving
up prices. High prices reduce local demand for imports, shift demand toward
local manufactures, and shelter local producers from the foreign competition
they would otherwise face. Local manufacturers can price their goods at levels
near the artificially-inflated prices of imports. Higher returns on the sale of

locally-manufactured goods can cover production costs that exceed those of overseas producers. Higher returns also translate into greater profits, thereby creating incentives for investment. Meanwhile, most African governments offer protection to manufacturers on the production side of the equation. They do this by granting monopolies or guaranteed market shares to new investors.

The higher returns generated by state restrictions on competition are what Robert Bates calls "noncompetitive rents."[25] Put most simply, the value of rents is equal to actual returns minus the hypothetical returns that would be generated if competitive market conditions prevailed. Through trade policy, governments determine the value of rents generated in the import-substitution industrial sector and in segments of the commercial sector tied to importation. Consumers pay the costs of these rents.[26] When import restrictions are imposed to protect a local textile industry, for example, consumers pay more for textile goods than they would if they were able to purchase on more competitive markets.

African governments use the promise of protection from foreign (and local) competition to attract investors in industry. Obviously what is at stake here is the bottom line—when competitive pressures diminish, manufacturers can expect more interesting rates of return. In many countries, levels of tariff protection are negotiated on a case-by-case basis with prospective investors. Bates offers several examples of how this works. He cites Steven Langdon, who analyzed negotiations between the Government of Kenya and potential foreign investors in local industry during the 1965–1972 period. Langdon found that "the demands most commonly made in . . . negotiations were for protection from foreign competition, either through tariff protection or physical restrictions on imports (53 percent of cases [considered by the government]). Over the period from 1965 to 1972, protection was granted to manufactured products in 90 percent of the cases. . . . "[27] Similar systems worked in Zambia, Ghana, and Senegal.[28] Protection from imports, often accompanied by government-enforced production monopolies or oligopoly arrangements, allows manufacturers to collect rents in the form of profits on sales of locally-produced goods. Distributors of locally-manufactured goods may also benefit from "noncompetitive rents" generated by monopoly or oligopoly control of markets.[29]

Through trade and tax policy, governments may also control the *allocation* of rents generated by the import restrictions designed to promote local industry. When governments rely on tariffs to protect local industry, the state collects a large share of the difference between the c.i.f. prices of imports and the local, wholesale prices of these goods. In many African countries, however, physical controls on imports play a more important role than tariffs in restricting import flows.[30] Import licensing regimes and foreign exchange rationing create administratively-generated scarcities of imported goods, and thus drive up prices of imports on the local market. Licensing and currency rationing allow governments to determine who, precisely, may import goods in controlled product categories and, thus, who may collect the rents generated by scarcity. In these situations, licenses and permits to import become valuable commodities. Licensed importers collect the premiums created by market scarcity and restricted competition. Bates calls these premiums "administratively-generated rents."[31]

Anne Kreuger's work indicates that rents generated in this way can be quite attractive from the standpoint of individual businessmen, and also quite substantial when aggregated and placed in a macro-economic context. Kreuger analyzed "returns" on import licenses in India and Turkey in the mid-1960s. In India, Kreuger found that import licenses were worth 100–500 percent of their face value, generating rents that totaled about seven percent of national income in 1964.[32] In Turkey, she estimated that rents created through import licensing accounted for 15 percent of national income in 1968.[33] These findings suggest how important the stakes may be in how governments allocate import licenses. Kreuger's analysis also indicates why the political process through which licenses are distributed can emerge as a central focus of entrepreneurial efforts to enhance the profitability of trading activity. In many African countries, the commercial rents generated through import licensing may be as high as they were in India and Turkey in the 1960s. The political dimension of the process is no doubt equally important.

Kreuger was interested in how businessmen compete for licenses. One of the ways in which they do this is by working to establish privileged personal relationships with the government officials charged with allocating licenses. Bates is interested in a corollary to this process; i.e., the political "returns" that these governments officials may reap by using the allocation of "administratively-generated rents" to attract supporters and allies. Both analysts show that state controls that produce commercial rents place government agents at the center of a competitive struggle organized around the distribution of commercial rents to particular individuals and firms. From the perspective of private economic actors, success in the market may hinge on the outcomes of this competitive struggle. "As Leith noted for Ghana, the import-license system . . . had virtual life-and-death powers over most industries."[34] For individual importers, access to licenses can produce "windfall" profits.

For African governments, the stakes in how political controls over trade are used can be just as high, for with independence came the pressures to promote economic growth and diversification, consolidate local bases of support and defuse opposition, and redress inequities of the past—including those built into colonial systems of trade regulation. Rents generated in commercial sectors became prime targets of political contention.

Throughout post-colonial Africa, indigenous merchants who had thrown their weight behind the struggles for independence lobbied new governments for measures that would facilitate their move into the urban retail trade, the agro-export circuit, wholesale operations, and the most profitable segment of the commercial sector—importation.[35] In many African countries, government banks began advancing commercial credits to local businessmen to make this possible.

By the end of the 1960s, some regimes had "reserved" segments of transport, retail, and wholesale sectors for indigenous traders.[36] Licensing systems became key instruments in efforts to accelerate the Africanization of trade. Licenses or permits usually regulated access to opportunities in reserved sectors. Through licensing systems that governed imports covered by quantitative restrictions (and lending programs), governments designated the privileged businessmen who moved into the import trade. Extensive state control over domestic and foreign trade allowed African governments, like the colonial administrations before them, to perform the "gate-keeper" function of deciding who could operate in the more lucrative niches of the commercial sector, on what terms, and when.

State controls over trading opportunities made it possible for governments not only to advance the interests of African businessmen in very concrete ways, but also to undertake such projects in ways that reaped political advantage.[37] The political dimension of the problem is relevant here, for it explains a great deal about how changes set in motion by decolonization could work over time to transform trading sectors organized to promote ISI. African traders and consumers had interests to promote or protect that did not necessarily coincide with the interests of owners of import-substitution industry. African governments had interests to promote that could not always be reconciled with their interest in enhancing the profitability of (often foreign-owned) light industry. In Senegal and elsewhere, domestic markets structured around ISI became arenas where such conflicts of interests were played out.

PART III: POST-COLONIAL COMPETITION FOR RENTS: THE CASE OF THE DAKAR TEXTILE INDUSTRY

While the drive toward ISI led governments to elaborate trading controls inherited from colonial administrations, political independence expanded the scope of competition for commercial rents and placed new and disparate pressures on regimes deciding how to allocate them. The post-colonial history of Dakar's textile industry shows that political cross-pressures that emerged could make ISI strategies based on extensive protection of local markets increasingly difficult to sustain. As local struggles over rents generated in the commercial sector intensified, the Senegalese government found it increasingly difficult to mediate competition in favor of foreign industrial interests. As a consequence, the government found it increasingly difficult to deliver on its promise of providing captive markets to local import-substitution industry.

The growth of the Dakar textile industry in the 1960s and early 1970s was predicated upon colonial patterns of control over trade. Although political independence gave rise to new rationales for and new expectations of the ISI strategy, the market controls designed to induce foreign private investment in Senegal's industrial sector were beefed-up versions of those the colonial administration relied upon in the 1950s. The import control regime was extended as tariffs were raised to protect new and expanding industries and as stricter bans and import quotas were introduced. Through the import-licensing system, the French trading conglomerates that had controlled the importation of basic consumer goods (including textiles) since the 1930s continued to dominate this segment of the commercial sector. Meanwhile, a generous investment code offered tax incentives to prospective investors. Production monopolies granted by the colonial administration were renewed and monopoly rights were extended to firms proposing large ISI ventures.[38]

Under this post-colonial investment and trade regime, Dakar's basic textile industry expanded. Employment in the two non-competing industrial groups which controlled the local production of staple textile goods grew from 1,400 workers in 1962 to 3,400 in 1975.[39] These firms supplied 10–25 percent of the local consumer market in 1960; in 1975 they covered almost half (46 percent) of officially-estimated local demand for staple textile goods.[40] A dozen smaller firms producing knits, blankets, and garments employed about 800 workers in 1974. Across the board, firms in the textile sector enjoyed extensive protection from competing imports. In the early 1970s, coefficients for rates of effective protection for firms in the textile sector were estimated to range from 1.99 to 3.29.[41] The government's efforts to use trade controls to foster the development of the local textile industry were successful over the course of the 1960–1974 period. In 1974, World Bank analysts viewed the textile industry as one of Senegal's most dynamic and diversified sub-sectors of local manufacturing.[42]

In Senegal, as in most of post-colonial Africa, foreign investors took advantage of most opportunities for large-scale investment in local manufacturing. Virtually all new investment in major import-substitution ventures in Dakar was undertaken by French firms in the 1960s. The lion's share of government assistance was targeted at these firms.[43] With better-established foreign capital dominating industrial investment, indigenous entrepreneurs in Senegal and throughout post-colonial Africa looked to the commercial sector to expand the scope of their operations. Under colonial rule, most had been confined to small-scale operations for want of capital, by the monopolistic and oligopolistic trade practices of the large import-export conglomerates, and by racist trade restrictions. After independence, African merchants expected, and in many cases demanded, government assistance to ensure them a fairer share of the commercial pie.

The Senegalese "merchant class" was weak compared to its counterparts in Anglophone West Africa in the 1960s. It included perhaps 300 medium-scale commerçants in semi-wholesale and a larger number of small-scale transporters and retailers in the rural areas.[44] The largest and most dynamic members of this group pressed the government for access to import licenses in the early 1960s. Although some were granted licenses and commercial credits to import government-controlled food staples (rice), only a handful of individuals and firms was allowed to import consumer goods that competed directly with the products of local industry.[45] By the end of the 1960s, frustrated elements within the Senegalese business community coalesced to press demands for government assistance more forcefully on the regime. In 1968, a new business association claiming 2,600 members criticized the government for pursuing economic policies that promoted foreign interests at the expense of local businessmen and "the national interest."[46] The group argued that "local private capital was forced to vegetate in marginal sectors of the economy," while foreigners [the French and Lebanese] controlled commerce, industry, banking, and the service sector. "Nationals control only 5–10 percent of the economic activity in this country. After 10 years of independence, this is not acceptable."[47] Government-backed foreign monopolies in the import trade came under bitter attack. The association demanded that Senegalese traders receive a share of import licenses and quotas allocated by the government. It pressed the government to "reserve" parts of the service sector for local businessmen and to promote local private share ownership in industry.[48]

Criticisms of the government launched by the local business sector were echoed in a broader wave of protest against the regime and its economic strategies that shook Dakar in 1968 and 1969. As the growth of the economy slowed and workers', peasants', and lower-ranking civil servants' standards of living deteriorated, the government came under fire for failing to "decolonize" the Senegalese economy and for pursuing an economic agenda that "offered so little to so few."[49] The leaders of the regime apparently concluded that one way to shore up their hold on power was to make selective concessions to mobilized social groups (unionized workers, students, local businessmen) and to spread resources under the command of the government more widely.

Beginning in 1969, the government moved to accommodate some of the demands advanced by Senegalese businessmen. The import-control system designed to protect local industry was put at the service of this cause. In the 1970s, the Ministry of Commerce began to "selectively insert" Senegalese businessmen into the import trade. The Ministry of Finance was authorized to draw up its own list of 100 individuals singled out for "special encouragement" through the allocation of import licenses. Other government agencies promoted their own candidates. By the mid-1970s, the bureaucratic process for allocating commercial rents was considerably less coherent and more diffuse than it had been in the earlier period. As bureaucratic prerogative over the allocation of commercial rents was decentralized, pressure for access to these rents intensified within the ranks of the bureaucracy and among clients of the regime. Government agents at various levels of the state hierarchy responded to this pressure and to political and economic incentives that encouraged state officials to promote their own business interests and those of their allies and dependents. As a consequence, the overall restrictiveness of the import-control system began to deteriorate.

By the end of the 1970s, the importation of light consumer goods such as textiles had been completely "Senegalized." Through this process, the colonial trading conglomerates lost their monopoly over heavily-regulated segments of the import trade. As the number of licensed importers with access to government credit grew, fraudulent importation and smuggling also began to increase. Fraud involved illegal and "extra-legal" manipulation of official regulations at one or more of the many stages of the importation process. Licenses were issued in excess of quotas; goods passed through customs untaxed; and import shipments were not invoiced correctly. Smuggling and fraudulent importation, like legal importation under license, were profitable because rates of domestic market protection were high. Importers—operating legally or otherwise—collected rents generated by artificially inflated domestic price levels. The rise of smuggling and fraudulent importation was most marked in the textile sector. In 1980, the government estimated that 70 percent of all textile goods sold on the local market were fraudulently or illegally imported.[50] The blatant and routine character of large-scale fraud and smuggling reflected the absence of concerted efforts to control it.

Expanding access to "noncompetitive" and "administratively-generated" rents in the commercial sector fueled the growth of long-established political machines within the government and the ruling party. State agents and politicians took advantage of new opportunities opening up in the commercial sector, either on their own or in partnership with full-time *commerçants*. At the same time, selective allocation of commercial rents worked to coopt restive elements of the local private sector into patronage networks linked to the regime. Bates summarizes the logic of the process that unfolded: "Market intervention establishes disequilibrium prices. These, in turn, generate rents. The rents . . . represent political resources—resources which can be used to organize political support and to perpetuate governments in power."[51] In Senegal in the 1970s, commercial rents became political resources that were used to strengthen the party bureaucratic machine and defuse challenges to the regime that emerged in the late 1960s.

As the restrictiveness of the import control regime eroded, the Dakar textile industry faced competition for the first time since the early 1950s. Full-blown crisis emerged in the industry in the late 1970s, as the long-protected local market was swamped with illegally and extra-legally imported textile goods. After 1978, the local market for made-in-Senegal textile goods virtually collapsed. The structure of vertical integration established in the mid-1960s disintegrated and most of the smaller firms in the textile sector closed. The largest firms teetered on the brink of bankruptcy. The government offered relief to these large firms in the form of production subsidies and loans, but refrained from launching a major crackdown on smuggling and fraud.

The forces that produced a marketing crisis in the textile industry affected the growing ranks of Senegalese textile importers as well. *De facto* competition emerged in the textile trade as the volume of imported textile goods available on the local market increased. This exerted downward pressure on rents generated at all levels of the trading circuit. The most powerful of the local importers began to press for reforms that would restrict access to import licenses to a narrower, more select, group of Senegalese businessmen. The Dakar Chambre de Commerce issued a call for the elimination of *faux commerçants* and trading intermediaries off all sorts from "anarchic" trading circuits encumbered and disorganized by a plethora of speculators, rentiers, and smugglers.[52] The Ministry of Industry made the same argument.

There is no doubt that many within the government remained entirely committed to restabilizing the local textile industry. The Ministries of Planning and Industry argued consistently from the late 1970s onwards that the government's goal of stabilizing the local textile industry" . . . will not be achieved unless fraudulent importation is suppressed. This requires rigorous measures at the level of import control and above all, a crackdown on those engaging in illegal trading activity (*répression vis-à-vis des fraudeurs*)."[53] The government committed significant resources in the form of subsidies to keep the largest textile manufacturers in business in the late 1970s and early 1980s, a time of great fiscal stress.[54] On paper, the trade regime governing imports became even more restrictive and the level of protective tariffs escalated.[55] Yet there was no move to reestablish *de facto* control over importation.[56]

What compromised the government's ability to respond decisively in favor of the textile industry and the largest textile traders (Senegalese and French) was political cross-pressure that it could not afford to ignore. At a time of general economic recession, rising external debt payments, and unrelenting pressure from external creditors to cut government expenditures, the government of Senegal was unwilling to alienate the segment of its political constituency that was rooted in the legal and illegal import trade. It would have done so at great risk of political backlash, which might have jeopardized its own survival. The political clout of what one Dakar journal termed the "smuggling lobby" was enormous.[57] Perhaps even more importantly, a crackdown on smuggling and fraud would have antagonized (and maybe provoked) Senegal's largest and most politically-alienated social group: the poor. Goods imported illegally into Senegal were generally less expensive than similar made-in-Senegal products, and less expensive than goods imported under the tax, tariff, and import quota regime. Textile goods sold on parallel markets clothed the urban poor, who were hard-pressed by inflation and the economic austerity programs adopted by the government in the late 1970s. In the rural areas, the peasants who sold their produce on parallel markets to escape government taxation purchased consumer goods like textiles on parallel markets for the same reason. Well-organized and extensive parallel market circuits also generated income for innumerable middlemen and retailers, thus providing desperately-needed urban and rural employment that neither the state nor the "formal sector" could offer. After the government raised the prices of bread, rice, oil, and urban transport in the late 1970s, one official considered the issue of suppressing illegal trading circuits and remarked, " . . . it is politically unwise to squeeze the people on all fronts simultaneously."[58] In 1978, a local union publication asked, " . . . in whose name, and on the basis of what justification, should we sacrifice [low-cost textile goods] for the benefit of *les industriels français de textile?*"[59]

Le Soleil, the progovernment Dakar daily, said that ''(b)ehind the textile war, enormous interests are at stake.''[60] *Le Soleil* was right. The struggle for control over the local textile market developed into a struggle over the legitimacy of an ISI strategy that promised captive, high-cost markets to foreign investors. The government became unwilling to jeopardize its own chances of political survival to deliver lucrative commercial rents to the narrow interests tied to local textile manufacturing. At the same time, the government was not prepared to allow the largest firms in the industry to fold. As the local market for textiles manufactured in Senegal collapsed, ever-mounting government subsidizies kept these firms open.

In 1980, the French firms that had owned and operated Senegal's largest textile manufacturing firms for almost three decades were ready to pull out. Government loans financed the complete buy-out of the basic textile industry by leading Senegalese businessmen. In exchange, these businessmen were to practice ''self-restraint'' in importing cheaper textile goods from abroad.[61] In spite of this arrangement, the market for made-in-Senegal textile goods contined to erode in the 1980s.[62]

PART IV: CONCLUSION

Trade and investment regimes that promoted investment in light industry in Dakar in the 1950s were shaped by efforts of French merchant and industrial firms seeking to retain a hold on colonial markets. Tariffs, taxes, bans on competing imports, production monopolies, and fixed purchase agreements created the local market conditions that made colonial investment in import-substitution industry profitable. Senegal's post-colonial regime was even more committed to ISI than its colonial predecessor. It elaborated trade controls protecting local industry in an effort to create markets—profitable markets—for foreign investors. This strategy was as much a reflection of already-established colonial patterns of market control, and of entrenched colonial interests, as it was the product of technocratic efforts on the part of the Senegalese government to promote growth. As the problems of the Dakar textile industry so amply illustrate, the strategy became increasingly difficult to sustain.

The government of Senegal was committed to sustaining patterns of state control over trade that guaranteed profits in the foreign-owned industrial sector. Simultaneously, it faced internal pressures to redress the inequities of an economic system established under colonial rule. Pressures to expand possibilities for local business—and to maintain the stability of the government in the context of a stagnant economy—eventually led to efforts to distribute rents generated in the commercial sector more widely. This shift in patterns of trade policy implementation generated new patronage resources for the government and helped to deflect restive elements within the local business sector away from more fundamental demands for economic restructuring. Once it began to tap commercial rents as a source of much-needed patronage resources, the government quickly perceived that forceful efforts to *contain* the scope of access to these rents would involve unacceptable political costs. This political problem was manifest in the government's unwillingness, or inability, to suppress smuggling and fraud.

The government of Senegal confronted what Tom Forrest calls the "recurring dilemma between tariff protection for industry and cost-of-living cosiderations."[63] In the context of general economic crisis and IMF-sponsored austerity programs, this dilemma emerged in Senegal in particularly acute form. It found concrete expression in the government's ambivalence and paralysis in the face of smuggling and in the resulting collapse of the domestic market for made-in-Senegal textile goods.

The problem of smuggling that emerged in Senegal was complex, revealing strains that permeated all sectors of the domestic economy and tensions built into the political order itself. In this sense, the factors that gave rise to and aggravated the smuggling problems in Senegal were not unique to that country. Throughout much of sub-Saharan Africa, the problem of smuggling grows out of three mutually-reinforcing processes. The first, and the most noted, is the rise of parallel markets for the export of agricultural commodities. When farmers find *de facto* taxes on their crops to be lighter in neighboring countries, they find ways to increase their returns by smuggling crops across borders. A reverse flow of cheaper imports may develop at the same time, as it did in Senegal. The second process reflects the powerful incentives for smuggling that are created by heavy import taxes and stringent trade restrictions. Profits generated by selling low-cost goods in markets with inflated price structures can be most attractive. The third is the complicity of some government officials in the illegal or quasi-legal import trade. Some state agents may use their positions to tap into rents generated in the import trade, either by offering political protection to importers or by manipulating bureaucratic controls in ways that neutralize the effectiveness of import restrictions.[64] When a government's hold on power is tenuous, and when direct material inducements are used to purchase political acquiescence, the actions of these state agents reflect deep weaknesses in political systems more than they reflect the predilictions of particular individuals. All three of these processes are likely to become more pronounced in the context of economic recession.

Import-substitution industries throughout Africa are vulnerable to smuggling. Governments have relied on trade restrictions and taxes to attract private investors to textile manufacturing. These measures raise the cost of goods legally available on local markets. Incentives for circumventing these controls may be powerful. Smuggling may be very profitable, and the "barriers to entry" into the smuggling business may be relatively low. Textile industries are particularly vulnerable. Consumer textile goods are high in value relative to weight, easing the logistics and costs of transport. Meanwhile, textile goods are basic necessities of life, and demand remains strong even in the worst of times. Textile manufacturers in Ghana, Nigeria, Kenya, Zambia and elsewhere confront smuggling as a recurring or chronic problem.

What are the implications of this situation for African policymakers and investors in African industry? It is clear that if African countries are to transcend the narrow limits, risks, and chronic bottlenecks of economies organized around the export of agricultural commodities and the import of manufacutured goods, then "import-substitution" industrialization in some form must play an important role. The goal of using state power to displace imports on domestic markets to create space for locally-produced goods is sound and necessary. The contribution that import-substitution industrialization has made to the development of Southeast Asian economies, Japan, and countries like Brazil suggests that what is at issue is not ISI *per se*, but rather the way in which this goal is pursued.[65] For Africa today, critical variables in determining the extent to which local industrialization can contribute to balanced and sustainable growth include the terms on which financing is secured, the deployment of profits, the choice of technology, and the linkages that are established among local consumer goods industries, other sectors of the local economy, and domestic demand.

More fundamentally, the observed problems of ISI in the African context do not provide grounds for sweeping attacks on government intervention in economies or sweeping calls for *laissez-faire* economics. The central and indispensable role of the state in promoting economic development is not only a historical fact in the cases of Europe and the United States, but also a necessary fact of development in the Third World.[66] "Withdrawal of the state" from industrial planning and promotion is neither desirable, feasible, nor practical in sub-Saharan Africa. What counts, ultimately, is the balance of social, political, and economic forces that condition how state power is used.

The central argument of this chapter is that domestic political forces that shape the implementation of industrial and commercial policy play a central role in determining the success and sustainability of broad industrialization strategies in sub-Saharan Africa. ISI strategies that have pitted the interests of foreign industrialists against those of large segments of local business classes and consumers tend to become increasingly difficult to sustain. In enforcing laws designed to enhance the profitability of light industry, African governments become the targets of conflicting political and economic pressures. These pressures may be resolved or managed in ways that diverge from the long-term interests of investors in light industry. When this happens, investors may find the returns promised by market protection and production monopolies increasingly difficult to collect.

To develop projects that are likely to be viable over time, direct investors in African industry must target opportunities that are not only viable from an economic point of view, but also provide a basis for building coalitions of shared interests with local producers, traders, and consumers. The development of such projects suggests, first and foremost, investment in industries that process local agricultural commodities for sale on local markets. Industry that delivers returns not only to firm owners, but also to local agricultural producers, consumers, and traders becomes the linchpin of a formidable political and economic coalition. This kind of coalition offers industrialists a durable form of "protection" that high tarriffs and *de jure* monopolies cannot guarantee.

NOTES

1. Anne Kreuger, "The Political Economy of the Rent-Seeking Society," *American Economic Review*, 64 (1974): 291–303; and Robert Bates, *Markets and States in Tropical Africa* (Los Angeles: University of California Press, 1981).

2. This part of the chapter is based on my own research on the Dakar textile industry, conducted in Paris and Dakar between 1984 and 1986. (C. Boone, "State Power versus Private Interests: Politics, Markets, and the Textile Industry in Senegal," Ph.D. dissertation, Massachusetts Institute of Technology, Department of Political Science, 1987.)

3. Studies of the "development of underdevelopment" in colonial and post-colonial Africa tend to focus on these dimension of ISI. I accept the broad description of ISI in Africa that is advanced in this work. See, for example, Colin Leys, *Underdevelopment in Kenya: The Political Economic of Neo-Colonialism* (Los Angeles: University of California Press, 1975), especially ch. 4.

4. For this perspective, see I.T. Little, T. Scitovsky, and M. Scott, *Industry and Trade in Some Developing Countries; A Comparative Study* (London: Oxford University Press, 1970).

5. See, for example, W.W. Rostow, "The Take-Off into Self-Sustained Growth," *The Economic Journal*, No. 66, August 1960. James H. Nolt stresses the support American and multilateral development agencies provided for ISI in the 1960s, and thereby places their current critique of ISI in correct historical context. See James J. Nolt, "Conditions for the Predominance of Import-Substitution Industrialization in the Post-World War Two Era: An International Class Analysis," M.A. thesis: Massachusetts Institute of Technology, Department of Economics, September 1983.

6. See Nolt, 1983.

7. See World Bank, *Accelerated Development in Sub-Saharan Africa: An Agenda for Action* (Washington, D.C.: World Bank, 1981), and Timothy Shaw's discussion of the *Agenda* and African governments' response to it. Timothy Shaw, "African Development and the International Division of Labor," in Adebayo Adedeji and Timothy M. Shaw, eds., *Economic Crisis in Africa: African Perspectives on Development Problems and Potentials* (Boulder: Lynne Rienner Publisher, 1985), pp. 267–284.

8. In 1978, the World Bank reported that in sub-Saharan Africa, "typically, three-quarters or more of industrial value added is in import substitutes, principally in relatively unsophisticated goods." World Bank, *World Development Report*, 1978 (Washington, D.C.: World Bank, 1979), p. 49, cited by Martin Fransman, "Introduction," in M. Fransman, ed., *Industry and Accumulation in Africa* (London: Heinemann, 1982), p. 8.

9. In Rhodesia, ISI was pursued in the 1940s and 1950s, with the Central African Federation of Northern Rhodesia, Southern Rhodesia, and Malawi as the intended market. (Rhodesia became the independent state of Zimbabwe in 1980.) In Nairobi, industrial production was aimed at the East African market of Kenya, Uganda, and Tanzania. Miles

Kahler, "Political Regime and Economic Actors: The Response of Firms to the End of Colonial Rule," *World Politics*, 33, 1 (October 1980): pp. 396–397.

10. The decolonization arrangement assured France continuing control over Senegal's monetary policy (the CFA franc remained tied to the French franc); ensured that tight trading links would be perpetuated; guaranteed the security of French investment in Senegal; and gave French technical advisors a great deal of say over economic planning. See Richard Joseph, "The Gaullist Legacy: Patterns of French Neo-Colonialism," *Review of African Political Economy*, 6, 1976.

11. See Jacques Marseille, *Empire Colonial et Capitalisme Français: Historie d'un Divorce* (Paris: Albin Michel, 1984).

12. This stance was not unique to French industrial and commercial interests. For a discussion of Lancashire's opposition to the creation of textile mills in Uganda from the 1930s to about 1950, see Mahmood Mamdani, *Politics and Class Formation in Uganda* (New York: Monthly Review Press, 1976), p. 254. For a discussion of British opposition to industrial investment in Tanganika in the interwar period, see E.A. Brett, *Colonialism and Underdevelopment in East Africa: The Politics of Economic Change, 1919–1939* (New York: NOK Publishers, 1973), pp. 266–282.

13. Ministère de la France d'Outre-Mer, Direction des Affaires Economiques et du Plan, "Comparison des prix Français et etrangeres d'articles de consommation courante dans les Territoires d'Outre-Mer," février 1954.

14. Gaston LeDuc, "Les Hauts Prix en Afrique Noire," *Industries et Travaux d'Outre-Mer* (janvier 1954), p. 49.

15. MM. Chafanel et Poncet du Haut Commissariat de l'AOF, Direction Générale des Services Economiques et du Plan, "Etude sur la structure des Prix et l'organisation commerciale en AOF," Dakar, janvier 1955.

16. Pierre Moussa, *Les chances economiques de la Communauté Franco-Africaine* (Paris: Armand Colin, 1957), pp. 122, 199.

17. Ministère des Colonies, Direction des Affaires Economiques, "Plan des moyens industriels correspondant au Plan Décennal d'Equipement Nationale, Exposé General," Paris, n.d. (1944?).

18. Moussa, 1957, pp. 154–155.

19. Conventional wisdom at the time held that the costs of setting up an industrial installation in the AOF were twice as high as the costs of creating a new firm in France. The initial costs of credit, transport, spare parts, capital goods, etc., were compounded by the high cost of operations in Dakar.

20. Tom Forrest, in discussing the emergence of import-substituting industry in Nigeria in the 1950s, makes a comment that holds true for French West Africa as well: "The extent to which merchant monopolies actually dropped their commercial activities for manufacture is easily exaggerated. Shifts in the structure of imports toward intermediate and capital goods favored these companies." (Tom Forrest, "Recent Developments in Nigerian Industrialization," in M. Fransman, ed., 1982, p. 325.)

21. Institut de Science Appliquée (ISEA), Les industries du CapVert: Analyse d'un ensemble d'industries legéres de l'Afrique Occidentale (Dakar: ISEA, janvier 1963).

22. CINAM et SERESA, Rapport général sur les perspectives du développement du Sénégal: une étude realisée à la demande du gouvernement du Sénégal en 1959, 1960.

23. See, for example, the case studies published in Adebayo Adedeji, ed., *Indigenization of African Economies* (New York: Holmes and Meier, 1981); Thomas Biersteker, *Multinationals, the State, and Control of the Nigerian Economy* (Princeton: Princeton

University Press, 1987); and Nicola Swainson, *The Development of Corporate Capitalism in Kenya, 1918–1977* (Los Angeles, University of California Press, 1980).

24. Fred Nixson, "Import-Substitution Industrialization," in M. Fransman, ed., 1982, pp. 45–46, 48.

25. Bates, 1981, p. 103.

26. Consumers are, of course, also workers, peasants, civil servants, traders, etc. In theory, the "excess costs" they pay purchasing goods on protected markets may be "returned" to them in a variety of ways. Local manufacturing may create jobs. It may expand markets for local producers of primary products processed by local industry. Local manufacturers may pay taxes that are used in ways that improve the lives of "consumers." Through taxation, governments may appropriate rents generated in the industrial and trading sectors and use these funds, for example, to subsidize the prices of basic foodstuffs. In practice, for most of sub-Saharan Africa there is little evidence to suggest that broad segments of local populations have benefited much from restrictions on trade designed to promote ISI.

27. Bates, 1981, p. 64. See also D.S. MacRae, "The Import-Licensing System in Kenya," *Journal of Modern African Studies*, 17, 1 (1979): 31, 33.

28. Bates, 1981, p. 64, 67; Boone, 1987.

29. Bates, 1981, p. 103.

30. Bates, 1981, pp. 63–64. MacRae reports that in Kenya from 1964–1972, "the prime function of import licensing was to protect local industries" (p. 31).

31. Bates, 1981, pp. 97–98.

32. Kreuger, 1974, p. 294.

33. Ibid.

34. Bates, 1981, p. 68.

35. For example, in early 1968, the Zambian African Traders Association sent a memo to the Vice-President that read as follows:

The government is in our hands and we expect the government to give us the same chances the previous government [i.e., the colonial administration] gave to its fellow white traders. We appeal to the government that 1968 should be the year to see African businessmen participate fully in commerce and industry backed by the government.

From Carolyn Baylies, "Zambia's Economic Reforms and their Aftermath: The State and the Growth of Indigenous Capital," *Journal of Commonwealth and Comparative Politics*, 20, 3 (November 1982): 239.

36. Leys, 1975, Ch. 5; Baylies, 1982; Mamdani, 1976; Adedeji and Shaw (eds.), 1985.

37. Bates, 1981.

38. In the mid- to late-1960s, Guy Pfefferman reported that 52 percent of Senegal's largest 160 firms enjoyed a monopoly position on the local market. Of the remainder, 22 percent were part of a coordinated oligopoly. He commented that "(t)here is virtually no competition in Senegalese industry." G. Pfefferman, *Industrial Labor in the Republic of Senegal* (New York: Praeger, 1968), pp. 58, 63.

39. These two firms invested jointly in a local weaving factory in 1966.

40. Ministère de la Coopération (France) avec le Ministère du Plan et du Développement (Senegal), *Le Secteur Textile au Sénégal* (Dakar, 1965); Gouvernement du Sénégal, SONED, *Recensement Industriel 1974* (Dakar, 1975), Tome 3:17.

41. World Bank (Bela Balassa), *Economic Incentives and Resource Costs in Senegal*,

1975: 41–44; World Bank, *Incentives and the Economic Efficiency of Resource Allocation in Senegalese Industry, 1971–1973*, Sept. 1985: 2.23–2.34.

42. World Bank, *Senegal: Tradition, Diversification, and Economic Development* (Washington, D.C.: World Bank, November 1974).

43. In East and West Africa, non-African investors who had generated capital at the intermediate levels of colonial trading circuits (the Lebanese, Indians, Greeks) took advantage of many opportunities for small- and medium-scale investment that opened up in the 1960s. In keeping with this trend, Lebanese immigrants created knitting firms in Dakar and thus contributed to the growth and diversification of the Senegalese textile industry in the 1960s and early 1970s.

44. See Samir Amin, *Le Monde des Affaires Sénégalais* (Paris: Editions de Minuit, 1969), especially pp. 66–68; 72; Majhemout Diop, *Histoire des Classes Sociales dans l'Afrique de l'Ouest, Tome II: Le Sénégal* (Paris: Maspero, 1972), p. 151.

45. Ibid.

46. On the formation and demands of UNIGES (Union des Groupements Economiques du Sénégal), see Sheldon Gellar, *Senegal: An African Nation Between East and West* (Boulder: Westview, 1982), p. 34; Ediafric, *La Politique Africaine en 1969* (Paris: Ediafric, 1970), p. 273.

47. UNIGES, "Rapport du Premier Congrès," Dakar, 1 juin 1968.

48. Ibid.

49. This is Donal Cruise O'Brien's phrase.

50. Ministère du Développement Industriel et de l'Artisanat, *Rapport du Groupe de Travail Textile*, 25 septembre 1981: Annexe 3, p. 37.

51. Robert Bates, *Essays on the Political Economy of Rural Africa* (Los Angeles: University of California Press, 1983), p. 129.

52. Chambre de Commerce de Dakar (CCI-RCV), "Note sur l'élaboration du Plan" (Dakar: mai 1983), p. 9. The Ministry of Commerce advanced similar arguments in the early 1980s (Ministère du Commerce, Direction du Commerce Intérieur et des Prix: Notes sur les mesures à prendre pour l'amélioration des circuits de distribution," Dakar: 5 avril 1982).

53. Gouvernement du Sénégal, Commission Nationale de Planification (n.B–6), Sous-Commission Textiles, *Rapport Provisoire*, 1982, p. 6. See also Ministère du Développement Industriel et de l'Artisanat, *Rapport du Groupe de Travail Textile*, 25 septembre 1981: 21–22.

54. For example, one spinning and weaving firm, Icotaf, received new tax breaks for the 1976–1979 period valued at 1 billion CFA francs. During the same period, it incurred 2 billion CFA francs in new debts to the state. In 1979, the government wrote off 1.4 billion francs of Icotaf's debt. During the same period, the government provided new subsidies on cotton, water, and electricity. The electricity subsidy cost the government 100 million francs in 1980 alone. (Le Gouvernement du Sénégal, *Mission du contrôle du contrat-programme Icotaf*, 2 Janvier 1982.)

55. In 1978, all textile imports—regardless of origin, nature, and value—were placed under a new, severely restricted licensing system. Under this system, all requests for licenses to import textile goods were subject to the review and veto of a textile commission composed of representatives of each firm in the industry. The commission met weekly and scrutinized requests on a case-by-case basis. Manufacturers were authorized to veto requests to import goods "likely to compete with locally-made textile goods." On the

operation of this system, see *Marchés Tropicaux*, 22 septembre 1978: 2511, and Gouvernement du Sénégal, SONED, *Le Textile au Sénégal*, Tome 1, 1978: 33.

56. The government argued that systematic surveillance and seizure of illegally imported goods was too costly. Manufacturers offered to finance seizure operations, but the government declined the offer. The government did not provide the Senegalese customs force with vehicles and petrol adequate to control smuggling along the borders. Textile manufacturers offered to equip the customs service themselves, but the government declined to accept.

57. *Liberté*, "Le textile: la mort en fraud," n.1, 1 mars 1985: 20.

58. Interview in Dakar conducted by the author, 1985.

59. *Taxaw*, "Textile, Halte aux manoeuvres contre les hommes d'affaires sénégalais," 12 aout 1978: 4.

60. *Le Soleil*, 7 novembre 1978: 1.

61. These arrangements are described in le Gouvernement du Sénégal, Commission Nationale de Planification (n.B–6), Sous-commission Textile, *Rapport Provisoire*, 1982.

62. One Dakar publication gives figures that indicate the magnitude of this recession. *Sopi* reported that over the course of the 1981–1988 period, firm closures and production cutbacks led to the loss of 1,800 jobs in the basic textile industry. These numbers represent over one-half of all jobs that existed in the basic textile industry in the mid-1970s. *Sopi*, "Misère du Textile," 26 aout 1988.

63. Tom Forrest in M. Fransman, ed., 1982, p. 333.

64. Werlin reports that in the early 1960s, bribes to obtain import licenses in Ghana ran about 5–10 percent of the face value of the license. Herbert Werlin, "The Roots of Corruption—the Ghanaian Enquiry, *Journal of Modern African Studies*, 10, 2 (1972): 252.

65. See Bruce Cumings, "The Origins and Development of the Northeast Asian Political Economy," *International Organization*, 38, 1 (Winter 1984), pp. 1–40; Alice Amsden, "The State and Taiwan's Economic Development," in Evans, Rueschemeyer, and Skocpol, eds., *Bringing the State Back In* (Cambridge: Cambridge University Press, 1979); and Peter Evans, *Dependent Development: The Alliance of Multinational, State, and Local Capital in Brazil* (Princeton: Princeton University Press, 1979).

66. See, for example, Alexander Gerschenkron, "Economic Backwardness in Historical Perspective," in B. Hoselitz, ed., *The Progress of Underdeveloped Areas* (Chicago: University of Chicago Press, 1952), and Stephen Skowronek, *Building a New American State: The Expansion of National Administrative Capacities, 1877–1920* (Cambridge: Cambridge University Press, 1982).

8

Manpower and Entrepreneurial Skill Shortages: Constraints to Private Sector Development in Africa?

KOFI APRAKU

Entrepreneurial ability is probably the most important scarce skill in sub-Saharan Africa.

OAU/ECA/ADB

Entrepreneurship can never be suppressed, only misdirected.

Ivor Peace

There is no doubt that the late 1980s can easily be classified as the era of public sector reform in Africa. All over the continent, governments are embarked on economic reform programs aimed at weakening the public sector, while strengthening and encouraging the growth of the private sector. The reforms have been manifested in large transfers of public ownerships of firms to private ownership (privatization), reduction of government subsidies to state-owned enterprises, management contracts, and lease agreements.

In this chapter, we will examine the numerous obstacles (political, social, economic, financial, manpower, and entrepreneurial skill, etc.) that constrain private sector development in Africa. Specifically, we will attempt to answer the question: Are the lack of manpower and entrepreneurial skills the major constraints to private sector development in Africa. We will also examine the observation of OAU/ECA/ADB quoted at the beginning of this chapter.

Our hypothesis is that it is the environment within which the African entrepreneur operates, rather than manpower and entrepreneurial shortages, that constrain private sector development in Africa. In analyzing this question, we rely on historical and contemporary evidence from various African countries, as well as on results of a survey recently conducted among African professionals living in the United States.

PRIVATIZATION IN ACTION

While privatization has been emphasized in the public sector reform programs, advocates of privatization concede that privatization is only one of many aspects of the public sector reform, and must not be viewed as an end in itself. Indeed, it is argued that it must be viewed only as part of a total package of liberalizing policies including the restructuring of markets (both formal and informal), devaluation, and rationalization of the inefficient bureaucracies. All these policies must collectively contribute to the development of the private sector as the major instrument for economic growth.

For many African countries (e.g., Ghana), these reforms are aggressively pursued as an economic necessity rather than as political ideology. Countries involved in the reform programs span the whole spectrum of political ideologies in Africa. For example, Nigeria has unilaterally slashed subventions to public enterprises by 50 percent and is considering several major privatization proposals. Other examples are;

- In Ghana, thirty state-owned enterprises (SOEs) have been put up for sale to private individuals (privatization).
- Kenya has sold some government interests to the private sector and has successfully contracted out road construction and maintenance.
- Côte d'Ivoire has transferred publicly-owned firms into private hands and has shifted some of its water supply network into the private sector.
- Mozambique, Tanzania, and Benin are relaxing their strict controls over private business activities, agriculture and trade, and are actively exploring ways to improve the performance of the public enterprises sector.[1]

However, it is privatization of previously state-owned enterprises that is leading the program for private sector development in Africa. Currently privatization efforts are under way in countries such as Gambia, Ghana, Guinea Bissan, Ivory Coast, Mali, Senegal, Somalia, Sudan, Tanzania, Tunisia, Nigeria, Uganda and Zaire, Togo and Malawi. Indeed, of the 400 privatizations carried out in the 1980s in LDCs, 160 occurred in Africa.

MOTIVATION FOR PRIVATIZATION

It is remarkable that all these countries are involved in privatization drives at the same time. Certainly, part of the reason is the common colonial experiences of these countries. Colonial regimes held back the development of the private sector for a long time. After the colonial period, African governments built extensive state industries. The development approaches of that era were based upon large governmental bureaucracies and centralized government control of the commanding heights of the economy. Having just emerged from independence, to protect the newly won independence from the "imperialist and multinational exploitation."

In addition, the poor state of infrastructural, social amenities development and the rising expectation of the population made it necessary for African governments to assume the role as the major instrument for economic development and the guarantor of social welfare and equity.

African governments were not the only ones who felt the need for an active involvement in the economy. The World Bank and other international organizations and agencies of donor countries often suggested, encouraged, and actively assisted in the creation of state-owned enterprises and the entrenchment of government in the economy. The result was that private sector development was ignored and public sector development was emphasized. This eventually made Africa the most statist region in the developing world. For example, as Table 8.1 shows, one group of thirty sub-Saharan African countries for which data is available created a total of nearly 3,000 state-owned enterprises. Even though these enterprises were corrupt, inefficient, and a drain on the economies of their respective countries, they were permitted to operate throughout the 1960s and early 1970s without any major reforms.

However, a number of factors had an effect on African economies during the 1970s that altered how governments viewed SOEs. Among these factors are the oil price shocks of the 1970s, the world economic recessions, increasing protectionism, and generalized world inflation. The results have been severe budget deficits, foreign exchange shortages, debt crisis, and general economic decline. Given the new economic realities, African governments unwilling or unable to support these economically draining SOEs have embarked on these reforms as an economic necessity.

Reflecting on this new economic reality in Africa, Barcar N'Diaye, the President of the African Development Bank (ADB) stated:

It is now generally accepted that over time the majority of public sector enterprises have not performed efficiently. Instead of accumulating surpluses or supplying services efficiently, a good number of these enterprises have become a drain on the national treasuries. Due to this poor performance coupled with the growing recognition of the cost of ineffective public enterprises in terms of foregone economic development and the scarcity of domestic and external resources for public sector expenditure, reappraisal of the strategy of heavy reliance on the public sector has become imperative. From this reappraisal, a view has emerged—the need for enhancement of the role of the private sector in development. . . . We in Africa are facing a great challenge. We believe that the creation of a conducive environment for the growth of the private sector, an important agent of economic growth, is essential.[2]

For African countries, privatization promises that private owners who are profit-motivated and subject to competition will have greater incentive to be

Table 8.1
State-Owned Enterprises in Sub-Saharan Africa[a]

Country	Year	Total
Benin	1982	60
Botswana	1978	9
Burundi	1984	51
Cameroon	1980	50
Comoros	1982	10
Congo	1982	75*
Cote d'ivoire	1978	147
Ethiopia	1984	180
Ghana	1984	130
Guinea	1980	181
Kenya	1982	176
Losotho	1978	7
Liberia	1980	22*
Madagascar	1979	136
Malawi	1977	101
Mali	1984	52
Mauritania	1983	112
Niger	1984	54
Nigeria	1981	107
Rwanda	1981	38
Senegal	1983	188
Sierra Leone	1984	26
Somalia	1979	44
Sudan	1984	138
Swaziland	1978	10
Tanzania	1981	400
Togo	1984	73
Uganda	1985	130
Zaire	1981	138
Total		2,959

*Excludes financial enterprises.
[a]Note some of these firms may be jointly owned by the state and private individuals and organizations.

Source: Adapted from John R. Nellis, ''Public Enterprises in Sub-Saharan Africa,'' World Bank Discussion Paper No. 1 (Washington, D.C., November 1986), p. 5.

efficient, to introduce new, lower cost technology and to be more sensitive to consumer needs and wants. Further, privatization promises that in a competitive economy prices will accurately reflect cost of production so that resource allocation will be efficiently channelled into the production of goods and services demanded by consumers. In addition, private ownership will be able to draw on more skilled entrepreneurial and managerial abilities available in the private sector so that the limited manpower in the public sector could be devoted to duties for which the private sector is unwilling or unable to undertake.

The World Bank and the United States Agency for International Development (USAID), in particular, have devoted considerable resources and efforts to broadening private sector initiative.[3]

The World Bank, for example, has for long urged African countries to provide adequate price incentives for farmers, to remove price controls in industry, to adopt market-based exchange and interest rates, to reduce the overgrown government bureaucracies, and to remove barriers to international trade. Now, in many African countries, privatization of inefficient SOEs has been added to the World Bank's standard economic reform package.

CONSTRAINTS TO PRIVATIZATION

As the public debate about the effectiveness of privatization as a cure-all for African economic problems has proceeded, it has increasingly become clear that Africa must overcome many social, institutional, economic, financial, political, and manpower, as well as technical, barriers if private sector development is to occur.[4] For example, in many African countries where privatization is going on, there are very few local business people with enough capital to purchase the privatized SOE. In these countries, this means that *de facto* equity privatization would lead to selling public property to foreign companies or minority groups, such as the Lebanese in the case of West Africa, or Indians in the case of East Africa.

Additionally, in many African states, SOEs have been a vehicle for providing employment opportunities for many people. Privatization often means reducing employment opportunities through shrinking the size of enterprises in order to make them viable. Even where there are local buyers and where privatization may not lead to significant unemployment, politicians may be reluctant to lose their control over the economy and the political patronage that these enterprises provide.

Again, in many African countries, capital markets are underdeveloped or unequipped to allow the conduct of a full-scale equity sale. Indeed, only Zimbabwe, the Ivory Coast, and Kenya have significant capital markets in sub-Saharan Africa. In addition, many African countries lack local firms with investment banking skills, facilities, and resources to arrange the sale of millions or even billions of dollars worth of public assets.

Above all, the entrenched civil servants who benefit from these SOEs will thwart any attempts to privatize them. Added to all these is the unstable political environment that creates additional uncertainty and lack of continuity in governmental policies. These, in turn, create fear that assets that are privatized by one government could be re-nationalized by a subsequent administration.

Also cited as a constraint to private sector development in Africa is the lack of manpower and entrepreneurial skills. While recognizing the above obstacles to private sector development in Africa, in the rest of this chapter, however, we will concentrate our analysis on examining whether indeed Africa's private sector development is constrained by lack of manpower and entrepreneurial skills or if it is the lack of an appropriate environment that has constrained private sector development in Africa. To proceed with our analysis, we will first define what the entrepreneurial process is, who is an entrepreneur, and the environment under which the entrepreneurial process can function.

THE ENTREPRENEUR AND THE ENTREPRENEURIAL PROCESS

In this section we provide only the definition of the entrepreneur and the entrepreneurial process needed to proceed with our analysis. Readers interested in detailed analysis of this topic are referred to the works of Joseph Schumpeter (1936), Frank Knight (1948), Isreal Kirzner (1973, 1979), and others who have done extensive work in this area.[5]

Unfortunately, there is no agreement among scholars as to what constitutes entrepreneurship or the entrepreneurial event. In the eighteenth century Richard Cantillion defined the entrepreneur as primarily the bearer of uninsurable risk. He argued that because of the risk-taking propensity, the entrepreneur became the balancing figure in the market, reacting to price movements that signaled shortages and surpluses. The idea of the entrepreneur as risk-taker was further developed and popularized in America in the writings of Frank Knight (1948).

However, to view the entrepreneur as only a risk-taker would be to limit the ability of the entrepreneur and to curtail the entrepreneurial process. As Edwin Hardwood (1982) demonstrates, there are many individuals and groups who assume uninsurable risks, but who do not necessarily perform the entrepreneurial function.[6] J. V. Say took the risk-bearer definition and developed it further, making the important distinction between the capitalist and the entrepreneur. The capitalist, or the financier, he argued, was one who supplied money and took a financial risk. This does not necessarily make the capitalist an entrepreneur, although the same person could also perform the function of both entrepreneur and the capitalist. Say's entrepreneur is a person who brought together the factors of production in such a way that new wealth was created. His entrepreneur combined the features of both risk-bearer and manager. Joseph Schumpeter and Isreal Kirzner's entrepreneurial process emphasizes the innovativeness and the alertness of the entrepreneur.

Michael Boskin (1984), on the other hand, defines the entrepreneurial process more broadly to include not only those in the business world taking risks to invent and promote new products and processes, but also those who are involved in the dissemination of new products and processes to new areas, whether locally, nationally, or internationally. He also includes the employees in the firms that are engaged in the new production process, as well as the scientists, the engineers, and others doing basic research, which generates new products and processes. According to Boskin, the entrepreneurial process is "a process by which new ideas, products, or processes are produced, generated, and disseminated to one or more markets."[7]

For our analysis we will adopt Boskin's definition because of its breadth and thus its applicability to the situation in Africa. However, for Boskin's entrepreneur to operate effectively and efficiently, what kind of political, economic, social, and legal environment must prevail? Are there some environments that are more conducive to its operation?

THE ECONOMIC ENVIRONMENT FOR ENTREPRENEURIAL DEVELOPMENT

Certainly, the economic environment has enormous implications for the development and the practice of the entrepreneurial process. As Binks and Coyne have commented, "It is evident that entrepreneurial skills may be more widely distributed in any population than is immediately apparent, but it requires a sympathetic economic environment to nurture and harness those skills in the creation of enterprise."[8] Indeed, the creation of an economic environment conducive to private ownership must precede everything. This involves implementing a tax system and property rights laws that protect value for owners. It involves a recognition on the part of the government that its role in the economy must be one of a facilitator and instrument for growth—providing the institutional framework that enables private entities to operate effectively.

Such a favorable environment must also include macro-economic reforms that offer appropriate tariff levels and tax structures that reward, not militate against, achievement and initiative and allow individuals to make and retain profits for engaging in risky enterprises. Government intervention in the economy to regulate prices, interest, and foreign exchange rates must be at a minimum.

However, the post-independence record of African governments' involvement in their economies have not facilitated either economic growth or the entrepreneurial process. Indeed, the disastrous record of such involvement has been widely documented and the evidence is quite convincing (World Bank, 1981; Young, 1982; Ravenhill, 1986; Hayden, 1983). The reasons that African states' involvement in the economy has failed to produce the desired results are many and varied. However, a review of the evidence strongly suggests that African states, instead of being instruments for economic growth and private sector development, have generally been regulatory states while some degree of involvement was necessary and needed. Given the poor post-independence economic state of most countries, the intervention has largely been excessive and inappropriate.

The overemphasis on SOEs not only discouraged private sector development, it also gave them unfair advantages and discriminated against private enterprise development. Policies such as government subsidies to SOEs, protection from both foreign and local competition, price controls, fixed foreign exchange rates, subsidized and concessionary interest rates, unfair tax structures, and poo r macro-economic conditions generally hurt the small businesses that operated in the private sector.

Given their generally limited resources, small businesses experience the effects of most governmental controls and regulations relatively more severely, requiring a disproportionately greater amount of time, labor, management, and money for compliance.

THE ENVIRONMENTAL IMPACT ON ENTREPRENEURSHIP—THE ROLE OF THE GHANAIAN COCOA FARMER

The case of the small peasant cocoa farmer of Ghana aptly demonstrates how such poor economic environments devastated the once resilient, creative, and innovative cocoa entrepreneurs. Cocoa has always played a dominant role in Ghana's economy.[9] Ghana used to be the number one producer of cocoa in the world; at one time cocoa accounted for more than 11 percent of Ghana's Gross Domestic Product (GDP) and 65 percent of all export earnings, as well as a sizeable proportion of government revenues. From its introduction to Ghana in the late nineteenth century, cocoa output increased consistently, reaching a peak output of 549,000 metric tons in 1964–1965—accounting for 31 percent of the world's supply of cocoa beans. However, since the 1960s, Ghana has gone from a position of dominance in world cocoa production to a distant third, behind the Ivory Coast and Brazil. Ghana's output reached a low of 180,000 metric tons in 1982–1983, accounting for only 16 percent of the world cocoa supply. This output change reflected the changes in both the absolute and relative price changes and government intrusion in the cocoa sector aimed at redistributing cocoa incomes in favor of industry and the government sector.[10]

Before April 1961, Ghana's economic policy had been a relatively liberal one that focused on the agricultural sector and emphasized free markets as the allocative mechanism of resources. However, in 1961, Ghana's development policy changed to one of forced industrialization, with the government as the main entrepreneur. Resources for the national industrialization program were to be extracted mainly from the agricultural sector and, thus, from the cocoa sector. To do this, national policy towards cocoa had to change to allow the government to tax the sector both directly and indirectly for its industrialization program.

While until 1939, the producer price of cocoa was largely determined by competitive market forces, with independent buyers competing for the output, by 1961 there was only one government agency authorized to purchase cocoa in Ghana. As a result, all competitive bidding for cocoa output ceased. With the government-created monopsonists came the "chit" system, whereby farmers were issued government "IOUs," rather than cash upon the sale of their produce. In addition to encountering corruption in this system, farmers also encountered delays in clearing these IOUs. The delays sometimes averaged six months and in some cases, payments were never made.

The heavy indirect taxes on the cocoa sector, the monopsonists' purchasing arrangements, and the price controls did not extend to food crop production. This situation encouraged the cocoa entrepreneurs (as it would have encouraged any entrepreneur) to rechannel their entrepreneurial abilities, as well as their productive resources, to food crop production.

As shown in Table 8.2, cocoa production became very unattractive relative to the production of other food crops that utilized similar resources and could be grown in the same ecological environment. As the table demonstrates, these small peasant entrepreneurs did not have much difficulty reacting to the strong positive correlation between cocoa output and real producer price, and the strong negative correlation between the real price of food crop and cocoa output.

The farmers responded to price signals and decreased the acreage under cocoa production. Indeed Manu (1974) reports that by 1965, the planting of new cocoa trees had virtually ceased in Ghana as a result of the economic conditions imposed largely by the government on the cocoa sector. Over time, many farmers abandoned their cocoa farms, while others cut down cocoa trees and replaced them with food crops.[11]

However, this was not the end of the demonstration of the entrepreneurial abilities of these small farmers. Soon these farmers, most of whom had never traveled outside their villages, were devising means by which they could smuggle their cocoa to such neighboring countries as the Ivory Coast, where the produce fetched higher prices. This underground economic activity, variously referred to as the "informal" or "parallel" market, became well developed. At some points in the late 1970s and early 1980s Ghana was losing an estimated 15 to 20 percent of its cocoa output to the Ivory Coast through smuggling.[12] A World Bank study of the cocoa sector in Ghana similarly concluded, "The Entrepreneurial skills and resources of the Ghanaian cocoa farmer, which had produced one of the highest living standards in Africa at the time of independence, had been drained by State Marketing Boards to finance ill-conceived public investment and to maintain an inflated bureaucracy."[13]

To stem the decline of the cocoa sector, on which the fortunes of the Ghanaian economy depended, and as part of its economic reform program, Ghana adopted a flexible exchange rate policy, liberalized its price control policies, and increased the producer price of cocoa. For example, the producer price of cocoa was raised from $57 a ton in 1957 and 1983 to $537 a ton in 1986. The response of the cocoa entrepreneurs was almost instantaneous. For example, cocoa output increased from 158,000 tons in 1983 to 230,000 tons in 1986. In addition, cocoa

Table 8.2
Cocoa Output and Real Producer Price Indices for Cocoa and Selected Food Crops in the 1970s

Year	Real Producer Price Index*	Output (Metric Tons)	Maize	Plantain	Cocoyam
1969	70.92	409.0	94.13	77.63	109.63
1970	64.73	386.0	87.87	104.87	110.11
1971	58.81	470.0	115.11	86.28	132.19
1972	62.47	422.0	104.56	128.31	130.08
1973	63.46	355.0	95.84	99.83	148.49
1974	61.10	382.0	92.42	93.67	111.74
1975	41.75	401.0	134.96	188.75	133.99
1976	24.11	329.0	130.17	121.00	163.79
1977	25.30	271.0	76.42	166.64	197.17
1978	32.88	265.0	70.41	148.85	136.67
1979	32.85	296.0	113.14	103.46	109.74
1980	15.18	258.0	109.43	101.15	117.71
1981	27.22	224.0	126.18	98.71	117.71

*1963 = 100

Source: Ghana Government: Ministry of Agriculture

smuggled to the Ivory Coast declined to 9 percent, or approximately 20,000 tons a year, from 15 to 20 percent in the early 1980s.[14] The story of the demise of the cocoa sector and the cocoa entrepreneur in Ghana can be retold for many African states. For example, Tanzania's total export of its major commodities (cotton, coffee, cloves, sisal, cashews, tobacco, and tea) declined by 34 percent between 1973 and 1980. This was due to a cutback in prices which, in turn, was caused by lower prices paid to the producers. The heavy indirect "taxes" paid by these export duties, combined with increasing marketing and administrative costs incurred by government marketing agencies, led to a reduction in the farmers' share in export earnings to below 50 percent. Reacting to this, farmers directed some of their crops (particularly coffee) into unofficial channels, neglected and, in some cases, abandoned some coffee trees and other crops, and shifted their resources into food crop production.[15]

IMPROVING THE ENVIRONMENT FOR ENTREPRENEURIAL ACTIVITY—REFORMS IN OTHER AFRICAN COUNTRIES

In spite of the many obstacles to its development, the resilience and the creativity of the African entrepreneur have been remarkable whenever an opportunity has offered itself. For example, when the Kenyan government permitted hitherto controlled and low prices to rise, corn production rose by nearly 50 percent in 1985.

Similarly, in 1981 the government of Zimbabwe introduced a package of support for small black farmers. That package provided price increases, credit availability, and proximity to input selling depots. The results were a significant increase in production. Since then, small farmers have increased their food production fifteenfold (much faster than White commercial farmers), and raised their market share of corn from approximately 7 percent before independence to approximately 66.6 percent in 1985.[16] Another example: since 1982 the government of Somalia has not only raised and liberalized prices, but has also provided newly-legalized, private marketing groups for sorghum and oil seed. The result has been a doubling of sorghum and oil seed production. Furthermore, currency devaluation, combined with farm output price increases, has led to increases in Somalia's corn output from 150,000 tons in 1982 to 350,000 tons in 1987. The cases reviewed above show that policies that favor entrepreneurial growth work in Africa the same way they work elsewhere. The cases also reaffirm the fact that entrepreneurs exist in Africa and will respond well to appropriate incentives.

Despite African governments' emphasis on the SOEs and fascination with foreign capitalists, the small African entrepreneur still remains the mainstay of most African economies. In Ghana small entrepreneurs still produce the main foreign exchange earner—cocoa. In the Ivory Coast, Kenya and Uganda, they produce the economic mainstays of coffee and cocoa. Indeed, in Africa, 60 percent of the food is produced by small peasant farmers—women. In Nigeria, small entrepreneurs produce the cloth, and everywhere in Africa they produce furniture, jewelry, shoes, and metal goods. They repair everything—cars, bicycles, chairs, tables, radios, and televisions.

Many of these entrepreneurial businesses are very small—almost half of them consist of one person, and 95 percent employ fewer than five people. Nevertheless, they provide two-thirds of the industrial employment in Africa, and what is more, they consistently generate more jobs on a per-capita investment basis than larger firms. They do not benefit from any of the concessionary and artificially low interest rates government provides to larger firms. Indeed, less than

5 percent of all the invested capital for these small entrepreneurs comes from government or bank loans.[17]

THE POLITICAL AND LEGAL ENVIRONMENT FOR ENTREPRENEURIAL DEVELOPMENT

Two other critically-related factors essential for private sector development are a legal environment in which property rights are well defined and legally enforced, and political stability. The literature on the economics of property rights shows that different property ownership rights give rise to different economic incentives and produce different economic outcomes. Private sector development depends significantly on the willingness of entrepreneurs to risk the investment of their funds toward the development of an enterprise in the hope that they will generate an acceptable rate of economic return. This willingness depends very much on the amount of faith they have in the legal system to protect this investment. Clear and simple laws, effectively and swiftly applied, are essential for building business confidence in a stable and supportive business climate. If the law does not contain enough safeguards for private ownership of property and for legal enforcement of contracts, backed by a fair, impartial, and accessible judiciary system, then entrepreneurship will not develop and grow.

An appropriate legal environment must recognize that private enterprises are owned by individuals who want to operate with the minimum interference within the limits of the law, and to use and exchange their property rights in the pursuit of profits. Entrepreneurs and capitalists operating in this environment must be free from fear and the uncertainty of government expropriation of their assets.

Unfair laws, excessive bureaucratic hassles, and intervention act only to suppress and re-channel the productive energy and the entrepreneurial skills from creative and innovative ventures into attempts to circumvent laws and controls, that is, to "beat the system." One result of such intervention is that "they reduce the flexibility of the private sector, raise its cost, and increase the uncertainty under which it operates. Often these interventions drive business 'underground' or into the 'informal' realm."[18] Indeed, in many African countries, tremendous amounts of energy, time, and effort are invested by individuals, entrepreneurs, small businesses, capitalists, and financiers in search of ways to get around numerous government controls, licensing rules, price controls, and unfair, illegal laws. In many cases the relevance and applicability of the law depend on who you know, and when you don't know anybody who is "important" and therefore above the law, one way to avoid the laws, the controls, and the bureaucratic delays is to choose to operate on the informal or the parallel markets.

OPERATING IN THE PARALLEL OR THE INFORMAL MARKETS

What exactly is this informal or parallel market? Why does it predominate in Africa, and indeed in many developing and command economies, such as China and the Soviet Union? Are the operators in these markets considered entrepreneurs according to our definition?

The parallel markets consist of highly organized systems of income-generating activities that are designed to circumvent the various government regulations, laws, controls, and licensing requirements. The common element among countries in which these markets prevail is the excessive involvement and intervention of the state in economic activities—through price controls, bureaucratic delays and red tape, numerous licensing requirements, high and unfair taxes, and government and official corruption. The parallel markets in Africa have developed generally in response to business attempts to avoid the regulations, controls, and high taxes imposed by the state. Some of the activities on these markets are illegal; others are quite legitimate in themselves, but are carried out in a manner that allows the entrepreneurs involved to avoid paying taxes, and to circumvent government controls and regulations. This sector of the economy consists of illegal gold and diamond mining and sales, ivory poaching, smuggling, hoarding, and speculation. Whether illegal or legitimate, the operators are simply responding to and taking advantage of market equilibria, and performing a market equilibrating function—buying when prices are lowest, selling when prices are highest, and seeking to balance the marginal gain from each proposed activity against the marginal cost.

In many instances, these activities are high-risk stakes, sometimes punishable by death. The operators in these markets fit our definition of entrepreneurs and are involved in the entrepreneurial process. However, in Africa, the entrepreneurs involved in these markets are perceived as disequilibrating forces—creating artificial shortages (hoarding) and charging higher prices. They are viewed as exploiters. In Ghana, the term "Kalabule," meaning economic saboteurs, has been coined for entrepreneurs involved in retailing and wholesaling. The implication of the term is that these entrepreneurs are somehow involved in activities that exploit society.

Many of the activities on the parallel markets, like the retailing and wholesaling in Africa, are carried out by women, and for very good reasons. Most of the activities are carried out without licenses, they do not require substantial amounts of capital investment (and thus no bank or government loans), they do not require compliance with bureaucratic regulations, controls, and record-keeping (and thus illiterates can operate freely in the market), and they do not require the permission of husbands (in countries such as Zaire, women are required to have their husband's permission to engage in certain economic and social activities).

Given this situation, the parallel and informal markets lend themselves to women's participation. The success of the women's group "Nana Benz" in Togo has been publicized widely as an illustration of the entrepreneurial acumen of West African market women. Nana Benz—so named because they are chauffeured around the city in Mercedes Benz—is a powerful group of Togolese market women who have succeeded against tremendous odds. As Mavi Franklin, one of the group leaders recounted, "You start very, very small. All you do at first is sit and wait for clients . . . you climb bit by bit.''[19] The women's success has been built on strong entrepreneurial abilities, shrewd business acumen, and an extraordinary ability to keep large and complicated accounts in their heads. Most of them have never had any formal education and are functional illiterates. Yet they have succeeded in the complex and risky political and economic environment of Togo.

As the Togolese economy has been deregulated and controls have been reduced, the Nana Benz group has sought to diversify. Recently, they have branched out into a wide array of business ventures, including restaurants, bakeries, boutique shops, trucking, taxis, canned goods, and real estate.[20]

Having succeeded and gained national prominence at a time when the private sector is being touted as the cure of the ailing Togolese economy, Nana Benz are using their new-found clout to pressure government to liberalize and to further deregulate the economy of Togo.[21] Like the peasant cocoa entrepreneurs of Ghana, the Togolese market women fared best when the economic environment allowed the development and full exploitation of their entrepreneurial abilities. Indeed, when private trading activities are legitimized, as the above example illustrates, the dual market structures prevailing in African countries can be merged and entrepreneurial energies directed towards improving the distribution systems. Benefits from such efficient distribution systems can be shared by both consumers and producers.

Closely related to the legal environment, in its effect on the private sector development, is the political atmosphere prevailing in a given country. The nonrepresentative and nondemocratic nature of African governments betrays one important requirement for private sector development—a degree of certainty and continuity in governmental policy. Wide swings in policy only exacerbate the risk inherent in the entrepreneurial process itself.

In most African countries the lack of basic political freedoms—of thought, expression, opinion—have hindered free and open debate on matters and policies that impact significantly on entrepreneurial decisions. Can we realistically expect a state to enact laws that protect private property rights, and respect and enforce these laws when individual private (human) rights are abused, curtailed, or denied? Did the Makola (one of the largest markets in Accra) market women have any property rights when the government of Jerry Rawlings ordered the market to be burned down because the retailers and wholesalers there had refused to comply with government price control guidelines? Where were their civil and human rights when they were insulted, whipped, and tried in ''people's courts,'' branded economic saboteurs, and all their goods confiscated by the state?[22] Obviously without political pluralism, economic pluralism becomes very difficult to achieve, and without economic pluralism, private sector development becomes a very difficult and, indeed, an unrealistic proposition in Africa.

Up till now, our analysis and discussions of the entrepreneurial process have deliberately been confined to the small African entrepreneurs—the peasant cocoa farmer, the market women, and the operators of the parallel and informal markets, who are largely illiterates. But however successful these small entrepreneurs may have been, many writers have argued that for African entrepreneurs to compete effectively in the increasingly complex global markets, they will need to sharpen their technical, managerial, and entrepreneurial abilities. The entrepreneurial process involves technological innovation and the introduction of new production processes and methods.

According to these authors, these skills are lacking in Africa's small entrepreneurs. For example, Beveridge and Oberschall (1979) observed that despite the achievements of Zambian entrepreneurs in building up modern enterprises employing large numbers of employees, there remained a considerable gap in terms of organizational efficiency between these indigenous firms and the majority of Asian and European firms in Zambia. The authors also observed that these local firms have not been successful in adopting any but the simplest technology, and have not advanced any management style that enables them to introduce effective, routinized systems of production control.

In his study of entrepreneurships in Nigeria, Schatz (1977) also observed the need for an entrepreneurial "leap." He stated that if Nigerian firms are to have any major impact on the local economy, "entrepreneurs must surmount three main hurdles: the ability to utilize high levels of technology with all that this involves in terms of quality control, training, and specialization; the attainment of a much greater degree of organizational competence—in particular the willingness to delegate authority and establish impersonal systems of control; and the management of wide-ranging market outlets based on an elaborate sales network and distribution."[23] Similar observations were made by Nafziger (1977) in his study of Nigerian entrepreneurship. He stressed that as the firm expanded and its output and quality of input requirements became more complex, so too the quality of managerial leadership and competence had to improve.

The consensus of these studies is that effective development of the entrepreneurial process in Africa requires a good supply of sceintists, researchers, engineers, technicians, and modern entrepreneurs who will not only develop new processes, methods, and sources of raw material supply, but will also transform the new discovery into actual production of goods and services. The question, then, is: does Africa have the requisite manpower and the entrepreneurial skills needed for the modern complex business operation?

Admittedly, Africa had very few trained personnel during the colonial period. However, since independence, Africa has made tremendous strides to train its people at all professional levels. For example, at the end of the colonial period, only one-third of African school children of the appropriate age were in elementary schools, less than 3 percent were in secondary schools, and an insignificant proportion was in the few colleges and universities that existed at the time. Since then, total enrollments have increased fivefold, and they tripled between 1970 and 1983 (growing at twice the rate for Asia, and three times that for Latin America).

Most African states provide free education up to university level, and a country on average spends approximately 20 percent of its gross national product on education. Furthermore, most African countries now have at least one national university, and the continent's total is up from six in 1960 to eighty today, with annual rates of enrollment growing at 14 percent.[24] Why, then, is there talk that Africa lacks enough manpower to carry the demands of privatization? The answer is simple. Despite the progress Africa has made in educating its people, it still has a long way to go. But even more important is that those that Africa has successfully trained are lost through migration to the developed world. Given the political instability, the lack of political, civil, and human rights on the continent, and an economic system that does not reward hard work, private initiative, and enterprise, many of Africa's educated personnel have left to seek economic and political freedoms elsewhere. Over the last two decades, thousands of highly-trained African professionals have migrated to the United States. During the summer of 1989, we conducted a survey of African professionals working in the United States—doctors, scientists, researchers, engineers, lawyers, economists, and technicians—to determine the factors that were most important in their migration decisions and to ascertain what would be required to get them to return to their respective countries.

The sample for the study was selected primarily from published professional directories and through contacts with private and public organizations. Based on these sources, one thousand three hundred names and addresses were selected. From this list, eight hundred were randomly selected and mailed survey questionnaires in June 1989. Postcard reminders were sent to nonrespondents in August. From these mailings we received 280 responses, of which 240 were usable for our analysis. After making adjustments for the high number of returns that were due to changes in addresses (for which no contact was made), our contacted response rate is calculated as 39 percent.

Despite the apparent low response rate, we feel that our sample is quite representative of African professionals in the United States, as manifested by the large number of African nationals who responded to our survey and by the wide geographical coverage of African professionals working in various states in this country. For example, our sample covers thirty-one African countries and had respondents from twenty-four of the fifty American states and the District of Columbia.[25]

An examination of the characteristics of our respondents provides useful insights for entrepreneurial and private sector development in Africa. The average age of the African emigrant in our study is forty years. The respondents are predominantly male (88 percent), married (77 percent), and have children (78 percent). They are highly educated—58 percent have Ph.D or M.D. degrees, and 19 percent have Master's degrees. And as shown in Table 8.3, these emigrants have professional specializations that span the whole spectrum of academic disciplines. Furthermore, more than 60 percent have acquired further education and training since their emigration to the United States. The average emigrant in our study has lived in the United States for 12.4 years.

Table 8.3
African Emigrants: Areas of Professional Specialization

Area of Specialitzation	No.	% of Responses
Accounting	5	3%
Architecture	2	1%
Business Administration Management	17	9%
Chemistry	3	2%
Computer Science	5	3%
Demography	2	1%
Medicine, Dentistry	16	8%
Economics	55	28%
Education	3	2%
Engineering	20	10%
Finance	13	7%
Political Science & International Relations	12	6%
Journalism, Language, Literature	24	12%
Law	5	3%
Philosophy	2	1%
Public Administration	5	3%
Statistics	3	2%
Others	6	3%
Total	198	100%

About 60 percent of the respondents had professional jobs in which they had six years of experience prior to their migration to the United States. In their home countries, most of them were college professors (18 percent), economists (11 percent), medical officers (8 percent), and engineers (7 percent).[26]

These emigrants maintain very strong ties with their families and home countries. Only 10 percent have not visited their home countries since their emigration. For 55 percent of the respondents, a trip home once or more in every 1 to 3 years is the norm, while 19 percent visit home once or more per year. Our results also show that 58 percent of the respondents currently have personal investment projects that they are financing in their home countries. Another indication of strong ties to their countries and families is manifested by the fact that 30 percent of the respondents plan to resettle permanently in their home countries in the next five years, while an additional 59 percent plan to resettle in their home countries sometime in the future.

The respondents are employed throughout the American economy, as is shown in Table 8.4. In this table, we see that the largest group, 43 percent, are employed in higher education institutions (college and university professors), 24 percent work for international development organizations (the World Bank, IMF, and

Table 8.4
Employment Categories and Positions of African Professionals in the United States

Employment Category	% of Respondents
Private Corporations	8.6
International Development Organizations	24.2
Higher Education	43.0
Medical Establishments	2.5
Federal Government	0.5
State and Local Governments	7.1
Self-Employed	7.1
Unemployed	0.5
Others	6.6
Total	100.1%*
No. of Respondents	198

Current Positions at Work	% of Respondents
Manager, Administrator	3.3
President, Vice President	3.3
Division Chiefs	2.2
Head of Department, Full Professor	7.7
Assistant, Associate Professor	31.7
Senior Engineer	2.2
Engineer	4.4
Senior Economist	3.8
Economist	5.5
Senior Medical Officer	0.0
Medical Officer	3.3
Research Officer	3.3
Financial Analyst	2.7
Other	25.7
Total	100.2*
No. of Respondents	183

*Due to Rounding Errors.

the UN), 9 percent work for private corporations, and 7 percent are self-employed.

The factors that were most important in the migration decisions of our respondents are shown in Table 8.5. As shown in the table, in their migration decision, an overwhelming majority (65 percent) indicated that the economic situation in their home country was either somewhat or very important in their

Table 8.5
African Professionals' Reasons for Migration to the United States

Reasons	Very Important	Somewhat Important	Not Important	N/A	Total %
Economic Situation in Home Country	31.8	33.0	19.6	15.6	100
Political Dictatorship and Lack of Freedom in Home Country	33.3	16.4	25.7	24.6	100
Civil Wars, Tribalism	11.3	12.5	28.7	47.5	100
Seek Further Training and Education	75.8	10.0	5.0	9.2	100.1

decision. For 76 percent of our respondents, the opportunity to seek further education and training (also related to improving their earning capability and living conditions) was very important in their decision. However, the reasons for the African migration are not merely economic. As Speare suggests, "In international migration, political factors are often more important than economic factors."[27] Granted that in the case of this study, our respondents ranked economic factors higher than political factors, nevertheless, 51 percent considered the political situation in their home countries to be either very or somewhat important in their migration decision.

Our analysis of the survey results confirms what we have already stated earlier—while Africa may be deficient in manpower and entrepreneurial skills supply, constraints to its private sector development can largely be attributed to poor economic, legal, and political environments that have acted to channel Africa's entrepreneurial talents and abilities, and have resulted in a large migration of its most highly skilled and trained professionals. For many African professionals, migration has become an alternative to operating in the parallel or the informal markets. The decision to migrate is itself an entrepreneurial decision. Indeed, most of our respondents, by choosing to migrate, were responding to the disequilibria that exists in the international labor markets. After all, international migration, among other factors, signifies, to a large extent, the inequalities in the level of economic development, employment opportunity, and, most of all, income and living conditions, between developed and developing countries.

Given that the average respondent has spent over twelve years in this country, that 60 percent of the respondents have acquired additional education and training in this country, that 7 percent work for themselves and, that an additional 9 percent work for private American corporations, we can safely conclude that these African emigrants have been exposed to the entrepreneurial and the capitalist culture of this country, characterized by creativity, innovativeness, competitiveness, personal achievement and success, limited government, personal freedoms, and civil liberties. Whether or not African businesses are organized along American lines, these Africans have had first-hand experience of the capitalist organization of business enterprises and have worked in an environment where personal responsibility, profit motive, quality, efficiency, and the bottom line are the essential ingredients of success. This exposure may be important for private sector development in Africa.

Indeed, when asked what they liked most about America, more than 75 percent of the respondents listed one or more of the following: political freedoms, civil liberties, private enterprise, the economic system, and economic opportunity. On the other hand, when asked what they resented most about their respective countries, more than 80 percent listed one or more of the following: the political dictatorship, the lack of political and civil liberties, corruption, economic mismanagement, civil war, and tribalism.

While 89 percent of our respondents plan to resettle eventually in their respective countries some time in the future, they will do so only after they see some fundamental changes in their countries, especially in the economic and the political spheres.

The factors cited by respondents as important in their decisions to return home are shown in Table 8.6. For an overwhelming majority of the respondents (94 percent), the desire to help the development of their country is important in their return decision. In a remarkable turnaround, we found that while the economic situation in their home country was of greater importance (cited by 66 percent of the respondents) than the political situation (cited by 50 percent) at the time of their migration, now the political situation in their country is given a greater weight than the economic situation in the return decision.

The restoration of political freedoms and civil liberties in their home countries was cited as being very important or somewhat important by 58 percent of our respondents, while 53 percent viewed better economic conditions in their country as somewhat or very important in their return decision. While this turnaround may be due to the economic success that our respondents may have achieved in America, it is also possible that their stay in America may have developed their appetite for more political freedoms and civil liberties.

Either way we interpret this turnaround, the fact still remains that while these professionals are willing to return to their respective countries in large numbers, they will not do so until their countries are willing to guarantee some degree of political and economic pluralism—two essential ingredients for the development of the entrepreneurial process and the private sector in Africa.

The unwillingness of these African professionals to return, given the political

Table 8.6
Factors Considered as Important for the Return of African Professionals to their Home Countries

	% of Respondents				
Factors	Very Important	Somewhat Important	Not Important	N/A*	Total
Desire to Help My Country's Development	70.0	24.4	4.2	1.8	100.4**
Racism, Discrimination in United States	19.6	27.2	39.2	14.0	100.0
Lack of Opportunities for Advancement in my U.S. Job	4.4	17.0	47.0	31.6	100.0
Family ties in my Country	6.6	25.8	7.0	1.2	100.0
Improved Economic Conditions in My Country	20.1	33.3	32.1	14.5	100.0
Freedom and Civil Liberties Restoration in My Country	41.1	17.1	26.6	15.2	100.0
Desire to Raise My Children in My Country	26.0	32.1	30.2	11.7	100.0

*N/A: Not applied
**Rounding Errors

and economic situation in their home countries, may have exacerbated the manpower shortages and contributed to the perception that Africa's private sector development is being constrained by lack of manpower and entrepreneurial shortages. Indeed, the return of all African professionals to their homes today would not necessarily lead to the development of the private sector. This fact has already been demonstrated in our discussion of the peasant cocoa farmer in Ghana, the market women in Africa, and the predominance of the parallel and informal markets in Africa. Our analyses have shown that it is not entrepreneurial talents or manpower shortages that afflict the private sector development in Africa so much as the political, economic, and the legal framework within which the entrepreneurial process must operate.

In fact, it is not only indigenous African entrepreneurs that are constrained by this poor business environment in Africa. For example, a survey of 233 industrial firms in the Federal Republic of Germany found that the most important individual constraint that they faced in doing business in Africa was the difficulty in dealing with government bureaucracy. Other obstacles cited by these entrepreneurs include: corruption, unstable political systems, and uncertainty about whether legal and contractual rights would be upheld in the courts.[28] Indeed, our results confirm this finding. We also find that the migration of African professionals abroad, like the rechanneling of entrepreneurial skills into the parallel and informal markets, is the inevitable result of the combined political and economic environments that militate against private initiative and enterprise.

CONCLUSION

Africa's current privatization drive is an important step toward developing its private sector. However, a fundamental prerequisite to the growth of the private sector in Africa is a favorable policy, political, and legal environment. This environment can be created through government reforms that remove the debilitating restraints on entrepreneurial activity.

The evidence reviewed in this chapter does not support the observation of OAU/ECA/ADB quoted at the beginning of this chapter. Our conclusion is that while Africa suffers from an inadequate supply of manpower, its inability to fully utilize its available manpower and entreprenuerial abilities is due to poor business, created largely by government intervention and the regulation of the economy. Our conclusion is supported by other studies. For example, a World Bank study also concluded: "The evidence demonstrates clearly that there is no shortfall of entrepreneurial spirit in Africa. The most critical limiting factor is not entrepreneurship, but weaknesses in the physical environment which inhibit effective investment."[29]

For a long time to come, Africa's private sector will continue to depend on small firms. While not all small firms are entrepreneurships, most entrepreneurs begin in small firms. It is generally agreed (Kent, 1984) that actions which encourage the formation of small firms also improve the entrepreneurial environment. Therefore, one of the greatest potentials for the blossoming of private enterprise lies in implementing policies that promote the growth and expansion of small business. The encouragement of small and, perhaps, medium-sized enterprises not only helps the development of an indigenous private sector, but also acts as a source for recruiting and training future entrepreneurs.

Another key task for Africa's private sector development is to find ways of harnessing the vast and creative energy of the informal and the parallel markets, bringing them into a restructured formal economy that may grow and develop.

Africa's private sector development, and, indeed, overall economic development, will continue to be constrained by an inadequate supply of skilled manpower and entrepreneurs. However, undertaking the necessary economic and political reforms that encourage the return of its highly skilled professionals is one important first step in relaxing the constraints.

Unfair and unjust laws, bureaucratic controls, delays, and regulatory policies of African states have tended to redirect the entrepreneurial abilities of Africans and have corrupted government officials at all levels. When corruption is combined with bureaucratic incompetence, we get the ultimate environment that chokes private initiative and enterprise.

It is for this reason that African governments should strive to be less regulatory, but more as instruments for the private sector development. Perhaps African governments may have something to learn from the historical experience of Japan. In his study of modern Japan, Chalmers Johnson states:

Looked at historically, modern Japan began in 1868 to be plan-rational and developmental. After about a decade and a half of experimentation with direct state operation of economic enterprises, it discovered the most obvious pitfalls of plan rationality: corruption, bureaucraticism, and ineffective monopolies. Japan was and remained plan rational, but it had no ideological commitment to state ownership of the economy. Its main criterion was the rational one of effectiveness in meeting the goals of development. Meiji Japan began to shift away from state entrepreneurship to collaboration with privately owned enterprises, favoring those enterprises that were capable of rapidly adopting new technologies and were committed to the national goals of development and military strength.[30]

Elsewhere, Johnson shows how Japan encouraged particular kinds of research and gave bonuses and contracts to companies that undertook research in state-preferred projects. The Japanese historical experience may have some relevance for Africa.

A sign that Africa may have already come to grips with the private-public sector role in the economy is reflected in the final communique issued at the 1986 Nairobi conference on private sector involvement in African economies. The communique summarized the emerging consensus among African governments, foreign and local firms, and the voluntary aid agencies. It called on business to make sure that its activities were consistent with national development priorities, to channel more resources into the training and assistance of small-scale entrepreneurs, and to be more sensitive to the social neeeds of workers and society in general. The communique also urged governments to move toward "freer markets and more realistic prices for foreign exchange, capital, products, and labor."[31] If African governments are willing to carry through the declarations in the the communiqe, there might still be a chance for an effective development of the private sector in Africa.

NOTES

1. *Africa Report,* July–August, 1986, p. 93.

2. Statement made at the International Conference on Privatization. February 17, 1986, Washington, D.C.

3. Since the early 1980s, the United States has been pushing for public sector reforms in the developing world. In 1986 USAID held a conference in Washington, D.C., at which delegates from thirty countries participated and talked about different techniques of privatization (*Washington Times*, February 28, 1986). Aid Deputy Administrator Jay F. Morris said AID had instructed its mission in forty countries to engage governments in discussions about privation and had set a goal "to be involved in an average of at least two privatization activities" in each of these countries by the end of 1987.

4. "The Public-Private Debate," *Africa Report*, July–August, 1986, p. 93.

5. Joseph Schumpeter, *The Theory of Economic Development* (Cambridge, Massachusetts: Harvard University Press, 1936), Frank Knight, *Risk, Uncertainty, and Profit*, Series of Reprints of Scarce Tracts in Economics and Political Science, No. 16 (London School of Economics and Political Science, 1948), Israel Kirzner, *Competition and Entrepreneurship* (Chicago: University of Chicago Press, 1973), and *Perception Opportunity and Profit* (Chicago: University of Chicago Press, 1979).

6. Edwin Hardwood, "Sociology of Entrepreneurship" in *The Encyclopedia of Entrepreneurship*, Calvin A. Kent et.al., eds. (Englewood Cliffs, N.J.: Prentice Hall, 1982), pp. 91–98.

7. Michael J. Boskin, *The Fiscal Environment for Entrepreneurship in the Environment for Entrepreneurship*, Calvin Kent, ed. (Lexington Books), p. 59.

8. Binks and Coyne, *The Birth of Enterprise*, p. 75.

9. The discussion in this section draws on the author's previous work, "Rationality of the Ghanaian Cocoa Farmer: Supply Response to Government Policies, 1933–1983," an unpublished paper.

10. J.C. Bethelemy and F. Gagey, "The Agricultural Supply Price: Elasticity in Africa," *European Economic Review*, 31: 1493–1507.

11. See Manu (1974) and a series of newspaper articles on the conversion of cocoa farms to food-crop farms, e.g., *Daily Graphic*, Accra, Ghana; March 4, 1981, p. 1, and July 8, 1981, p. 1.

12. See *Daily Graphic*, May 2 (1982) and May (1985).

13. Kith Marsden and Therese Belot, *Private Enterprise in Africa* (World Bank: Washington, D.C., 1988), p. 62.

14. *Africa Report*, September–October, 1988, p.28.

15. See *Accelerated Development in Sub-Saharan Africa: An Agenda for Action* (World Bank, 1983).

16. Jennifer Seymour Whitaker, *How Can Africa Survive?* (New York: Council on Foreign Relations Press, 1988), p. 163.

17. Data cited in this section are from Whitaker, op. cit., p. 190.

18. See *Developing the Private Sector: A Challenge for the World Bank Group* (World Bank, 1989).

19. See *Africa Report*, May–June, 1986, p. 47.

20. Ibid.

21. Ibid.

22. See *News Watch*, February 2, 1987, p. 15, and *West Africa*, October 4, 1982, p. 2571.

23. S.P. Schatz, *Nigerian Capitalism* (Berkeley, California: University of California, Press, 1977), p. 78.

24. See Whitaker, op. cit., p. 175

25. African countries involved in the survey include: Algeria, Tunisia, Egypt, Mo-

rocco, Sudan, Chad, Niger, Djibouti, Ethiopia, Somalia, Kenya, Uganda, Tanzania, Mozambique, Malawi, Zambia, Botswana, Zaire, Rwanda, Gabon, Cameroon, Togo, Nigeria, Benin, Ivory Coast, Ghana, Liberia, Guinea, Senegal, Sierra Leone, and Gambia.

26. This section draws from earlier unpublished work of the author.

27. See A. Spear, Jr., ''The Relevance of Models of Internal Migration for the Study of International Migration,'' in *International Migration*, G. Tapinos, ed. (Proceedings of a Seminar on Demographic Research, 1974).

28. See Kith Marsden and Therese Belot, op. cit., p. 16.

29. Ibid., p. 47.

30. Chalmers Johnson, *MITI and the Japanese Miracle* (Stanford: Stanford University Press, 1982), p. 23.

31. Peter Robbs, ''Privatization in Africa: Neither Pox nor Panacea,'' *Development International,* March/April 1987, p. 28.

9

Gender and Entrepreneurship: Issues of Capital and Technology in Nigerian Small Firms

MARY J. OSIRIM

As a result of the economic crises of the early 1980s in Africa, many states are attempting to "disengage" themselves from the economy in an effort to promote greater "laissez-fairism." These actions have largely been encouraged by the major international lending agencies, such as the World Bank and the IMF, in the hopes of creating leaner, more efficient economies that will attract multi-national investment. At the same time, privatization is also designed to provide investment opportunities for local entrepreneurs. In the wake of rising unemployment and poverty in African societies today, scholars have increasingly attempted to examine the informal sector, since it is the principal sphere of economic activity for the masses in the region. The informal sector has been defined by the International Labor Office Report on Kenya by: "its ease of entry, reliance on indigenous resources, family ownership of enterprises, small scale of operations, labor-intensive and adapted technology, skill acquired outside the formal school systems, and unregulated and competitive markets."[1] In addition to clearly defining this field of activity, a rigorous study of the informal sector has become essential, since several predictions and stereotypes regarding African economies have not materialized, namely: (a) Despite the recommendations of the international lending agencies and the austerity measures that most often accompany their loans and debt-restructuring programs, a significant increase in multinational investment has not occurred in many African states such as Nigeria; and (b) the stereotypes of the informal sector as consisting of *traditional* activities bearing very little, if any, relationship to the formal economy is untrue (Portes and Walton, 1981; Afonja, 1981). Given the realities of African development, it has become exceedingly important that we understand the composition, contributions, and articulation of small-scale activities to the formal sector and to the national and global economies.

METHODOLOGY

This study is based on the results of two independent samples of entrepreneurs who began small firms in southwestern Nigeria. The first of these investigations sought to identify "who the entrepreneurs really are" and the characteristics of "successful" entrepreneurship among firms in the bakery and furniture industries in Lagos and Benin, Nigeria. Fifty entrepreneurs (twenty-five each in Lagos and Benin) were randomly selected and interviewed about the following issues: (a) their personal background characteristics, (b) their operation of the firm, and (c) the use of institutional support services in their enterprises. Only *five* of the respondents in this study, conducted in 1982–83 were female (Osirim, 1986). A second survey of entrepreneurs was undertaken in June/July, 1988. This research sought to analyze women's roles in the small-scale sector by intensively interviewing participants in three fields where women were highly concentrated— as traders (of cloth and foodstuffs), as hairdressers, and as seamstresses. Fifty-four women in Lagos and Benin were questioned about: (a) their personal background characteristics, (b) their current family life, and (c) the operation of their business, in an effort to discover if the long history of economic independence manifested by these West African women translated into greater equality in the domestic sphere. (Earlier sociological and anthropological studies have recognized this contradiction—see Sudarkasa, 1981; Sanday, 1974; Afonja, 1981.) In addition, this research attempted an analysis of the relationship of the informal to the formal sector, and a look at the possibilities for an expanded involvement for women with the emergence of new economic opportunities.

FEMALE AND MALE IN BUSINESS: THE CASE OF ENTREPRENEURSHIP IN LAGOS

As previously stated, two studies of entrepreneurs who began small firms in Lagos were conducted independently—one from November 1982 to February 1983 and another in June to July 1988. Although twenty-five entrepreneurs were interviewed in the first of these samples, only twenty-two respondents will be included here; the three female participants in this earlier study will be excluded so that an all male sample can be compared to the all female sample of 1988. The bakery and furniture industries were selected for the first project since those industries contained a large number of firms in both Lagos and Benin. Ten bakers and twelve furniture manufacturers were interviewed for this work. In the second study, seamstresses, hairdressers, and cloth sellers were chosen precisely because these firms contained a high concentration of women as entrepreneurs. A subsample of twenty respondents has been selected for examination here. These participants were distributed as follows: (a) four cloth sellers, (b) eight hairdressers, (c) seven seamstresses, and (d) one combination hairdresser and seamstress. Due to time constraints in the second study, the interviewing was restricted to the town of Suru-Lere, a largely middle-class section of Lagos.

Ethnic homogeneity was more apparent among the male than the female entrepreneurs. The vast majority of males were Yoruba (nineteen) compared to almost half the female sample (nine). The remaining male population consisted of one person of mixed Hausa and Yoruba origins, one Edo, and one member of a small minority group. The female entrepreneurs also included four Ibos, three Edos, and four persons from smaller ethnic groups within their ranks. Although Lagos is located in Yorubaland, it has the distinction of being the commercial capital and, to some extent, still remains the center of political life, since the permanent relocation of the national government to Abuja is still under way. Thus, given the position of Lagos as the major urban center of the country, it is more likely than many other areas to experience ethnic heterogeneity in business. With respect to commerce, this character is readily seen in Suru-lere, a more middle-class area of the city with a bustling small business sector. Of particular interest here was the seemingly high proportion of diplomats' wives, who established businesses in this area. This population does include wider ethnic variation within its ranks.

Significant variation was noted in the mean and median ages of the firms examined. Enterprises owned by men had a mean age of 22 years and a median age of 22.5 years. The women's firms were much younger in comparison—they had a mean age of eight years and a median age of 6.5 years. Several of the furniture businesses and bakeries included here are among the oldest and most successful in Nigeria. In fact, at least three of the businesses (one bakery and two furniture companies) are considered among the most successful in West Africa. It is not surprising that the female businesses are considerably younger than the male firms, given the history of women and work in Nigeria. Historically, trading was the most predominant occupation among working women (in addition to farming). In fact, in this study, two of the three oldest businesses here were cloth sellers. In addition, the typical "double duty" that women experience makes it especially difficult to establish a firm and "stay in business," particularly in the face of structural obstacles provided by cultural constraints and lack of support services for businesses. Further, the economic crisis of the 1980s has made survival for small firms increasingly difficult and, when coupled with the realities facing women, it is a wonder that many have been in their respective businesses this long.

Educational attainment was higher among women than among men in this study. While the vast majority of women had completed primary school (nineteen of the twenty participants), among the men just sixteen of twenty-two had completed elementary education. Among the latter, three had no formal training. Sixteen of the women and twelve of the men had at least begun secondary school. Thirteen of the female entrepreneurs completed secondary school, while only six of the men did. Of greater interest with respect to their business concerns is the choice made to pursue technical training after secondary school. In this regard, options in both formal and more informal educational spheres exist. Colleges of technology exist in Lagos, providing some skills training, while apprenticeship programs exist more unofficially within small enterprises. All eight dressmakers and five of the beauticians attended these programs—with the majority of them receiving their training from other firms. Thirteen male entrepreneurs, most of whom were in the furniture industry, had also received specialized training, with the majority receiving this instruction through formal schooling. Formal training was almost nonexistent for the bakery trade—generally potential entrepreneurs learned their craft from relatives.

It is interesting to note the different institutions providing skills to women and men—the latter are finding the formal sphere more specifically meeting their needs, while women have been more reliant on the informal, small firms to provide them with training. Although apprenticeship training has long existed as an important "training ground" for future Nigerian entrepreneurs,[2] it is only recently that the government is beginning to officially recognize this valuable resource. A system to provide some remuneration to firms engaging in these programs has very recently been instituted. However, it is the opinion of this author that knowledge about this program is very limited among small entrepreneurs. (Discussion of this program will follow.)

Finally, some participants in these studies did attend institutions of higher learning. Two women completed their A-levels before attending more specialized programs (one in fashion design, as referred to above, and another the Nigerian School of Journalism), two attended nursing school, while another received an Associate's Degree from an American university, and the last a Bachelor's Degree from a Nigerian university. One male entrepreneur completed his A-levels in Britain, while another went on to complete a Bachelor's Degree and an M.B.A. in the United States. In general, higher levels of educational attainment can be explained by the younger ages of the women and the relatively more affluent backgrounds that many of them come from. Age is a significant factor here because younger members of this sample had enhanced opportunities to attend school, generally because of the gradual spread of "free education" compared to older Nigerians, who most often would have to pay for every level of school they attended. Despite the fact that the entrepreneurs' fathers had a wide variety of occupational backgrounds, more female entrepreneurs had fathers employed as upper-level Civil Servants, including Directors of Ministries. While women often achieved lower levels of educational attainment than men,[3] some of these women were especially privileged in that several of them came from more affluent backgrounds. Thus higher education was a greater possibility for them.

For the majority of entrepreneurs in this study, starting their own firms was not their first jobs. Of those businesspersons interviewed, 83 percent (thirty-five) had previous positions before establishing their enterprises. Of those men who lacked previous work experience, one was a carpenter and the other a baker.

For the most part, those who pursued furniture manufacturing had a wider range of training options available to them—they could study the trade in secondary and in vocational schools, serve as an apprentice in an already established firm, or obtain employment in one of the many furniture companies that existed. Among bakers, however, learning one's craft was more difficult. Nigeria offers very few formal opportunities to learn the bakery trade, and such possibilities were virtually nonexistent before the last two decades. Consequently, these entrepreneurs learned the trade largely from relatives who are in the business (or who just had experience baking for their families), by serving as an apprentice to another baker, or by training abroad, most often in England. (This latter option was pursued by only two bakers in this study.) Thus, many bakers in Nigeria *lack* formal schooling or on-the-job training in the bakery business. Consequently, many of them enter the trade having had more varied work experiences than those in the furniture industry. In fact, the bakery business is viewed as one with few barriers to entry and is perceived as a lucrative business, especially after retirement or for those who have largely become dissatisfied/disillusioned with their work, e.g., civil servants.

Among the female entrepreneurs, five of the women had no previous work experience. Three of these women started their business when they were quite young: (a) a cloth seller had learned trading from her mother and had been engaged in this as her only job for the past thirty years, (b) a woman who learned sewing as an apprentice and established her own business after that program over eighteen years ago, and (c) a hairdresser who opened her business full-time while still in secondary school. The remaining two women were in situations where their husbands did not want them to work or did not want them to work in a field of their choosing, such as nursing. The opportunity appeared for one of these women after her sister-in-law died, leaving a shop to her husband, which she later transformed into a hairdresser and seamstress business. The woman who did not pursue nursing because of her husband's wishes had taken a course in hairdressing in the United States and a refresher course later in Lagos. Once they were resettled in Lagos (after many years abroad), she set her cosmetology skills to use and began a beauty salon. As previously stated, the female entrepreneurs in this study demonstrated exceptionally high levels of educational attainment, especially specialized training in their fields.

Under what circumstances did the entrepreneurs decide to start their businesses? For the majority of these businesspersons, starting their particular firm was not a desire during childhood or adolescence. (Some exceptions to this existed among furniture manufacturers and traders, who essentially learned how to market their wares as one of the earliest examples of socialization from their mothers (see Adeokun, 1983). Several male entrepreneurs and one female in particular remarked that they would have liked to pursue one of the professions, e.g., medicine or law, but that they were unable to obtain these goals because their families were unable to pay for their educations. This situation was especially acute before 1976 (when the Universal Primary Education Scheme was passed) in families where the father died while the child in question was in primary or secondary school, and, in either case, such a child might have had to be removed immediately. Further, if this child was not the first born (and/or not a son), her/his chances of continuing in school were also limited.

An interesting level of gender differentiation can be noted when one examines the *reasons that* an entrepreneur decided to establish an enterprise. While the most commonly-cited reason given by women and men for beginning their firms was "the need to be on one's own," the factors behind this decision were different for women vs. men. Many males viewed owning a business as the only viable means (outside of the professions) of adequately supporting one's family.

My family did not have much money. I was determined to work hard and get rich and provide everything for my children—I do not want them to suffer as I had to. I wanted to work so hard, to be on my own, to be able to provide for my family.[4]

For some male businesspersons, entrepreneurship was the road towards developing one's country.

I wanted to be known for my contributions to the economy—and for my contributions to the country and to politics. Maybe because I grew up in the slums, I always looked forward to the day that I could change the life of these people. The first aim of this business is to provide employment.[5]

An entrepreneur who began a bakery after retirement from the civil service stated:

If I am to provide food for people, how could I improve hygiene and food for people . . . and above all, what share [am I] taking in the burden of unemployment in my country?[6]

For several female entrepreneurs, the "need to be on one's own," was frequently a desire voiced by their husbands for them. While women in this study (and historically in West Africa) have a long history of providing for their families, these women often wished to pursue different career paths meeting this goal. Conflict around this issue was frequently expressed by women who had trained as nurses, clerical workers, and occasionally cloth sellers, especially those who once travelled abroad to purchase materials. In general, the husbands of these women urged them not to start, or in some cases to discontinue, this work because it was too difficult to maintain while raising a family. Oftentimes, husbands found the hours that such work entailed too irregular to successfully handle one's family responsibilities.

My husband would not allow me to do office work—I must wake up early in the morning, etc.—[I] forgot all about nursing . . . doing sewing meant I could have something of my own.[7]

Furthermore, since several of these women considered their families to be middle class, it was often the case that the husbands travelled frequently for state or private business. Thus, "being on one's own" was more accommodating to the husband's career.

My husband wanted me to do something that would not take me from my children— couldn't leave the children to go work in an office . . . I travel a lot with my husband— I would like to open schools [in sewing], teach people, share experiences.[8]

Thus men believed that if their wives started their own firms, the women would have greater flexibility and be able to more effectively combine the roles of mother, wife and worker. At the same time, they would be able to assist in the support of their families, have control over their firms, and be flexible enough to delegate responsibility or "close up shop," if their husbands' careers necessitated that they relocate.

Women's choices to start firms in this study also have to be understood in the wider context of the gender-based division of labor and job segregation by sex. While many Nigerian families do have some assistance with housework and child care because of the contributions of live-in extended-family members, "househelps" from one's village, or from the ECOWAS [The Economic Community of West Africa] states, the reality remains that women are *responsible* for these tasks. This responsibility remains with women in the vast majority of cases, despite their well-documented roles as wage-earners. The labor market further offers few opportunities for women. As of 1979, women were very underrepresented in administrative and managerial positions in the professions, and in technical and clerical work. See Table 9.1.

This list does not account for women's very major role in agricultural production in the country which, while formally documented as 22 percent, is very likely to be higher, given the long history of women's more "invisible labor" here. Women more frequently produce for domestic consumption, while the males are more likely to be involved in the more lucrative cash cropping.[9] An examination of the table does demonstrate how women are concentrated in positions considered women's work—e.g., sales/trading and teaching, rather than a more diversified range of activities within the formal sector. This situation is exacerbated by the few positions in vocational/technical schools available to women in traditionally male fields, such as carpentry and welding. Thus, given the limited opportunities for free education before 1976 and real limitations in the range of education and job opportunities, it is little wonder that for many women, entrepreneurship provides the major alternative to farming or trading.

Table 9.1
Proportion of Women in the Labor Force by Sector

Occupations	% of All Employed Women[9]
Clerical	.5
Professional and Technical	1.5
Administrative, Managerial	6.0
Crafts and Production Process	12.0
Sales	39.0
Teaching	
University	10.0
Secondary	19.0
Primary	23.0

For some women life in nontraditional fields in the formal sector proved to be highly problematic. In fact, in two such cases in this study, issues of sexual harassment and the lack of long overdue promotions led these two women to leave their positions as a bank manager and television producer to establish their own firms—one as a cloth seller, the other as a seamstress. This is not to imply that women should be discouraged from entering nontraditional fields, but rather to suggest that serious obstacles still exist to restrict women's entry and mobility within these spheres.

ACCESS TO CAPITAL

Figures and sources of start-up capital available to each of these firms again reveal some interesting gender differentiation. Among the male entrepreneurs studied, figures for the amount of start-up capital were only available in nineteen firms; among the women, this information was provided in sixteen cases. Although the male firms were nearly three times older than the female businesses, the latter firms began on the average with significantly less capital than the male firms at their inception. Mean figures for start-up capital among the male firms was ₦ 10,816, compared to ₦ 6369 for female businesses (begun about eight years ago).[10] The picture is far less dramatic when the median figures are com-

Table 9.2
Start-up Capital: Lagos

Source	Female	%	Male	%
		Number of Entrepreneurs		
Own Savings	3	18.75	10	52.63
Relatives (spouse)	4	25.00	0	0
Spouses and Gifts from Relatives	1	6.25		
Spouses and Own Savings	1	6.2		
Relatives (other)	4	25.00	3	15.79
Relatives and Own Savings	3	18.75	1	5.26
Bank	0	0	1	5.26
Combined Bank Loan and Savings	0	0	1	5.26
Combined Bank Loan and Gift from Relatives	0	0	3	15.79
TOTAL	16	100	19	99.9 = 100

pared—among male entrepreneurs, ₦ 2000 was the median; among female entrepreneurs, ₦ 1500 was the median.

Of particular interest here is the source of capital and to what extent this differs between women and men. The greatest single source of capital for male businesspersons was their personal savings (10), while for women, the greatest source was their husbands (6). (In two of the latter cases, the husband was assisted in this task by either the entrepreneur or the wife's parents.) See Table 9.2.

The extent to which personal savings and gifts from relatives were major sources of capital here is not surprising. Previous studies on Nigerian entrepreneurship have maintained that these are the major sources of start-up capital (Kilby, 1965, 1971; Harris, 1967, 1971; Schatz 1964, 1977). What is noteworthy here is that five of the male entrepreneurs did receive some assistance in the form of a bank loan to establish their firms and none of the women did. In fact, women were highly likely to turn to their husbands or other relatives for financial assistance in starting their firms. While both women and men admitted that banks do discriminate against potential Nigerian borrowers by frequently employing policies based on foreign standards, as earlier noted by Schatz (1977), women generally felt it was highly unlikely that they would receive loans, and many would not even apply.

I know banks can help, but I haven't gone to them for help—I think they won't give me a loan. I don't like being turned down, so I haven't been there.[11]

Getting the loan, it depends on your relationship with the Bank. If you know people, it is not hard.[12]

When one considers the myriad of activities that women are responsible for in both the public and private spheres, and the fact that women have little or no contact with business assistance programs or other formal business organizations (to be discussed below), it is no wonder that they are in an especially disadvantageous position vis-à-vis men in obtaining loans. Further, these data reveal that as husbands' occupations and beliefs about their wives' needing to be self-employed played a major role in women beginning small firms, men/husbands maintained a very important role in this start-up phase by providing the capital. Once the business was established, women generally controlled the profits but they were much less likely than men to have sufficient savings to begin these endeavors, given the difficulties in the labor market and the domestic sphere earlier explained. When one considers the intensifying economic crisis in Nigeria, it becomes apparent that relying upon relatives to provide start-up capital will become increasingly problematic and for women is likely to retard the movement toward greater empowerment.

Beyond the start-up phase, male Lagos entrepreneurs continued to utilize commercial and development banks for loans and overdraft facilities. Five additional loans were given to ten businesspersons, and eight of them had overdraft facilities. The majority of them used the latter, especially to assist them in meeting the cost of materials for a job before receiving the client's payment, or to pay wages.

Women, on the other hand, have had little interaction with the banks. Only one woman in the sample obtained a bank loan for ₦ 10,000 (she paid it off on time) within a three-year period. She is a well-educated seamstress, with specialized training in her craft from the United States. Further, her business was flourishing at the time of her loan application—she has a shop and a factory and estimates the value of her business to be in excess of ₦ 200,000. Another woman, however, has twice applied for a bank loan and was denied on both occasions. She wanted to add to her fashion design business and stated, "I was turned down [by the bank]. I'm not from a rich family."[13] This businesswoman also had attained higher education (an Associate's Degree from an American university), had received specialized training, and had been in business for approximately the same amount of time at the point of application as the previous female entrepreneur. This respondent specifically referred to the issue of discrimination in borrowing, and claimed that social class and/or ethnic group affiliation were important variables in deciding who gets a loan. Being a woman only complicated matters.

ACCESS TO TECHNOLOGY

Although a discussion about technology in the context of entrepreneurship could involve an inventory of highly sophisticated machinery, taking such an inventory is not my intention here. Rather, this section will focus on access to the channels, those networks that facilitate one's knowledge of and access to modern technology.

Both women and men were largely satisfied with their machines—many of the male entrepreneurs had modernized their factories with the use of profits, overdraft, and loan money, particularly during the oil boom of the 1970s. For the most part, the female entrepreneurs in this study were satisfied with their machinery—only one woman claimed she wanted a facial machine but actually lacked the training to use it. With respect to machinery, both women and men expressed a need for generators (power shortages in Lagos are a common oc-currence) since businesses were paralyzed without them for significant periods of nearly every day.

What was most revealing about the issue of gender with respect to technology was the differential knowledge and access to further information about it available to them. Included in the discussion here is knowledge about government and/or private sector programs that might provide assistance to businesses—technical and management training programs, apprenticeship support, and unions and associations. While previous research has indicated that the existence of these services is insufficient to adequately meet the needs of Nigerian entrepreneurs (this problem was especially acute in extension services), knowledge about the existence of such institutions is the first step in gaining access to these resources (Osirim, 1986). Further, these institutions frequently began to involve an entre-preneur in the network of additional support services for business.

When asked if any institutions and/or services exist in Nigeria to assist their business, 100 percent (twenty two) of the male entrepreneurs answered in the affirmative, while only 45 percent (nine) of the females gave this response. Of this latter group, 20 percent (4) specifically cited commercial banks as sources of business loans, although only *one* woman had ever received a bank loan for her firm. Three other women listed Seamstress Unions and Associations of Hairdressers/Cosmetologists as possible sources of assistance. These associations served as referral agencies for the entrepreneurs, providing them with names of potential workers, especially during the peak holiday periods when more seam-stresses were needed, for example. One businessperson cited the role of the Association of Cosmetologists as a group that could help an entrepreneur obtain hair and beauty products at reduced rates. Only two female businesspersons mentioned the names of government or private sector programs concerned with training—both mentioned a program sponsored by the National Directorate of Employment that gave entrepreneurs ₦ 100 per year per student to provide them with apprenticeship training. This program also gave the student a living stipend and gave a national exam to certify one's competence in the subject at the end of the course. Despite the knowledge that women had gained about these business assistance programs, only one entrepreneur had ever used these services, beyond applying for a loan. One seamstress, formerly a television producer, with a business valued at ₦ 250,000, attended a Management Training Program sponsored by ICON Merchants Bank in January 1985.

By contrast, male entrepreneurs were very familiar with the existence of business assistance programs, as stated above. In addition to the fact that more of them had used commercial and/or development banks for loans, they could list several more management training and technical assistance programs and associations—ranging from the Nigerian Industrial Management Board, the Small-Scale Industry Board, and the Nigerian Institute of Management to the Lagos Chamber of Commerce and the Federal Institute of Industrial Research. Although they possessed this knowledge, only 23 percent (five) of the males in this sample used any of these services beyond the banks. Those that were used included technical training programs in Britain and management and technical training programs in Nigeria. In fact, one of these technical training programs was actually offered by a firm in this study.

While use of these programs (other than the banks) was limited among women and men, women generally remain in a more disadvantaged position with regard to any benefits that might accrue from these programs. In large part, government and the private agencies offering these services are to blame for their extremely limited advertising of such programs. Some male entrepreneurs noted seeing ads for some services in the newspapers or on television. Other men knew about the existence of these programs because of membership in the Chamber of Commerce and/or their affiliation with particular Development Banks. Thus one can readily understand the positive value that might emerge from belonging to such a network. Access to loans, overdraft, and information on the latest technology in one's field can result from these associations. Unfortunately, women's access to these potentially valuable resources remains blocked, largely because of their "double" and "triple" duty responsibilities to their children, their husbands, and their enterprises.

CONCLUSION

This chapter has attempted to demonstrate the continued importance of the study of entrepreneurship in Third World development. By examining case studies of entrepreneurship in Lagos, Nigeria, this chapter also revealed gender differences with respect to reasons for starting their firms and access to capital and technology. Although serious limitations exist in Nigeria with regard to occupational choices, obtaining bank loans, and the availability of institutional support services for many businesses, women were found to be in a *more disadvantageous* position in these areas.

While Nigerian women have experienced a long history of economic independence, playing a significant role in supporting their families, this sample of women (who considered themselves largely middle class) were frequently encouraged to start their firms by their husbands. Furthermore, their husbands were a major source of start-up capital for their firms, unlike the male businesspersons in this study, who were more dependent upon their savings and banks. Many husbands in this study maintained that self-employment not only enabled the women to be "on their own," but best allowed them to fulfill their duties in both the domestic and public spheres. In addition, since many of these men were in administrative, professional, or semi-professional positions, which frequently required them to relocate, self-employment for their wives meant greater flexibility and fewer problems for their families. As a consequence, women's businesses generally occupied a subordinate role to men's activities in these families. Although female and male entrepreneurs themselves most often controlled the resources and decided how profits from their firms would be used, husbands did assist in decision-making, especially during the start-up phase and periods of further expansion and/or diversification. Wives of the male businesspersons did not fulfill a similar role.

With regard to outside institutions, female entrepreneurs were much less likely to even "think about them" as sources of assistance. There was a major discrepancy between women and men in identifying such sources and in considering them as support services for their enterprises. This discrepancy is especially problematic in Nigeria at this time since: (a) knowledge of these services generally leads to inclusion in other business associations/networks that provide one with more information regarding technology, management training, and loan programs, and (b) given the dismantling of many former parastatals and a move toward greater privatization of the economy, indigenous entrepreneurs might be standing at the threshold of expanding their activities and/or investing in some of these areas. Female entrepreneurs in this study expressed strong desires to expand their firms and increase their profits, mainly to provide higher education for their children. At this juncture, the potential for contributions to the local and national economy, and empowerment as indigenous entrepreneurs seems to *remain with men.*

NOTES

I am greatly indebted to Sydney Howe and Rhonda Evans, who worked with me as Research Assistants on this project. This research was supported by grants from the Bryn Mawr College Africa Fund and The Dorothy Danforth Compton Fellowship.

1. International Labor Office, *Report on Kenya*, as cited in Nici Nelson, "How Women and Men Get By . . ." in Bromley and Gerry's *Casual Work and Poverty in Third World Cities.*

2. A. Mabawonku, "An Economic Evaluation of Apprenticeship Training in Western Nigerian Small-Scale Industries," *African Rural Economy Paper*, #17, Michigan State University, 1979.

3. Educational Attainment in Nigeria as of 1975 was: Age 6–11—of all girls, 32 percent, of all boys, 45 percent (primary school); Age 12–17—of all girls 14 percent,

of all boys, 24 percent (secondary school). Higher education—no statistics available. Literacy in 1977 was estimated at 6 percent of all women and 25 percent of all men. Cited in Robin Morgan's *Sisterhood Is Global*, 1984.

4. Interview with Mr. Kenny, Lagos, Nov. 24, 1982 (Baking).

5. Interview with Mr. B., Lagos, Dec. 8, 1982 (Furniture).

6. Interview with Mr. Gameliel, Lagos, Dec. 2, 1982 (Baking).

7. Interview with Ms. N., Lagos, June 29, 1988 (Seamstress).

8. Interview with Ms. D.I. Sports, Lagos, June 28, 1988 (Seamstress).

9. Robin Morgan, *Sisterhood Is Global*, 1984, section on Nigeria.

10. The Nigerian N(naira) has experienced massive devaluation in the last few years. In early 1983 ₦ = $1.60; in June 1988, ₦ = $.33.

11. Interview with Ms. Belo-Osagie, Lagos, June 29, 1988 (Hairdresser).

12. Interview with Ms. Lawal, Lagos, June 30, 1988 (Seamstress).

13. Interview with Ms. Moreen, Lagos, July 7, 1988 (Seamstress).

10

The Market System and the Transformation of the Peasant Mode of Production in Africa

KIDANE MENGISTEAB

The peasant sector in Africa is the largest sector in terms of the size of the population that is employed. Forced to live under the precarious subsistence mode of production, the peasant sector is also increasingly facing a decline in its standard of living. The transformation of this sector into a surplus-producing exchange economy is thus essential for African development, and it is the most formidable challenge African countries face. This transformation challenge has been a subject of debate for quite sometime. Yet our understanding of the peasantry, what impedes its transformation, and what the appropriate roles of the state and the market are in this endeavor remains incomplete.

With the rise of the new orthodoxy, which associates state intervention with economic inefficiency, the debate on the appropriate roles of the state and the market has been brought to the forefront again. The new orthodoxy has produced the IMF-World Bank-sponsored structural adjustment programs (SAPs). These programs have dominated development policy in the 1980s and are likely to continue to do so in the early 1990s. Among the basic tenets of the new orthodoxy are: (1) that the market is more efficient than the state in resource allocation and thus in generating economic growth, (2) that the state is not any more redistributive than the market (Sender and Smith, 1984), and/or distributional objectives are best served by economic growth, and (3) that the prevailing economic problems such as slow or negative growth and internal and external imbalances are attributable to state intervention. When applied to African conditions, this doctrine suffers from two flaws. One is failure to understand the nature of the peasant mode of production. The other flaw is its failure to distinguish between different qualities of state intervention, which has led to discounting the potential contribution of the state in developing countries. These two flaws have led to a reductionist explanation of the causes of Africa's economic crisis and also to inappropriate and/or unrealistic prescriptions.

This chapter aims, first, to analyze the basic flaws with the rationale upon which SAPs are built. Second, it attempts to prognose the impacts of some of the major components of SAPs on the transformation of the peasantry by ana-lyzing their implications for the peasantry's access to resources.

MISDIAGNOSIS OF THE PROBLEM

Assuming that the market does better than the state in "getting factor prices right" and thus in a more efficient allocation of resources, one would expect that it would enhance economic growth, which is highly desirable in Africa. However, one has first to establish that the peasantry is part of the market system and that if state intervention is reduced or eliminated, its replacement would be the market system.

The African peasantry is a heterogeneous group ranging from the market-oriented middle-income segment to the subsistent and low-income majority. The first segment is largely integrated into the market system. The subsistence seg-ment, however, is, as Hyden points out, still largely independent (1980). Both the market and the state have increasingly encroached on the peasantry. The peasantry has, for instance, come to rely on the state for some services such as health care and some educational facilities. The peasantry is also a source of cheap labor and sells limited quantities of food and livestock products and buys farm inputs and a small group of basic consumer goods. At times, it may even appear that the village or small town markets, where the peasantry participates, are close to perfectly competitive markets as they are characterized by freer competition among large numbers of sellers and buyers. Yet the production of this overwhelming majority of the peasantry is essentially use-value-oriented and thus such markets have a limited role in the allocation of resources. In other words, the nature of these markets is different from the nature of the market in a capitalist system. For a subsistent peasant, providing for the needs of the family, not considerations of exchange value, determine allocative decisions. The subsistence segment of the peasantry is thus, to a large extent, outside of the domains of the market system, although it is integrated enough to suffer from unequal exchange with the modern sector. The independence of the large peasant sector from the modern sector makes the latter more or less an enclave that is deprived of a domestic market and has to rely on the international market. Excessive dependency, of course, weakens the bargaining power of such econ-omies and makes them vulnerable to international shocks.

African economies are thus the most disarticulated since the peasant mode of production is the most predominant. Their modern sectors are also the most dependent and the most vulnerable to international shocks. The deepening of Africa's crisis since the mid-1970s is, for instance, better explained by the vulnerability of African economies because of their disarticulated nature than by the magnitude of state intervention. This crisis has been, to a large extent, instigated by international shocks such as declining commodity prices, rising interest rates, and declining inflows of resources. There is little evidence that African states have become more interventionist since the mid-1970s than they were in the 1960s and early 1970s, when their economic performance was somewhat better.

As claimed by the new orthodoxy, the public sector in most African countries is generally larger than those of other countries in the Third World. By some estimates, its share of total output is 15 percent, compared to 3 percent in Asia and 12 percent in Latin America. Its share of investment is estimated at 25 percent, while in Asia and Latin America they are about 17 percent and 19 percent, respectively (World Bank, 1989a:25). The public sector also accounts for as much as 40 to 50 percent of the manufacturing value added, while public sector employment in Africa in 1980 was estimated at 50 to 55 percent of the nonagricultural wage, compared to an average of 36 percent in Asia, 27 percent in Latin America, and 24 percent in OECD countries (Diamond, 1987:573).

African states also intervene in the marketing of agricultural inputs and produce. They subsidize fertilizers, farm machinery, seeds, credit, and even land (Bates, 1981:52–53). Most of them also attempt to control producer prices through the activities of their marketing boards (Bates, 1981:12). However, the impacts of state intervention on the subsistent peasant sector is often exaggerated. As Ghai and Smith note government pricing, for instance, affects "only a limited percentage of the total quantity of the commodity being produced and traded" (1987:66). The magnitude of state intervention and the poor performance of African economies have led proponents of SAPs to deduce that state intervention explains the poorer performance of African economies relative to the economies of other developing areas (Balassa, 1984:338; Landau, 1984; Marceau, 1987). Some have even claimed that empirical evidence supports the hypothesis that economic performance is inversely related to the degree of state intervention (Balassa, 1984; Landau, 1984; Vengroff and Farah, 1985).

The quality of data on Africa is simply too limited to provide reliable tests for such a hypothesis. Furthermore, Africa is not different from the other regions of the developing world only in the magnitude of state intervention. Historically, Africa, more than any other continent, was pillaged by Western Europe during the colonial and pre-colonial era. The slave trade clearly marked the watershed of such pillage. Africa also benefited the least from colonialism. By the advent of political independence African economies were generally among the least diversified in the Third World. As Mkandawire (1988:11–12) points out, manufacturing accounted for less than 6.8 percent of GDP in sub-Saharan Africa. Africa, as Goran Hyden points out (1980:218), is still the only continent where the peasant mode of production is predominant. Human resource limitations are also more severe in Africa (Eicher, 1984). Technological progress has also been much more slower (Ghai and Smith, 1987:45). Moreover, Africa is in the process of nation-building, which involves civil strife, while the other regions have, by and large, passed this stage.

All these factors have contributed to the poor performance of African economies. The predominance of a peasant mode of production is perhaps the most critical of them all, as it implies the disarticulation of the economy as already noted. The diagnosis of the new orthodoxy that views state intervention as the key explanatory variable of African economic problems is thus a gross oversimplification. It also reflects a failure to understand the peasant mode of production and its implications, since state intervention cannot provide a sufficient explanation of the economic stagnation of the peasantry when the peasantry is, by and large, outside of the reach of state intervention. Furthermore, when the peasant mode of production is predominant, reducing state intervention does not necessarily lead to expansion of the market system.

Despite this weakness, the doctrine of the new orthodoxy would still be relevant if theoretically and/or empirically it can be shown that promoting the market system at the expense of the state would enhance the transformation of the subsistence sector to a surplus-producing exchange economy. To do this one would need to demonstrate that market allocation of resources facilitates the peasantry's access to resources more than that of the state. However, in this regard the new orthodoxy also fails to discriminate between states. Instead it compares the performances of bad states with ideal market conditions. In so doing, it not only discounts the potential contribution of the state but also precludes the possibility of an effective cooperation between the state and the market in the transformation of the peasantry.

UNDERESTIMATION OF THE ROLE OF THE STATE

State intervention in agriculture takes essentially two forms. On the one hand, there are policies that have negative effects on agricultural development because they result in the extraction of surplus from the sector. Such policies include producer price controls, maintenance of overvalued currencies, heavy export taxes, and import controls. On the other hand, there are policies such as subsidies of land, fertilizers, pesticides and other inputs, subsidies of credits, and tax breaks that attempt to infuse capital to agriculture. The impacts of state intervention on the peasantry thus depends on the net differences between the amounts of the extractions of surplus and the infusions of capital. Given the political commitment to transform the condition of the peasantry and the competence to implement policies, the state can provide the peasantry with access to productivity-raising resources and other incentives and thereby promote agricultural development. Zimbabwe is one country that has achieved a modest success in this regard (Cornia and Stewart, 1987:123–24).

In most cases, however, because of the lack of state commitment, the inability of the peasantry to influence policymaking (despite its size), and attempts by African governments to extract surplus from agriculture in order to industrialize, state allocation of resources have seldom represented the interests of the peasantry or that of the agricultural sector. Public expenditures in agriculture per capita of agricultural population and the share of public expenditure in agriculture

Table 10.1
Average Public Expenditures in Agriculture, 1975–1984

COUNTRY	A	B
Botswana	16.3	0.67
Cameroon	2.5	0.16
Cote d'Ivoire	7.0	0.23
Ethiopia	1.9	0.19
Ghana	5.1	0.18
Kenya	6.5	0.23
Liberia	7.0	0.19
Malawi	4.0	-
Mali	2.2	0.18
Mauritius	30.2	0.44
Niger	1.4	0.22
Nigeria	2.8	0.12
Senegal	3.0	0.26
Sierra Leone	4.9	0.25
Sudan	6.0	0.26
Swaziland	15.6	-
Tanzania	4.0	0.20
Zaire	0.5	0.06
Zimbabwe	13.0	0.57

A = Public Expenditures in Agriculture Per Capita of Agricultural
    Population in U.S. $ 1970

B = The Share of Public Expenditure in Agriculture Relative to
    Its Share in GDP $\frac{TPEA/TPE}{AGDP/GDP}$

Source: FAO, *The Impact of Development Strategies on the Rural Poor.* Rome: 1988.

relative to its share in Gross Domestic Product ((TPEA/TPE)/(AGDP/GDP)) clearly show the deprivation of the agricultural sector (see Table 10.1).

In the 1980s African states have, in different platforms, expressed change in policies and promised to pay more attention to their agricultural sectors. The OAU's Priority Program for Economic Recovery, from 1986–90, for instance, established a consensus for African states to allocate 20–25 percent of aggregate public investments to agriculture (ECA, 1985b). However, there have not yet been any notable efforts to transform the subsistence peasantry.

The benefactors of state allocation of resources have essentially been the state itself (those who control the state), the bureaucracy, and to a certain extent the industrial sector (which, with low food prices, can keep wages low), and the urban consumers, who have a stronger political voice than the peasantry (Bates, 1981:11–44). The net impact of state intervention on agriculture and the farmers has thus been essentially negative. The different segments of agricultural producers are also affected differently. The large-scale commercial farmers seem to lose the least while the subsistence farmers seem to suffer the most from intervention. Large commercial farmers benefit from subsidized inputs, including land. They also receive tax breaks from governments that try to promote investments, especially those from foreign sources. However, it is likely that the overall net impact of intervention on this social group is negative since, as Uma Lele (1984:442) points out, the subsidies provided to the agricultural sector do not compensate for the high rates of taxation through price controls.

Overvalued currencies may also hurt the commercial farmers by lowering the domestic currency value of their export earnings and by reducing their competitiveness at the international level. And when they engage in production for the domestic market, overvalued currencies subject them to competition from cheaper foreign imports. Even the subsidies of imported inputs of fertilizers and machinery that this group benefits from are largely made possible by extracting surplus from the cash-crop-exporting producers that suffer from overvalued currencies and export taxes. The net loss from intervention is, however, likely to be less for this segment of agricultural producers than for the peasantry, since its cost of production is likely to be lower because of its higher access to subsidies and productivity-raising and cost-reducing technology. In other words, the surplus extracted from this group is largely plowed back to the same group through subsidies.

Like the commercial farmers, the middle-income farmers also suffer from the negative aspects of intervention. This group often withdraws "from ventures that have been rendered unattractive" by state controls and shifts its production mix to "alternatives that are clearly second best" (Bates, 1987:83–87). This group's access to subsidized inputs is also more limited than that of the commercial farmers. It is thus likely that this group suffers more than the commercial farmers from intervention.

The impact of intervention on the subsistence peasantry is more complex. The subsistence farmers, for a variety of reasons, including lack of knowledge, lack of political influence to overcome the bureaucratic red tape, and inability to meet many of the conditions for obtaining the subsidies, such as making the necessary down payments and providing collateral, have the least access to state-subsidized resources. Many studies have pointd out (Bates, 1981:55; Lele, 1984:442) that subsidies on interest rates, fertilizers and other inputs largely benefit the already better-off farmers. No more than 5 percent of African farmers have, for instance, access to institutional credit (Gonzalez-Vega, 1984:120).

Since the production of the subsistent peasantry is essentially use-value oriented, the marketed portion of its output is limited. Nevertheless, it also is affected by the negative aspects of intervention, for instance, by price controls although, as already noted, the magnitude is often exaggerated. The peasantry sells limited quantities of food products during good harvest years. It also sells livestock and livestock products and buys a small group of basic consumer goods and some farm implements. Therefore, even for this segment of the producers, price controls mean negative terms of trade with the modern sector and, unlike the middle-income farmers, this group has little flexibility to change its production mix in reaction to price changes since production is primarily directed by use-value, soil conditions, and availability of rain. Price controls are also harmful to the peasantry because they deprive it of incentives to transform itself from its subsistence mode of production. During sub-normal harvest years, which, due to recurrent droughts, have become increasingly more common in many parts of Africa, large parts of the subsistence farmers have become unable to produce enough food to feed themselves. It thus appears that they would benefit from low food prices during the lean years. However, because of their lack of purchasing power, their benefit in this regard is also often limited.

The subsidized land offered to large-scale commercial farmers and investors is also made at the expense of the peasantry. In some cases, peasants are forcibly evicted to make room for commercial farmers and if they are not evicted, they are left with less land for pasture with the expansion of commercial farming. The subsistent peasantry thus clearly suffers some surplus extraction from state intervention. However, even when the degree of direct extraction by the state is limited, the peasantry, except in a few countries such as Zimbabwe, suffers from lack of access to productivity-raising resources necessary for its transformation. In other words, the problem of the peasantry has more to do with its deprivation of access to resources than extraction of surplus by the state.

Some studies have claimed that little or no relationship exists between state expenditures and performance in agriculture (Vengroff and Farah, 1985). Data on Africa, as already pointed out, is too poor to provide conclusive results. Nevertheless, a test of the relationship between government expenditures and food self-sufficiency ratio and growth of agricultural production for sixteen sub-Saharan African states for the years 1980–85 supports the findings of Vengroff and Farah. These results (see Table 10.2) show that the relationships between public expenditures and food self-sufficiency ratios, as well between public expenditures and agricultural growth, are insignificant. However, the absence of a strong relationship between state expenditures in agriculture and agricultural performance does not necessarily reflect that public expenditures are not useful. The absence of a strong relationship may very well be because these expenditures are too small to make a significant difference (see Table 10.1).

The modest successes of Zimbabwe and Botswana also indicate that the state can be an agent of transformation of the traditional sector. Outside the African continent, some of the successful transformations of the peasantry in countries like Japan, Taiwan, and South Korea were accompanied by active state intervention (Hayami, 1979; Dore et al., 1959). The generalization that state intervention is negative thus needs to be qualified. Governments can certainly bring about the transformation of the peasantry by providing it access to resources, even though many usually fail to do so. Differentiation has thus to be made at both the state and policy levels because whether intervention is good or bad

Table 10.2
Results of the Regression Model*

		Dependent Variables	
Independent Variable	Coefficent	Y_1	Y_2
X_1	B_1	0.573	5.522
F Value		3.045	0.033
Adjusted R^2		0.120	-0.069
Intercept		84.990	0.109

X_1 = Public expenditures in agriculture per capita of agricultural population in U.S. $. (Average 1980-84).

Y_1 = Food self-sufficiency ratio, average 1980-1985 (%).

Y_2 = Growth of agricultural production, average for 1980-1985.

*The sixteen countries included in the study are: Botswana, Cameroon, Cote d'Ivoire, Ethiopia, Ghana, Kenya, Liberia, Mali, Mauritius, Nigeria, Senegal, Sierra Leone, Sudan, Tanzania, Zaire and Zimbabwe.

depends on the nature of the state, its commitment to transforming the peasant mode of production, and its competence to select appropriate policies and to implement them.

Furthermore, despite the common failure of the state to transform the peasantry, in Africa, as in many other low-income developing countries, socioeconomic development is unlikely to be achieved without state intervention. As Caporaso (1982) points out, the weak linkages between economic sectors that limit their ability to benefit from external economies, the fierce competition the developing countries, as newcomers to industrialization, face in the international economic system, the inability of the private sector to raise large sums of capital necessary to start certain industries, the high population growth that undermines their economic standards, and the high expectations and severe deprivation of large segments of their populations that threaten their social order make state intervention unavoidable and essential.

A number of factors also make state intervention necessary for the transformation of the traditional sector. The traditional sector lacks the purchasing power to have access to private health services and educational facilities. The private sector is too weak to provide the peasantry with the resources it needs to raise its productivity as well as its marketing capabilities on a long term credit basis. The peasantry's lack of transportation facilities, research services, and protection from pre-harvest and post-harvest grain losses to pests are unlikely to be overcome by initiatives of the weak private sector alone. Another area where the peasantry requires state intervention is in the protection of its environment. Peasants in many countries have faced severe deterioration of their environment, partly because of the overmining of forests. The private sector in Africa does not have the organizational capability or the resources to mobilize the peasantry and help alleviate this problem.

The transformation of the peasant mode of production into a surplus-producing exchange economy is one of the most important external economies the modern sector in Africa needs. Such a transformation would provide it a domestic market to grow upon and to fall back to during periods of international shocks. The modern sector (state or private) has so far been essentially unwilling or unable to pay for the costs of such a transformation. Relative to the private sector, the state is more capable of providing some of the resources necessary for the transformation. It can also coordinate the private sector to contribute for this effort. Contrary to the proposition of the new orthodoxy, the involvement of the state is critical for the transformation of the peasant mode of production. The relevant question is thus how to bring about political reforms to ensure the commitment of the state for the transformation of the peasant mode of production. Reforming states is certainly not an easy task. However, if the state can be induced to implement SAPs, as the new orthodoxy expects, there is no reason that it cannot be induced to undergo political reforms.

According to the new orthodoxy, redistributive objectives are best served by economic growth, which is promoted best by market allocation of resources. We now turn to the question of what happens to the transformation of the peasantry if state intervention is replaced by the market, as required by SAPs. Specifically we examine the subsistence peasantry's access to resources and its socioeconomic transformation under SAPs. Analyzing the implications of all the policy recommendations of SAPs is beyond the scope of the chapter. The analysis is thus limited to the implications of removal of subsidies, price decontrols, privatization, devaluation and decontrolling imports for the transformation of the peasantry.

IMPACTS OF REMOVAL OF SUBSIDIES ON THE PEASANTRY

In view of their debt burden and their declining commodity prices, African states cannot help controlling their expenditures. There have already been some reductions in public expenditures in many African states (see Table 10.3). The different types of subsidies to agricultural producers have also seen reductions in many countries. The commercial and the middle-income farmers are negatively

Table 10.3
Public Expenditures in Education and Health in Selected African States (As Percentage of Total Expenditures)

Country	Education 1972	Education 1987	Health 1972	Health 1987
Malawi	15.8	10.8	5.5	7.1
Tanzania	17.3	8.3	7.2	5.7
Burkina Faso	20.6	19.0	8.2	5.8
Uganda	15.3	15.0	5.3	2.4
Kenya	21.9	23.1	7.9	6.6
Losotho	22.4	15.5	7.4	6.9
Nigeria	4.5	2.8	3.6	0.8
Ghana	20.1	23.9	6.3	8.3
Liberia	15.2	16.2	9.8	7.1
Botswana	10.0	18.4	6.0	5.9
Mauritius	13.5	12.4	10.3	7.6

Source: World Bank, *World Development Report 1989* (New York: Oxford University Press).

affected by deflationary policies. Nevertheless, these groups can be expected to manage to get access to productivity-raising inputs without government subsidies.

The peasantry, however, lacks the purchasing power to replace any losses of resources due to deflationary policies. Despite its limited access to subsidies, it suffers the most from deflationary policies. SAPs do not dictate the areas for public expenditure reductions. It would thus seem possible to simultaneously reduce public spending and create access to resources for the peasantry. Given the political will, this might be possible, especially with improved international conditions such as higher commodity prices, debt relief measures, and the increased inflow of resources to Africa from abroad. There are little indications for such improvements. Moreover, considering the power structure in Africa and the inability of the peasantry to safeguard its interests by influencing policymaking, it is unlikely that the peasantry will be protected from public spending cuts. SAPs thus cannot be viewed as politically neutral since the peasantry is the first victim of deflationary policies and SAPs have no safty mechanisms to protect it. Proponents of SAPs, with their disdain of the state, would not expect the state to protect the peasantry. They may argue that deflationary policies would, through a more balanced and fine-tuned economy, promote economic growth. Even if this were to happen, however, there is no clear mechanism to benefit the peasantry other than the questionable trickle-down mechanism process.

IMPACTS OF REMOVAL OF PRICE CONTROLS

The impact of price controls on Africa's agriculture in general, and the peasantry, in particular, is often exaggerated as already noted. Nevertheless, removal of price controls is one policy that can have important consequences on the producers, as well as on agricultural development, since fixing producer prices at low levels is an important mechanism of taxing agriculture. However, decontrolling prices has a differential impact on farmers. In the case of the large scale commercial farmers, as well as the middle-income farmers, higher producer prices would increase their income since the higher prices are likely to more than compensate for the higher costs of inputs and consumer goods caused by reduction of subsidies and by devaluation.

In the case of the subsistence peasants, price decontrols would have only marginal impacts since the marketed portion of the output of this social class is rather small. It may marginally improve their income by marginally improving their terms of trade with the modern sector. For more reliable and more significant improvement to take place, price decontrols need to be accompanied by extension services that would increase their productivity, storage and transportation facilities, and marketing capabilities.

A comparison of two cases provides some evidence in this regard. Ivory Coast is one of the few African states that paid its producers favorable prices. The IMF actually is said to have constantly prodded Ivory Coast to cut its guaranteed prices to its farmers (Bourke, 1988:11). This incentive, however, has not spared Ivory Coast from agricultural crisis. Its average annual agricultural growth rate and food self-sufficiency ratio for the period 1980–85 have, for instance, been − 1.1 and 96.2 percent, respectively (African Development Bank, 1986).

Zimbabwe's rare success, on the other hand, is attributed to a combination of factors including favorable pricing, increased access to credits, inputs, technical assistance, marketing facilities, tools, grain depots, health and educational services, and a political climate that mobilizes the producers to improve their own conditions (Cornia and Stewart, 1987:123). Zimbabwe's average agricultural growth and food self-sufficiency ratio for the years 1980–85 has been 3.7 and 111.2, percent, respectively (African Development Bank, 1986). The experiences of these two countries thus suggest that price decontrols are necessary but not sufficient conditions for the transformation of the peasantry and that they need to be accompanied by other support mechanisms.

PRIVATIZATION

Privatization is another reform proposed by SAPs. Many African states have dismantled some of their parastatal firms or their monopolies over the production and marketing of some products. Somalia, for instance, terminated the monopoly in maize, sorghum, and imported goods in 1986. The government of Madagascar eliminated its food-marketing bodies in 1985. Nigeria also eliminated its marketing boards in June of 1986 (ECA, April 1987).

Among the reasons that proponents of SAPs expect privatization to promote agricultural development is that it eliminates the government monopolies and monopsonies of the marketing of farm inputs and outputs, which they anticipate to promote competition. This, together with producer price decontrols, is then expected to lead to a more efficient allocation of resources. The degree of competition in the less-diversified economies is limited because of the small number of firms. Nevertheless, there would be more competition under private firms than under state monopolies. Another reason is that private firms that depend on their efficiency to survive are expected to be more efficient than the bureaucracy of parastatals in the timely distribution of inputs to the farming community, as well as in the purchase of products from farmers. While the lack of strong competition undermines the efficiency of private firms, they are likely to be more efficient than the centralized government bureaucracy.

Privatization, thus, because of the relative efficiency it engenders, can be expected to generate faster economic growth, as claimed by many (Landau, 1984; Vengroff and Farah, 1985), although the evidence on its growth impact is not yet conclusive. However, even if its growth impacts were positive, its distributional impacts in general, and its impacts on the peasantry in particular, are likely to be negative, at least in the short run. There is evidence that the supply of credits in Senegal and crop collection, and fertilizer and pesticide supplies in Nigeria were disrupted with the dissolution of marketing boards and other parastatals (Harsch, 1988:12–13).

Peasants, especially the poorer subsistence farmers, are unlikely to attract private investments that tend to flow to where money (purchasing power) is more plentiful. Private schools and hospitals are unlikely to expand to the subsistence rural areas. Private banks are also unlikely to extend credits to subsistence farmers without collateral, which the farmers often fail to provide. If privatization is extended to land ownership and the communal land tenure pattern, which is predominant in most of Africa, is dismantled, as implied in the arguments of some (Marceau, 1987), peasants would face large-scale evictions and their condition would certainly deteriorate.

IMPACTS OF DEVALUATION

Presently, many sub-Saharan African states are suffering from severe debt and current account crises and, consequently, from import strangulation. Proponents of SAPs attribute these problems, at least in part, to overvalued currencies, which they view as discouraging the production of exportables and import-competing domestic products (UNCTAD, 1988:46). Devaluation is expected to overcome the deficit problems by raising the prices of imports and reducing their demand and by lowering the international prices of exports and thereby raising their volume and, consequently, their value. Agriculture is also expected to benefit from devaluation since, in Africa, it provides the bulk of the exports (Norton, 1987:34).

There has been little empirical evidence to determine the magnitude of the overvaluation of African currencies and its impact on the balance-of-payment problems of African states. In the absence of such information, it is difficult to determine the extent to which devaluation could be used as a remedy for their imbalances. The argument that overvaluation discourages the production of import-competing domestic products is also not convincing. Some degree of overvaluation, which lowers the cost of imported inputs for import-competing industries, in company with infant industry protection measures, can promote import-substitution industrialization.

Whether or not devaluation leads to higher export earnings also depends on a number of factors (Robinson, 1980). One important factor is the price elasticity of the export products at the international market. As Godfrey (1985:168–179) points out, most African exports have rather low price elasticity. A study by Scandizzo and Diakosawas (1987) also estimates the elasticities of world demand for cocoa, coffee, and tea, three of Africa's most important exports, at –0.300, 0.230, and –0.250 respectively. It is thus unlikely that devaluation would significantly raise the export earnings of African states. Another factor is the supply elasticity of the traded commodities. Some of Africa's exports have limited supply elasticity because of the international quotas that they face. Some products, such as coffee and cocoa, also require up to five years between planting and harvest.

In addition, devaluation impacts agricultural producers differently. In the case of the commercial farmers and middle-income farmers, who already use fertilizers, pesticides, and other imported agricultural inputs, devaluation would make these inputs more expensive and might lead to a decrease in their demand if the increase in producer prices, reduction in export taxes, and weaker competition from cheaper imports, as well as the gains from devaluation, if any, do not sufficiently compensate for the increases in input costs. For the subsistence peasants, who already have little access to modern inputs and whose benefits from producer price increases are marginal, however, devaluation is likely to make imported inputs even less accessible. Subsistence peasants are also unlikely to benefit from devaluation since their produce is essentially use-value-oriented and their supply elasticity is limited by their productivity constraints. Thus devaluation is unlikely to help them. It may even contribute to their continued exclusion from access to modern inputs.

The peasantry, which benefits only marginally from higher producer prices, also suffers from the inflationary conditions prompted by devaluation. The Mozambican experience with devaluation confirms the negative impacts on the poorer classes of society. There were three steep devaluations in Mozambique between January 1987 and January 1988. The official exchange rate against the U.S. dollar was slashed from MT40 to MT450 (*Africa Recovery*, March 1988:9). The prices of imported products rose sharply and availability has increased because of import decontrols. Businessmen, traders, and better-paid officials have benefited from the reduction in direct controls and the general increase in availability of goods. However, lower-paid urban consumers, wage-earners, and the subsistence peasantry have suffered a sharp decline in living standards. Workers' wages rose by about 70 percent, while overall prices rose about 210 percent (*Africa Recovery*, March 1988:12). In rural areas the middle-income farmers, who benefit from higher producer prices, also benefit from the availability of more goods. However, the impacts of devaluation on the subsistence farmers are similar to those on the wage-earners.

THE IMPACTS OF IMPORT DECONTROLS

Decontrolling imports is another policy which may have two negative impacts. One, as recent experiences of Nigeria, Tanzania, and Ivory Coast suggest, the reduction of trade barriers, can bring about a flood of cheap imported products, undercutting local producers (Harsch, 1988:14). In Ivory Coast alone the number of workers employed in textiles dropped from 12,000 in 1982 to 8,000 in 1987 (Harsch, 1988:14). In Nigeria closures have become rampant and manufacturers have blamed their difficulties on the reduction of protectionist barriers and on the sharp cost increases for imported raw materials and spare parts brought about by devaluation (Harsch, 1988:14). A decline or stagnation of the industrial sector impairs the transformation of the traditional sector by not expanding alternative employment. Import decontrols would also subject African farmers to difficult competition from cheaper imports. This problem cannot be overcome by further devaluation, which will further push up the prices of imported capital goods and raw materials and may also reduce the value of exports due to the low-price elasticity of African exports.

CONCLUSION

SAPs attempt to shift the balance of power from the politically dominant segments of society, who are benefactors of the state-dominated political economy, to the wealthy, who benefit most from a market-dominated political economy. SAPs would thus improve the conditions of the commercial and middle-income farmers who already have access to resources and the purchasing power to effectively participate in the market system.

The subsistence peasantry is neither politically nor economically influential. Such a shift thus does not clearly represent the interests of this sector. SAPs do not provide any clear and direct mechanisms that enable the peasantry to have access to resources. Even the World Bank (1989c) recognizes that SAPs do not directly benefit the lower economic classes, including the peasantry. SAPs are thus clearly a disguised trickle-down approach to rural development, since any benefits to the subsistence peasantry from SAPs occur essentially indirectly through a trickle-down process from the expected econpomic growth.

However, the most formidable challenge to the socioeconomic development of Africa cannot be left to indirect mechanisms. The trickle-down mechanism did not produce satisfactory results in the 1960s when it was the predominant development strategy. In 1972, the then president of the World Bank, Robert McNamara, for instance, warned that without rapid progress in small-holder agriculture, there is little hope either of achieving long-term stable economic growth or significantly reducing the levels of absolute poverty (1973). In addition, the U.S. Congress, in its 1973 Foreign Assistance Act, called for the end of the trickle-down approach to development and concentration on the lower 40 percent of the population of the less developed countries (Cohen, 1987:36). There is also very little basis for expecting the approach to work in the 1980s and 1990s.

Furthermore, it is not clear that SAPs are dynamic enough to lead to significant and sustainable economic growth, which is not likely without the transformation of the peasantry. The problem of African economies is thus a vicious circle. They cannot grow significantly without the transformation of the peasantry, and they need economic growth to transform the peasantry. There is a need to strike a delicate balance between growth-oriented and redistributive policies. And this, in turn, requires another delicate balance between the efficiency of the market and the redistributive authority of the state.

Some of the reforms SAPs introduce, such as decontrolling prices, can improve the condition of the peasantry when accompanied by extension services, but the conditionalities of SAPs do not make such provisions. As we have already seen, the self-serving state has not provided the peasantry with notable access to resources. However, dismissing the state altogether amounts to throwing out the baby with the bath water. Changing the nature of the state is a prerequisite for the transformation of the subsistence mode of production. It is not sufficient to replace some of its roles by the market when the limitations of the market are obtrusively conspicuous.

PART III

PROSPECTS AND ALTERNATIVES

11

Aspects of
Vertically Integrated Corporations

ADHIP CHAUDHURI

INTRODUCTION

The objective of this chapter is to present a simple theory of backward integrated mining multinational corporations, and then to analyze the implications of their behavior on the welfare of the *host* countries. The focus of the chapter is thus on the question: Is it better for mineral-exporting countries to have multinational corporations undertake production in their countries through subsidiaries, or is it better to have the mines under national ownership? Naturally, the question is of greater interest to less-developed countries, because of their special need to earn foreign exchange and to mobilize resources for domestic development. Within the less-developed countries, the problem might be more important to African countries than those from Asia and Latin America. For countries like Zambia, Nigeria, and Niger, mineral resources constituted, respectively, 96, 94, and 81 percent of total exports in 1986.

For the better part of the twentieth century, mineral resources in less-developed countries were extracted and exported by multinational corporations from the industrial countries. The multinational corporations conducted their business, more or less, like sovereigns, with no interference from the host governments. But from the 1960s onwards, there have been increasing interventions by the host governments in the operations of multinational corporations. This change ushered in an era of conflict and strife between the multinational corporations and the host governments, including several expropriations.

The conflict between the multinational corporations and the host governments from the less-developed countries was basically over the "returned value" from the mineral resource exports. The "returned value," from the point of view of the host country, consists of taxes paid by the multinationals, and the expenditures by the multinational corporations on local inputs and factors. Both these inflows are generated from the export revenues, and hence, they are received in the host country in the form of foreign exchange. Generally speaking, the returned value is greater when the multinational pays a higher price for the resource and produces a larger quantity. Because mining multinationals are vertically integrated corporations, the prices, which the parents pay to their mining subsidiaries, are, strictly intra-firm or internal prices. They are better known as "transfer" prices. The governments of several developing countries have, for a long time, believed that the transfer prices paid by the multinational corporations have been too low. Similarly, the governments of many less-developed countries have complained that the multinational corporations have not produced a desirable level of output, at least in their respective countries. Such complaints have been the strongest from countries that have had multinational corporations present in their countries for a considerable period of time.

By the late 1960s and early 1970s, several less-developed countries, including Zambia, nationalized several subsidiaries of the multinational corporations in order to control their own economic destinies. Unfortunately, except for petroleum, nationalizations in most other mineral resource industries have been judged to be "failures" [e.g. Moran (1974) and Shafer (1983)]. They are so considered because after the nationalizations, the countries in question typically encountered a decline in their export prices as well as quantities.

There have been a number of attempts to analyze and explain these failures in the literature of political economy. In a case study dealing with Zaire and Zambia, Shafer (1983) concluded that the expropriations there had failed because once those countries broke away from the multinational networks, they lost the protective "insulation" provided by the multinational corporations. That is, they lose, among other advantages, the long-term supply contracts that provide for stable exports and commodity prices through the international oligopolistic networks.

Shafer's study is in the tradition of the "bargaining school," which was first articulated by Moran (1974) in his analysis of the evolution of the relationship between two copper multinationals and the Chilean Government, culminating in the expropriations of the Allende administration in 1971. Moran's thesis is that the power and the ability of the Chilean Government to extract benefits from the multinational corporations was increasing over time, and hence, it was a mistake to expropriate. Moran recommends that mineral-exporting countries are better off staying within the oligopolistic network of the multinational corporations and bargaining hard for greater shares of their profits. However, in the opinion of this author, the bargaining school does not have a satisfactory *economic* explanation for why host governments should not go all the way and expropriate the subsidiaries of the multinational corporations.

The objective of this chapter is to use microeconomic tools to analyze the respective advantages and disadvantages to the host countries of exporting mineral resources through multinational corporations, as opposed to national firms. The plan of this chapter is as follows: In section 2, the notations and the assumptions of the basic model are presented. In the basic model an assumption is made that the parent of the multinational corporation is a *monopsonist* in its industry. All the suppliers to the monopsonist are assumed to be the subsidiaries of the multinational corporation. The equilibrium transfer price and the profit-maximizing output of a subsidiary are determined, using the standard analytical techniques from the literature of transfer pricing [e.g. Hirschleifer (1857)]. In section 3, we allow for independent suppliers to the monopsonist multinational, in order to determine a new profit-maximizing equilibrium for the multinational firm. The analysis in this section draws heavily on Krugman (1983), which itself is an extension of some innovations in monopsonist theory Perry mode (1978). In section 4, I examine the policy implications of the Perry-Krugman theory to the problem at hand. The conclusion is presented in section 5.

THE MODEL

Consider a multinational corporation in which the parent, denoted by the subscript p, does all the processing of a mineral resource in the home country. The subsidiaries of the corporation, denoted by the subscript s, are the mines which extract the mineral resource in their respective host countries. The parent of the multinational corporation is assumed to be a monopsonist of the mineral resource and hence is the sole buyer of the outputs of the subsidiaries. The parent is, consequently, a monopolist in the final product market. Prices are denoted by P and quantities by Q. The final product is measured in the same unit as the input with a suitable conversion; for example, pounds of aluminum can be measured by the equivalent tons of bauxite. Thus the quantity of the finished product, Q_p, is taken to have the same unit of measurement as the quantity of the input produced by a subsidiary, Q_s.

We further assume that the multinational corporation does not have any *a priori* reason to manipulate declared profits, either at home or in any of the host countries. In other words, the multinational corporation follows "national neutrality." Moreover, we assume that the tax rates are identical in all the countries and also that the government of the home country gives a credit for taxes paid by the subsidiaries before profits are remitted to the parent. There is no restriction on profit remittances by the subsidiaries. Lastly, we assume that there is free trade in the mineral resource.

All the assumptions made in the previous paragraph *de facto* rule out any effects of public policy on the over-all profitability of the firm, making it possible to concentrate on the intrinsic properties of the private decision-making process of the multinational corporation. Now, given our assumption of national neutrality, profit-maximization for the multinational corporation will consist of maximizing the simple sum of the profits of the parent and the subsidiaries. Also, given the assumption that the parent is a monopsonist, such a maximization will be subject to the constraint that the sum of the outputs of all the subsidiaries is exactly equal to the amount purchased by the parent. The objective function of the multinational corporation will be the following Lagrangian:[2]

$$L = P_pQ_p - C_p - P_sQ_s + P_sQ_s - C_s - k(Q_p - Q_s) \qquad (1)$$

The first three terms on the right-hand side of (1) give the profits of the parent's operation. They represent, respectively, the total revenue obtained from selling the final product, the processing cost of transforming the mineral into the final product, and the amount paid to the subsidiary for the purchase of the input. The subsidiary's profits are, in turn, given by the difference between its sales receipts from the parent, P_sQ_s, and its own costs, C_s. The last term in (1) represents the monopsonist constraint, with k denoting the Lagrangian multiplier.

The profit-maximizing output for the parent will be given by:

$$\partial L \backslash \partial Q_p = MR_p - MC_p - k = 0 \qquad (2)$$

where MR_p stands for the marginal revenue from the final product market and MC_p for the marginal cost of processing for the parent. The difference between MR_p and MC_p is the Net Marginal Revenue (NMR). The net marginal revenue function of the parent, NMR_p, represents the parent's derived demand for the input of the subsidiary, derived from the final product market. This function will have an inverse relationship with Q_p. This is so because the parent, which is a monopolist in the final product market, faces a declining marginal revenue curve from the sale of the final product, while its marginal cost rises as it produces more. The profit-maximizing output for the parent is determined where

$$NMR_p = k \qquad (3)$$

The profit-maximizing output of the subsidiary is, in turn, given by

$$\partial L \backslash \partial Q_s = -MC_s + k = 0 \qquad (4)$$

that is, where the marginal cost of the subsidiary is equal to the shadow price of the resource, k. Thus, the profit-maximizing solution for the multinational corporation as a whole is determined by:

$$NMR_p = k = MC_s \qquad (5)$$

Equation (5) is illustrated in Figure 11.1. In the figure, the optimal input price, k, is determined where the NMR_p and the MC_s schedules intersect.

Given our assumptions, there is no incentive for the multinational corporation to use any other price and therefore business between the subsidiary and the parent will be conducted through this internal or "transfer" price. But, it should be clear from Figure 11.1 that a lower input price, P', raises the profitability of

Figure 11.1

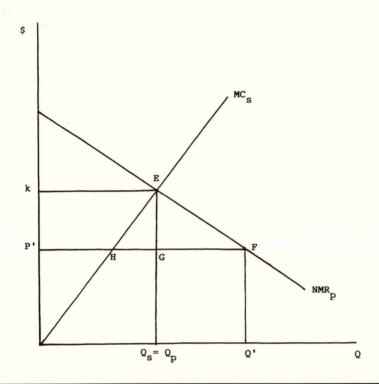

the corporation as a whole because the gain in the parent's consumer's surplus, kEFGHP', is greater than the loss of producer's surplus of the subsidiary, kEHP', by the area EFGH. Of course, P' is not feasible unless there are *independent* suppliers to the parent, because at input price P' the parent wants to buy $Q_{p'}$, which is greater than $Q_{s'}$, the amount that the subsidiary will produce at P'. Hence, the difference will clearly have to be made up by the independents.

The presence of such independents will also help explain why a lower price for the input leads to an increase in the profits of the corporation as a whole. Again, from Figure 11.1 we can see that the net gain to the multinational corporation from a lower input price, P', given by the area EFGH, can be broken up into two parts, EGH and EGF. The area EGH arises from the lower price P' for the quantity HG, which used to be bought from the subsidiary at a higher price, k, but now is bought from the independents at lower price P'. Similarly, the net gain represented by the area EGF arises because now it is profitable for the parent to buy additional units of the input, GF, over and above the old equilibrium Q_p^*.

Clearly, if there were independents, then the price would indeed fall because now the world supply curve would be the horizontal summation of the marginal cost curves of the subsidiaries, as well as of the independents. Even though this curve is not drawn in Figure 11.1, one can imagine it going through the point F on the parent's demand curve for the input, NMR_p. In the following section, the independents are explicitly introduced into the model.

THE MODEL WITH INDEPENDENTS

We still retain all the assumptions of the previous section, but now we allow the processing parent to buy the input from mines which are not owned by the multinational corporation, namely, the independents. We denote the variables relating to the independents with the subscript i. The profit-maximizing equation for the multinational corporation will now be:[3]

$$L = P_pQ_p - C_s - P_sQ_s - P_iQ_i + P_sQ_s - C_s - m(Q_p - Q_s - Q_i) \quad (6)$$

It can be easily checked that the profit-maximizing solutions for the parent and the subsidiary will be the same as (3) and (4) above. We only need to consider the quantity which the monopsonist will buy from the independents and the price which it will offer:

$$\partial L \backslash \partial Q_i = -[(dP_i \backslash dQ_i).Q_i + P_i] + k = 0 \quad (7)$$

The interpretation of the term $dP_i \backslash dQ_i$, the change in the price charged by the independent with a change in the quantity purchased by the multinational, is the key to understanding (7). Because the parent of the multinational corporation is a monopsonist, it believes that the independents will raise their offer price if it increases its purchases from them. Thus, $dP_i \backslash dQ_i$ will be positive. This "monopsonist effect" suggested by Perry implies that the multinational corporation will misread the supply curve of the independents in the sense that it will believe that each unit supplied by the independents will cost it more than MC_i. Now, if $dP_i \backslash dQ_i$ is positive in (7) above, then the price paid to the independents by the monopsonist, P_i, will be less than the shadow price k. The difference between the two prices is the term $(dP_i \backslash dQ_i).Q_i$, which is the wedge that arises because of the monopsonist effect.

The implication of the monopsonist effect is that the multinational corporation will pay too low a price (relative to the shadow price k) to the independents and hence end up buying too little from them too. Clearly then, in the presence of both subsidiaries and independents, the utilization of the mineral resource by the parent of the multinational corporation will be below the efficient level. The remarkable thing about Perry's analysis is that the situation where there is a coexistence of some mines which are owned by the multinational corporation and some which are not, is not a stable equilibrium. It will be beneficial to the

Figure 11.2

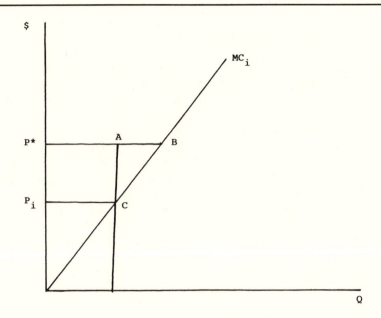

multinational corporation to acquire the independents and make them into sub-sidiaries, and at the same time it will benefit the independents to merge with the multinational corporation.

The reason that the independents will gain is that once they are part of the multinational corporation, the monopsonist effect will disappear and they will be able to sell higher quantities at higher prices. This will earn them a higher producer's surplus on the intra-marginal units that they used to previously sell to the monopsonist as independents. The corporation as a whole will benefit, because even though the parent will have to pay a higher input price on the intra-marginal units to the old independents, which are now the new subsidiaries, such payments are now *internal* to the corporation. Hence, these additional payments will cancel out, just like P_sQ_s did for the old subsidiaries in (1) above. Moreover, the net gain in producer's surplus which will accrue to the newly-acquired subsidiaries from producing more than they previously used to, as independents, will also be part of the over-all profits of the multinational corporation. All these ideas are illustrated in Figure 11.2.

In Figure 11.2, P_i represents the price that the former independents received as a solution to (6). The higher price, P^*, is the price that will prevail once all the producers have become part of the multinational corporation. In that sense it is analogous to the equilibrium price k in Figure 11.1, except that P^* is less than k because of the addition of the new subsidiaries. The gain in producer's surplus of the new member of the multinational corporation is given by the area $P*ABCP_i$, which is greater than the area $P*ACP_i$, representing the parent's additional payments on the intramarginal units relative to the old purchase Q_i. The net gain to the corporation is, therefore, the area ABC, which is the extra producer's surplus of the new subsidiaries, now internalized by the corporation.

What is happening to the older subsidiaries? When there were no independents, they could expect to get a price k, as shown in Figure 11.1, but once independents come on board, the price which the subsidiaries will receive will fall below k, and hence their production levels will also fall to obtain the equality between the lower price with lower marginal costs. But the subsidiaries will still receive a higher price than the independents because the subsidiaries are not susceptible to the monopsonist effect. However, once the independents are merged with the multinational corporation, the equilibrium price P* will be even lower than what the old subsidiaries were receiving. Thus, during the Perry-Krugman process, the multinational corporation as a whole benefits, but only at the expense of the older subsidiaries. What is even more unfortunate is that if the host government chose to nationalize a subsidiary, then the monopsonist parent would pay it an even lower price because the old subsidiary would then take on the status of an independent.

IMPLICATIONS OF THE THEORETICAL ANALYSIS

Even though the theoretical analysis was conducted for a monopsonist multinational corporation, while the real world corresponds more to oligopsonists, it is still possible to use the analysis to explain some of the facts relating to relations between less-developed countries and multinational corporations. One of the puzzling phenomena has been that while one or more less-developed countries would be confronting the multinationals in a particular industry, at the same time there would be other less-developed countries that would be courting the multinationals to start mining in their countries in the same industry. An easy explanation of this phenomenon would be to use the different political ideologies of the governments of the relevant less-developed countries. Thus we have a nationalistic government like Zambia expropriating its copper mines in the 1970s, while at the same time the Philippines, under a pro-Western Marcos, was laying down the red carpet for the Western copper multinationals. But I believe that such divergent attitudes towards multinational corporations can also be explained by the analysis presented above.

We saw in the previous section that it is better for any new mine that is coming on board to be a part of the multinational corporation, rather than becoming an independent supplier. The multinational corporation buys more at a higher price from its subsidiaries than the independents. However, we also saw that as the multinational corporation adds more and more subsidiaries, the older subsidiaries lose, both in terms of price and quantity. Hence, it is not surprising that by the early 1970s the older copper-mining countries like Chile, Zaire, and Zambia were very unhappy with the copper multinationals because of falling export revenues and market shares, while, at the same time, those in the Philippines, Canada, and Australia were very eager to join the multinational network.

It might seem, at first, that a necessary implication of the Perry-Krugman model to sub-Saharan Africa is that it is *always* better for a host country to export through subsidiaries rather than independents. That is, if a host government chose to nationalize a subsidiary and make it an independent supplier to the multinational corporation, it would always be economically detrimental to the host country. But that is not true, even within the confines of the monopsonist model presented above. It all depends on the objectives of the host country government.

Consider first the objective of maximizing income tax revenue. For the same tax rate, which strategy yields more revenue depends on who earns a greater profit, the subsidiary or the independent, that is,

$$P_s.Q_s - C_s \gtreqless P_i.Q_i - C_i \qquad (8)$$

Because a subsidiary fetches a higher price and sells more to the parent, its revenues will always be higher, but so will be the cost, as long as the law of diminishing returns holds. Thus, the subsidiary will always make a greater profit as long as the level of operation is such that the average cost is falling. If, on the other hand, a subsidiary is operating at a level beyond the minimum point of the average cost curve, then a cutback in output, with a lower price, which is what would happen with nationalization, *may* actually increase (taxable) profits. One might conjecture, though, that the kind of operations we are talking about are characterized by high fixed costs and thus increasing returns to scale. Thus, a higher output level, which accrues to the subsidiaries, will more often than not fetch higher taxable profits.

If the only objective of the host country is to maximize employment from the relevant operation, then also subsidiaries, with greater levels of output, would fare better than the independents. This is so simply because the subsidiary produces more than the independent. But if the only or the primary objective of the host country is to maximize foreign exchange earnings, then the subsidiary may indeed be the worse of the two alternatives. Let us assume that the subsidiary remits all the after-tax profits to the parent. Then the foreign exchange earnings of the host country are reduced to what the parent sends back as its liabilities to the host country entities, namely, taxes to the host government and remunerations to all the local factors (including labor) employed. If, however, production and exporting are conducted by the independents, then the total revenue earned is all in the form of foreign exchange. The algebraic difference in the foreign exchange earning potential of the two strategies is presented below, with t standing for the tax rate on subsidiary profits,

$$t(P_s.Q_s - C_s) + C_s \gtreqless P_i.Q_i \qquad (9)$$

The above equation can be rewritten as follows:

$$tP_s.Q_s + (1 - t)C_s \gtreqless P_i.Q_i \tag{10}$$

Clearly, we cannot say which side is greater without specifying actual demand and cost functions. But (10) substantiates the intuitive idea that a lower total revenue earned by the independents could still bring in greater foreign exchange than higher total revenues minus remitted profits.

We can derive some policy implications from (10) above. From the left-hand side of (10) we can see that increasing the tax rate, t, does increase the portion of the subsidiary's revenue that can be retained by the host government, but at the same time the portion of the local costs which the multinational corporation can retain also increases. Thus, requiring higher taxes on profits is not the surest way of maximizing foreign exchange earnings. Add to this the greater possibility of the multinational corporation manipulating the transfer price, P_s, in the face of higher tax rates, and we can make a case for discouraging the use of this policy instrument for the purpose of maximizing the inflow of foreign exchange. From (10) above, we can see that for the same tax rate, t, a higher value of C_s does increase the inflow of foreign exchange. Thus, pressing the multinational parent to increase the local value-added, C_s, is a superior policy in this context. How obliging the multinational corporation will be in this regard will depend on the bargaining power and skills of the host government.

CONCLUSION

We believe that simple economic analysis can provide quite robust explanations of the experiences of several African countries that chose to nationalize their mining industries. Clearly, mines operating outside the multinational network receive lower prices and get to sell less than the subsidiaries. Yet, as has been pointed out in the fourth section, the returned value might still be greater from nationally-owned firms. But pure economic analysis can only be a part of the overall picture. One has to take into account political factors if the mine is not only national, but also in the public sector. There can be macro-economic problems also. For example, if the nation's credit rating is low, it might have problems getting hard currency loans, which may be needed to import capital goods for the mines. Thus the intrinsic economic forces analyzed in this chapter, can, at best, be considered to be the starting point for helping choose between going national or multinational.

NOTES

1. *World Development Report 1988* (New York: Oxford University Press, 1988).
2. For notational ease, I shall conduct the mathematical analysis for one subsidiary only. There is no loss in generality in following this simplified procedure.
3. Again, for notational simplicity, I shall conduct the mathematical analysis for one subsidiary and one independent.

12

Investment and Capital: A Development Strategy for the African Environment?

MYLES F. ELLEDGE AND LOUIS A. PICARD

In 1985 the factory was abandoned. The windows were broken. The roof had caved in. What was left of the outer walls was a dirty yellow. The huge grounds were empty, as was the building itself. It sat along side the road from Dar es Salaam to Morogoro, a lumbering giant corpse, a relic, it might have seemed, from another century.

Twelve years before the sight had been different. The neatly landscaped, sparkling clean Friendship Textile Mill of Tanzania was bustling with energy. The state-owned enterprise employed over 3000 people at its peak. It had been set up by the People's Republic of China as a turnkey industry. The purpose of the factory was to produce printed textile products using local cotton. This locally-produced cloth would replace expensive African print made in the Netherlands (Rweyemamu, 1973: 124).

The Friendship Textile Mill has its counterparts all over Africa: Derelict hulks of buildings in abandoned industrial centers, collective farms and decaying central business districts. All of these stand as evidence of the misplaced optimism that donor agencies and LDC states placed in public enterprises and collective production units.

These expensive experiments now account for much of the debt burden carried by most African states. This burden of international foreign debt for developing countries is one of the critical reasons that academics and policymakers are once again focusing on capital formation in Africa. This perceived need for capital formation for development has led scholars and practitioners to the study of international sources and plans for encouraging foreign direct investment (FDI).

THE ISSUE OF INVESTMENT

The issue of investment is a neglected part of the literature on development management. One current text on development managment (Bryant and White,

1982) does not even discuss the problems of investment or capitial formation. When discussions of investment do occur, LDCs are portrayed as being "bled . . . exploited directly by the great multinational corporations which dominate a growing proportion of the economic and social life of the third world" (Harrison, 1981: 346).

Our discussion of investment in this chapter will center upon an approach for attracting foreign direct investment known as "Build, Operate and Transfer" or BOT. The focus on BOT in this chapter offers some insight into a (relatively) new method for encouraging and managing foreign direct investment and explores its potential applicability in the political and economic environment of Africa. BOT is an interesting concept in that it is posited as an alternative to the traditional host-country foreign-investor relationship. That relationship pits the two actors in an antagonistic relationship, filled with suspicion for each other. The concept of build, operate, and transfer is particularly attractive, at least at first glance, when set against the frailty of the African private sector and the crucial intervening variable of the capacity of Africa's bureaucracy to manage development. The administrative constraint is largely one of capacity. Third World bureaucracies often lack the capacity to plan, manage, and evaluate (development) projects that are not of an infrastructural nature (Picard 1986: 126).

The decline in foreign capital investment in many developing countries over the last ten years has led many of these countries to search for ways to increase foreign direct investment inflows. The situation has been most dramatic in Africa where in real terms, net resource flows to Africa have been falling dramatically over the last decade. The net flow of hard currency into sub-Saharan Africa, measured in 1986 prices and exchange rates, indicates flows in 1986 and 1987 well below 1985 levels. The figures also show a fall-off in direct private sector investment in Africa, where investments dropped from $1.5 billion in 1981 to about $400 million in 1986 (*Financial Times of London* 1988: Section III, p. IV). Measures to alleviate some of the debt burdens and to stimulate capital transfers are critical to halting economic and social erosion in Africa.

Build, Operate, and Transfer

This chapter examines the strategy for investment entitled "Build, Operate and Transfer (BOT)" and whether the concept offers a workable strategy for boosting foreign direct investment in Africa. First, the discussion will examine how BOT works and explore why it is put forth as an attractive method for encouraging foreign direct investment. The latter is essentially a cost-benefit assessment of the approach. Finally, we raise a number of fundamental questions that arise when considering BOT in the context of African economic development.[1] Fundamentally, does the economic, political, and bureaucratic environment in Africa offer the possibility for the success of a BOT-type project? Can the foreign investor charge enough to recover the investment, plus a profit? Can a BOT project be negotiated, financed, and managed in the context of a "soft state''? (Myrdal, 1968).[2] The answers are not readily available, but the environment for foreign investment appears to raise doubts about both the potential as well as the prospects for BOT's success in Africa.

Why consider BOT?

The attitude toward foreign direct investment (FDI) among policymakers in less-developed states has moved away from hostility and suspicion. FDI has become more attractive in Asia and the Middle East as host governments have gained confidence in dealing with international firms and as state-sponsored development schemes have fizzled. For example, both Iraq and Syria are comfortable with foreign direct investment in spite of their traditional ideological concerns about overseas corporations. African elites, however, have been less able than their counterparts in other parts of the world to separate political rhetoric from economic decision-making.

Foreign direct investment is again being considered a desirable economic development mechanism because of recent trends in foreign direct investment (which are more sensitive to the political needs of LDC elites) and because of the negative impact of the debt crisis. In the past decade, LDC governments have concerned themselves with placing requirements for performance on the firm, rather than focusing on gaining complete control of the foreign-financed project. Similarly, the use of these performance requirements in FDI projects has facilitated the host government's ability to enter into re-negotiations and to seek new terms for the continued operation of the foreign enterprise (Moran, 1988: 120). The BOT concept follows in this trend.

What is BOT?

The BOT concept is similar to a traditional turnkey operation (the transfer of ownership after construction of a manufacturing unit that is ready to operate as soon as the occupant turns the key) insofar as both involve the construction of a project by a private contractor that in turn passes the operation over to the host for pre-arranged terms.[3] The key difference in ''BOT'' is that there is an important second phase not found in the traditional turnkey operation. In the BOT concept, the ''transfer'' of operation/ownership does not occur until the foreign investor has successfully operated the enterprise for a number of years. This phase is designed to allow the investor to recover the investment, plus profit. The method also allows the host country policymaker to test and examine the quality of workmanship that has gone into the project. The BOT concept is enticing because it puts forth a method by which there is a built-in incentive for the host government to allow the foreign firm relative freedom of operation, but with a closing clause that squeezes out the foreign firm over time. A variation on the concept suggests a build, lease, and transfer model in which the investing company works out a leasing arrangement not dissimilar to a rent-to-purchase arrangement at the consumer level.

In both cases, the incentive is initially on the contractor to make the project operable and profitable before ultimately being forced to bow out of the operation. A critical question is whether this is good enough for the potential investor or not. For the host government the advantages are clear. It gains a capital investment project but maintains ultimate control.

Conceptually, the components of BOT are the following. The construction or building of the project offers profit potential and market exposure for the investor, and the long-term physical presence of a (mutually-agreed-upon) desired project for the host government, with up-front monetary cost. ''Build'' is both desirable for the host and the investor. ''Operate'' places the initial burden on the investor to manage the project well in order to re-coup the costs and make a profit. In so doing, the host government or its affiliated enterprise is relieved of the immediate responsibility for management. The final ''transfer'' phase relieves the investor of the lasting responsibility for management of the project while satisfying the host's needs for maintenance of control of an enterprise erected within its borders. For privatization purists, of course, the problem is whether or not BOT will contribute to a further bloated public sector, since many of these operations will end up as parastatals. For the public choice theorist, the problem of public enterprise development is the displacement of investment by public consumption and administrative transfer (Rogowski, 1988: 323; Bates, 1981: 12–19). Post-transfer management problems will likely involve those common to public enterprises.

Charles Oman offers the term ''new forms of investment'' as a label for ''a broad heterogeneous range of international business operations that all have a common denominator: for an investment project in a host country, a foreign company supplies assets, but it does not own the project itself'' (1988: 131). BOT would seem to fit broadly within the categorization. Oman's purpose is to make a distinction between the traditional form of FDI that ''involves transactions whereby corporations based in one country acquired or created firms in other host countries'' (1988: 131). The key point in a BOT-like project is that a different type of relationship is created. This is a relationship that keeps ultimate ''control'' in the hands of the host government but also fulfills the fundamental needs of the foreign investor, i.e., to gain market exposure and make a profit.

HOST AND INVESTOR OBJECTIVES

Managing Benefits and Costs

For the host government, the goal is to attract foreign capital and obtain sovereign status and avoid having scarce resources further depleted. Foreign capital has the potential to fulfill an important need: that is, to bring investment funds (where there are none) to bring about the development of desired enterprise or the construction of some infrastructure. Thus, the desired entity is constructed without drawing upon the national budget or taking valuable foreign exchange. Secondly, the investment offers the potential of providing a needed service or creating a domestic operation that may directly or indirectly generate income, employment, and foreign exchange. Third, assuming that a tax holiday has not been granted, taxes gained from the foreign investor help gather financial resources for other development projects. Fourth, the host country may gain use of and interaction with technology, management, and entrepreneurial skills not found in the country.

The host government also must guard against the dangers of attracting foreign investment as it minimizes the costs to the investor. This includes insuring that: (a) the project is indeed an appropriate one for the country's economy, (b) local labor will be utilized, and (c) profits and services generated will not totally escape the host country. To the extent possible, policymakers must ensure that the powerful foreign investor will not exert its control over local assets or jobs and depress local initiatives. In spite of the demands made by the IMF and the bilateral donors to avoid state intervention in the economic sector, pressures remain on local elites to ensure that the host government does not completely lose power and persuasion over economic activities within its boundaries.

For the foreign investor, the goal is essentially twofold: to gain market exposure through carrying out an operation outside of its normal terrain, and to make a profit. One must constantly see reality, in that foreign direct investors are, generally, for-profit private enterprises. While they may have concern for the plight of developing nations, concessional financing is not their business. For an investor to venture to Africa, and forego opportunities in safer investment climates, the project must offer monetary reward. Within the African context, a reward that is 30–40 percent over cost is not unreasonable. Simply put, the benefits, market exposure and profit, must exceed the cost. The foreign investor must have reasonable assurances that a stable environment will persist for the life of their involvement. This includes the ability to act somewhat free of host government regulations and the opportunity to charge enough to recoup its investment.

Managing Conflict: Host v. Investor

Few areas of development theory arouse as much controversy and are subject to varying degrees of interpretation as the question of the benefits and costs of private foreign investment. Often underlying in this debate are differences over the nature of and ideology surrounding the development process. The arguments, linked to dependency theory, traditionally pit the neo-classical economists promoting foreign investment against the economic and philosophical arguments claiming foreign investment as exploitative. Thus dos Santos complains about the "remittance abroad of high profits" (dos Santos, 1984: 98) without indicating whether or not low profits are acceptable. Beyond this, dependency theorists treat investment as a given, something that can be regulated by the LDC state (Wallerstein, 1982: 275–277) without reference to the perceptions of decision-makers in international corporations as to the desirability of such investment. Most important, questions have been raised recently about the assumptions that dependency theorists have made that foreign investment impedes economic growth in less-developed states (Jackman, 1984: 211).

Classically, foreign direct investment (FDI) is seen by economists to hold three essential benefits for the host country's economy: 1) employment expansion, 2) technology transfer, 3) saving and earning of foreign exchange (Gillis et. al., 1987: 382–384). Each of the benefits promised results from the infusion of foreign capital. The counterarguments stress that such foreign inputs are incapable of fulfilling their neo-classical promise, given the structure of the North-dominated international economic system within which the South is forced to operate. Further, there is some question about the extent to which privileges granted to foreign investors, such as that given under BOT, might displace possible indigenous investment, where that exists, which does not receive similar privileges (Popkin, 1988: 269).

It is the concepts of power, control, and profit that seem to be the center of arguments on foreign investment in LDCs. The BOT concept is offered as a model for a controlled and equal exchange negotiation in which both host and foreign investor are able to meet their objectives. As both sides specify their objectives to each other, they are better able to negotiate how these goals can be achieved within the same operation. History has shown that trouble tends to arise when neither side includes profit and control as part of the contract negotiation. As a result of this neglect, the host feels exploited and the investor suffers a backlash of host government policy or, worse yet, expropriation.

Beamish's survey work on joint ventures in LDCs is instructive and can be applied here to provide support for the BOT concept (Beamish, 1987). Beamish's findings indicate that when there is a mutuality of interests built into a joint venture project between a foreign investor and a LDC enterprise, the project is more likely to be successful. The survey findings point to the fact that the perception of mutual long-term needs between partners was paramount in successful joint ventures; short-range and one-sided attitudes towards profit and control proved detrimental to the long-term success of the venture (Beamish, 1987: 25). This is a valuable point for the BOT methodology, as a BOT project by nature is structured to account for the fundamental objectives on both sides of the negotiating table.

BOT in Africa

Simply put, for foreign private capital to be attracted into Africa, there must be a perception that the key ingredients for profit-taking are present. This is a very difficult proposition to sell to African states, and African states are very difficult to sell to the international private sector. As Goran Hyden points out,

Western businessmen are much less interested in investing capital in Africa today than they were a decade ago, not so much because of politically-motivated nationalizations as the general absence in many of these countries of the key ingredients for money making. To many foreign businesses eager to find new markets and new wealth, Africa has become a pit that swallows their money with little or no return. (Hyden, 1983: xi)

The economic institutions and administrative capabilities needed to attract and manage investment have either been absent or have deteriorated.

BOT is an attractive process for foreign investment management and has been successfully applied in other parts of the world, notably in Turkey and in parts of the Middle East. In Turkey, the Bechtel Corporation has negotiated a framework to build two Export Processing Zones (EPZs) employing the BOT financing arrangement. Bechtel is responsible for financing and constructing a $220 million EPZ and deepwater port at no cost to the Turkish government, with cost recovery and profit achieved by the Bechtel-led private consortium over a zone transfer period of less than twenty years.[4]

Unfortunately, BOT's success in the Middle East does not necessarily translate to success in Africa. One of the marked legacies of colonial rule in Africa is the inherited system of law-and-order bureaucracy. This colonial baggage has generally precluded the establishment of ''developmental'' administrative systems capable of managing economic development. The BOT strategy requires a state structure which can negotiate and monitor the construction and operation of the project and ensure a transfer which is financially viable in the long run. Fundamentally the issue is one of capacity (Picard, 1986: 126); the administrative capacity needed to guide a BOT-type project is absent in many African countries.

The Limits of Investment in Africa

The problem of BOT style investment in Africa is threefold. One, because of the low level of administrative development, the economic pie has not been expanded, and in some cases not even sustained. Political and administrative leadership in economic development policymaking is terminally injured as it has limited resources from which to operate. This situation closely parallels Hyden's argument that it is the economic realm that puts limits on progress; ''the economic conditions provide the parameters within which progress can be made'' (Hyden, 1983: 4).

The second problem is that limited development administrative capabilities, like those found in Africa, constrain economic development possibilities. The skills needed to manage development projects are often absent or checked by a ''soft'' bureaucratic system. African civil servants and parastatal managers are meant to be neutral managers within their developing economies. Too often the civil service is in a unique position to manipulate and exploit public policy because of administrative position, while encouraged to act to preserve their own economic class standing (Hirschmann, 1981, p. 471).

Thirdly, political instability leads to constraints on the capacity of the state policymakers to make effective decisions that are in the broadest interests of macro-level economic development. Decisions are instead made in the interests of narrowly-based groups and/or individuals.

In the context of BOT and foreign direct investment, these political-economic ("environmental") problems in Africa create nearly unsurmountable constraints. Foreign investors are not apt to be attracted to an environment where profit-making opportunities are limited and civil servants are lacking in technical and management skill to facilitate project development.[5] The lack of administrative and management skill will discourage negotiation of BOT-type financed projects.

Similarly, economic conditions greatly hinder prospects for BOT project-financing arrangements. The development cost of a BOT arrangement is significant. Such projects inevitably require support in the form of investment and export credits from the foreign investors' government. Yet such support is difficult to secure, given the economic and political environment in Africa. This environment does not lend itself to the prospects for the foreign investor being able to charge a high enough user fee to recover cost plus profit. In all likelihood, the billing of fees deemed appropriate by the foreign investor would result in political suicide for the host country's political and administrative leadership.

The BOT arrangement calls for advanced financing mechanisms, capable public sector organizations, and development management skills. Foreign capital divorced from bilateral and multilateral lending agencies is highly desirable. However, the lack of capacity to manage foreign private direct investment creates an undesirable environment for FDI in much of Africa.

CONCLUSION

The presence of many "white elephant" projects in Africa, such as the Friendship Textile Mill in Tanzania, encourages the pursuit of alternative methods for attracting foreign capital investment and nurturing productive industrial and infrastructure development. The "Build, Operate and Transfer" concept has been experimented with in Latin America and in Asia and is gaining wider consideration as an attractive method for garnering and managing foreign capital in developing countries.

BOT encourages consideration of important issues for the establishment of joint ventures between multinational firms and host country governments. BOT calls for attention to issues of host country control and viability of investment end-product, balanced against the interest of the multinational to have a safe environment in which to invest and recover cost plus profit.

However attractive the BOT concept appears, it seems far less promising in the context of the African "soft-state." Significant constraints are found in the African environment including: (1) limited administrative and management capacity, (2) limited administrative capacity that places parameters on the economic possibilities for development, and (3) political instability that facilitates the operation of a "soft" state in which decisions are made by and for a few. Given these constraints, BOT is less than a promising development strategy for the African environment.

NOTES

1. The use of the term economic development refers to economic development policy and is defined as an innovative process that increases the capacity of individuals and organizations to produce (and support the production of) goods and services, thereby creating wealth and jobs.

2. Myrdal (1968:845–897) describes the "soft state" as an institutionalized pattern of government having the following characteristics: 1) a systematic circumvention of laws and regulations by officials and the inconsistent application of policies and laws; 2) secret collusion between civil servants and politicians whose task it is to supervise the implementation of policies; 3) the use of corruption to secure objectives other than those officially stated.

3. "Turnkey" as defined here relates to a project in which a private contractor completes the building/installation to the point it is ready for operation; the finished product is then passed on or "sold" to the customer.

4. A BOT agreement between Gulf and Western and the Government of the Dominican Republic has led to the development of a successful export processing zone, airport and resort facility (The Services Group, 1979:4). The World Bank has also endorsed the BOT idea and has proposed taking a stake in a BOT project in Pakistan for financing a dam (World Bank Watch, 1989:5). Information of BOT was also provided by Sy Tobenblatt, Washington representative of the Bechtel Corporation in an oral interview with one of the authors (Elledge) in Orlando, Florida, on May 15, 1989.

5. Discussions with Bechtel representative Sy Tobenblatt revealed that though each individual nation presents a unique situation, there are a number of common shortcomings present in Africa that would hinder the initiation of a BOT-like financing scheme: Poorly written investment laws, lack of bureaucratic development, limited management organizations in the private sector, corruption, serious deficiencies in communications, poor transportation services and the absence of indigenous subcontracting capacity. Oral interview, May 15, 1989.

13

Money Control, Investment and Output in a Developing Economy: The Case of Nigeria, 1973–1985

FELIX NDUKWE

This chapter examines the structure of the Nigerian economy and monetary policy during the 1970s through the early 1980s. The first section presents an overview of the changing structure of the economy during the decade of the 1970s. Following this overview is a description of the Nigerian Financial System. Section three reviews the institutional practices of the Central Bank of Nigeria (CBN) and its impact on investment and growth in the economy. Section four offers an appraisal of the monetary policy of the central bank and reviews the performance of selected macroeconomic variables during the period. The last section summarizes the main conclusions of this chapter.

THE STRUCTURE OF THE NIGERIAN ECONOMY

In the aftermath of the Nigerian Civil War (the Nigeria-Biafra War, 1967–1970), which ended in January 1970, the Nigerian economy entered the 1970s with high expectations for economic expansion and sustained growth and development. Output was rising and the inflation rate was quite moderate. As a member of the fledgling oil cartel, the Organization of Petroleum Exporting Countries (OPEC), Nigeria realized windfall revenue following the dramatic increases in the price of oil in 1973 and 1974. Both the federal and state governments embarked on several projects aimed at developing the economy's infrastructure. These projects, it was hoped, would provide the impetus for sustained economic growth. Initial results were very encouraging as the growth rate of the economy rose through 1976. By the end of the decade, however, the economy faced a set of seemingly intractable problems: recurring military coup d'etats that made the economic environment risky and uncertain, erratic fluctuations in the price of Nigeria's major foreign exchange earner (oil), sluggish economic growth, high unemployment, and spiralling inflation. These problems were aggravated by balance-of-payment deficits and rampant corruption in government circles.

The Economy: An Overview

Two basic documents are crucial to understanding the Nigerian economy. These are the National Development Plan (the plan), and the Annual Budget (the budget). The plan gives a medium- to long-term perspective of the economy. The budget, on the other hand, gives a short-term perspective and it is used to implement, revise, and update the plan on an annual basis. These set the objectives and strategies of the economy. The first Independence Budget in 1960 spelled out the objectives as: "The achievement and maintenance of the highest possible rate of increase in the standard of living and the creation of necessary conditions to this end."[1] Subsequent plans have expanded, elaborated, and highlighted aspects of these objectives. For instance, the objectives of the third plan were "to establish Nigeria firmly as a united, strong and self-reliant nation, a great and dynamic economy, a just and egalitarian society, a land bright and full of opportunities for all citizens and a free and democratic society."[2]

The plans and budgets also specify the policy thrust for achieving the set objectives. Broadly, these are fiscal and monetary policies. Although the two policies are analytically different, they have a common objective of influencing aggregate economic activity.

The plans and budgets further classify the Nigerian economy into sectors. Table 13.1 shows the absolute contribution of each sector to the Gross Domestic Product during the sample period. Table 13.2, on the other hand, shows the percentage contribution of the sectors.

Throughout the entire period, the agricultural sector of the economy witnessed a steady decline. Although the sector employs about 70 percent of the country's labor force, its contribution to the GDP has declined steadily, from about 70 percent in 1960 to approximately 22 percent in 1981. While the agricultural sector has always been perceived as having major potential for growth and development, its realization has been limited by the several factors. Among these are inadequate supply of qualified manpower, lack of improved technology, insufficient supply of agricultural inputs, poor feeder roads, a water shortage, bureaucratic inefficiency within the Marketing Boards,[3] and a debilitating land tenure system.

The importance of the mining and quarrying sector derives from the fact that it is the engine of growth and the mainstay of the economy. The sector's immense mineral resources include petroleum, which accounts for over 80 percent of Nigeria's foreign exchange earnings and 95 percent of her exports. This heavy reliance on the sector has, however, been a source of instability in the economy as projections of foreign exchange earnings have been reduced to guesswork by the fluctuations in the price of petroleum. The sector's instability is clearly illustrated by the volatility of its contribution to the GDP. This has risen from

Table 13.1
Nigeria's Gross Domestic Product at 1977/78 Factor Cost (000 naira)

Sectors	1973	1974	1975	1976	1977	1978	1979	1980	1981	1982	1983	1984	1985
Total (All Sectors)	24.285	26.7001	28.2841	29.148	32.119	29.179	29.132	30.235	29.907	29.55	27.36	25.854	26.472
Agriculture/ livestock	7.024	7.752	6.947	6.838	7.305	6.674	5.786	6.071	6.139	6.965	6.58	6.691	6.903
Mining/ Quarrying	6.435	7.967	8.277	7.696	7.905	7.074	8.24	7.407	5.339	4.68	4.497	4.875	5.014
Manufacturing	0.993	0.96	1.187	1.464	1.555	1.778	1.908	2.245	3.163	3.807	3.629	2.968	3.111
Utilities	0.078	0.079	0.0861	0.085	0.937	0.11	0.137	0.143	0.171	0.192	0.201	0.205	0.209
Building/ Construction	2.779	2.935	3.039	3.628	4.072	3.95	3.856	4.147	4.23	3.373	3.105	2.477	2.403
Transpprt/ Communication	0.891	0.897	0.935	1.006	1.039	1.0834	1.162	1.311	1.461	1.506	1.149	0.878	0.856
Wholesale & Retail	4.8445	5.0131	5.397	6.02	6.771	6.031	5.652	6.432	6.342	5.643	4.973	4.559	4.696
Govt. Services	0.893	0.549	1.644	1.641	1.676	1.651	1.584	1.687	2.141	2.27	2.148	2.184	2.216
Others	0.346	0.548	0.772	0.77	0.859	0.828	0.806	0.791	0.92	1.114	1.075	1.015	1.062

Source: The Bullion, Publication of the Central Bank of Nigeria, Vol. 10, No. 3, September, 1986.

Table 13.2
Sectoral Distribution of Nigeria's Gross National Product (percent)

Sectors	1973	1974	1975	1976	1977	1978	1979	1980	1981	1982	1983	1984	1985
Agriculture/ livestock	0.29	0.29	0.25	0.23	0.23	0.23	0.20	0.20	0.21	0.24	0.24	0.26	0.26
Mining/ Quarrying	0.26	0.30	0.29	0.26	0.25	0.24	0.28	0.31	0.18	0.16	0.16	0.19	0.19
Manufacturing	0.04	0.04	0.04	0.05	0.05	0.06	0.07	0.09	0.11	0.13	0.13	0.11	0.12
Utilities	0.00	0.00	0.00	0.00	0.03	0.00	0.00	0.01	0.01	0.01	0.01	0.01	0.01
Building/ Construction	0.11	0.11	0.11	0.12	0.13	0.14	0.13	0.17	0.14	0.11	0.11	0.10	0.09
Transpprt/ Communication	0.04	0.03	0.03	0.03	0.03	0.04	0.04	0.05	0.05	0.05	0.04	0.03	0.03
Wholesale & Retail	0.20	0.19	0.19	0.21	0.21	0.21	0.19	0.26	0.21	0.19	0.18	0.18	0.18
Govt. Services	0.04	0.02	0.06	0.06	0.05	0.06	0.05	0.07	0.07	0.08	0.08	0.08	0.08
Others	0.01	0.02	0.03	0.03	0.03	0.03	0.03	0.03	0.03	0.04	0.04	0.04	0.04
	100%	100%	100%	100%	100%	100%	100%	120%	100%	100%	100%	100%	100%

Source: The Bullion, Publication of the Central Bank of Nigeria, Vol. 10, No. 3, September 1986.

a modest 13 percent in 1970 to a historical high of 31 percent in 1980. Since then, it has fluctuated and stood at 19 percent in 1985.

Nigeria's manufacturing sector showed promise during the decade. The sector grew by about 12 percent in 1973 and rose to a high of 16 percent in 1978. The growth rate decelerated in 1980 because of an acute shortage of industrial raw materials, spare parts, an erratic supply of electricity, and the troublesome problem of smuggling. By the end of 1981, most operations in the sector had either shut down or operated at a low level.

Other sectors whose share of the GDP are shown in Tables 13.1 and 13.2 include utilities, which, because of excess demand, experienced chronic power outages; transportation and communication, which supported the growth and development of agriculture, commerce, and industry with the movement of people and material.

An important feature of the contemporary Nigerian economy is the over-dependence on a single commodity, oil, for both foreign exchange earnings and government expenditures. In the early 1970s the oil boom influenced the pattern of investment in the construction and service sectors, the import of luxury goods, and the abject neglect of the agricultural sector. The economy experienced shortages in food production and large population drifts from the farming areas to the urban centers. Consequently, structural unemployment became rampant in these densely-populated urban centers. The mass population drift created an acute shortage of housing in the large cities. The oil glut, which began in 1978, imposed a severe constraint on government finances and, given the predominant role of the public sector, slowed the pace of economic activity. Faced with rising budget deficits, the government resorted to large-scale foreign and domestic borrowing. Borrowing not only increased the size of debt/debt-service payments from the shrinking foreign exchange earnings; however; it also resulted in the crowding-out of private investment in the economy. Finally, the heavy dependence of the manufacturing sector on imported raw materials and spare parts limited the ability of the sector to supplant imports during this period of foreign exchange scarcity. By the end of the decade, the economy was mired in a doldrum of decline with several structural problems that seemed impervious to policies designed to control them.

Such was the state of the Nigerian economy at the beginning of the 1980s. The country, which entered the 1970s with bright prospects for economic development and sustained expansion, closed the decade with dismal statistics for most indicators of economic activity.

THE NIGERIAN FINANCIAL SYSTEM

The Nigerian Banking Environment

The legal environment for commercial and merchant banking in Nigeria is provided by the 1952 Banking Act. Until the promulgation of the Indigenous

Enterprise Promotion Decree in 1972, all three major banks with nationwide branches were private and foreign-owned. The decree set the stage for the government "to get intimately involved in commercial banking activities so as to guide them to operate to the maximum benefit of the economy."[4] By 1977, the Federal Government had acquired 60 percent controlling interest in the three major foreign-owned banks (Barclays Bank, Standard Bank of West Africa, and the United Bank for Africa). These acquisitions had the immediate effect of transforming banking into a public sector industry since, with few exceptions, all the banks in the country were now either wholly owned by the state governments or predominantly owned by the central government.

The legal framework for central banking in Nigeria is provided by the Central Banking Ordinance of 1952 and the Central Banking Act of 1958, which formally established the Central Bank of Nigeria (CBN). The Bank, which replaced the colonial West African Currency Board, opened for business on July 1, 1959. Since then, however, a number of Amendment Acts and Decrees have been passed which have profoundly changed the status of the Central Bank. For instance, while the original Act empowered the central bank to issue the nation's legal tender and promote monetary stability with several provisions for the Bank's independence from political interference, subsequent decrees eroded the bank's authority and independence. In addition, the 1968 decree specifically requires the Board of Directors of the Bank to "keep the Minister of Finance informed of the monetary and banking policy pursued or intended to be pursued by the Bank."[5] It further requires that, in the event the minister disagreed with the Board on the monetary policy pursued or intended to be pursued by the bank, the minister should notify the bank of the disagreement and may then submit the matter to the Federal Executive Council whose decision shall be final and binding on the Central Bank.

The Institutional Environment

The institutional environment of banking is the Nigerian Financial System, which is illustrated in Figure 13.1. At the apex of the Financial System is the Federal Executive Council, or the Supreme Military Council, which has the final word on monetary policy issues. For all intents and purposes, however, the monetary authorities are made up of the Minister of Finance and the Central Bank of Nigeria as co-players at the helm of the Banking System. Next to the Central Bank are the banks, the nonbank institutions and the Security and Exchange Control. For operational purposes, however, the institutional relationships are as follows:

Banking Institution	*Supervising Institutions*
Central Bank	Ministry of Finance
Nigerian Industrial Development Bank	Ministry of Commerce
Nigerian Bank of Commerce & Banking	Ministry of Commerce

Figure 13.1
The Nigerian Financial System

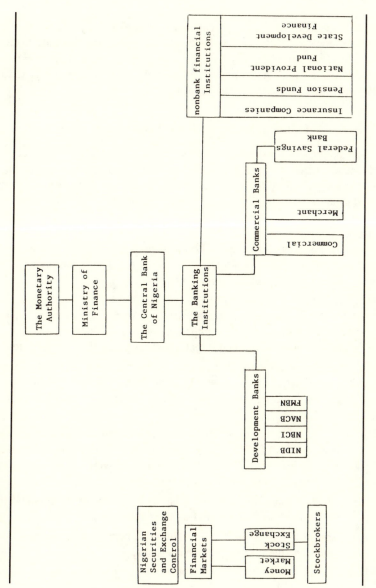

Source: Bullion, Central Bank of Nigeria, Volume 10, No. 3, September 1986.

Nigerian Agricultural Credit Bank	Ministry of Agriculture
Federal Savings Bank	Ministry of Finance
Federal Mortgage Bank	Ministry of Works
Commercial Banks	Central Bank

Apart from the Central Bank, which has Branches/Currency Centers in all states of the Federation, by the end of 1985 a total of forty-five banking institutions existed in the country. These consisted of twenty-eight commercial banks, twelve merchant banks, four development banks, and a federal savings bank. Collectively, there were a total of 1401 branches.

MONETARY POLICY AND THE ECONOMY

The banking environment influences the economy through monetary policy instruments. However, because of an undeveloped financial market, the traditional monetary policy technique of open market operations has not been employed as an instrument of policy in Nigeria. Instead the Central Bank has used a variety of other, more direct, techniques to influence the quantity and direction of credit in the economy. The basic thrust of monetary policy is provided in the Central Bank's annual Monetary Policy Guidelines, in which it outlines the monetary policy objectives and the instruments through which policy is implemented. The main characteristic features of these Guidelines usually include:[6]

1. The reserve requirements, which usually consist of the cash ratio, liquidity ratio, special deposits, and stabilization securities. Alteration of any or all of these have immediate and direct effect on the banking system liquidity.

2. Ceilings on overall expansion of credit determined on the basis of specified assumptions on the levels/growth rates of important macro-economic variables such as the domestic prices, money supply, gross domestic product, and balance of payments.

3. Sectoral and sub-sectoral ceilings for credit allocation in accordance with the desired objectives of policy. For this purpose, sectors/sub-sectors are categorized into "preferred" and "less preferred," with loans to the preferred being minimal and those to the less preferred being maximal.

4. An interest rate structure for the system including the lending and borrowing rates, as well as the discount and treasury bills rates.

5. A rediscount policy of the Central Bank with respect to central bank lending rates to the commercial and merchant banks.

6. Loans to indigenous borrowers, which in 1985 was prescribed at 90 percent of total loans and advances of commercial banks.

7. Stipulations that define the proportion of deposits mobilized from rural areas under the Rural Banking Program Scheme that must be invested in those rural areas.

8. Provisions for sanctions and penalties against noncompliance.
9. Exchange rate policies/controls to be in effect during the year.

In essence, the Guidelines is a policy channel through which the CBN conveys to the banking system monetary and credit policies and the interest rate structure for the year. It also provides the Central Bank the opportunity to emphasize to the commercial and merchant banks the lending ceilings to observe during the year, and the sectors to emphasize in terms of preferential or concessional treatment in their lending decisions.

Investment in Nigeria

The government of Nigeria supports and encourages foreign and domestic investment in the country. It also offers incentives to all investors to strengthen those sectors of the economy that the government believes contribute most toward economic development. At the same time, however, the government strictly regulates the establishment and operation of foreign businesses through laws and decrees.

Two main laws, the Companies Decree of 1968, and the Nigerian Enterprises Promotion Decree of 1977, stipulate and strictly regulate the sources and control of investment in Nigeria. The primary objective of these laws is to regulate and guide the economy to self-sustaining and indigenously-controlled development. Under the Nigerian Enterprises Promotion (Indigenization) Decree of 1977, the minimum level of Nigerian equity participation in any business establishment is 40 percent. The decree, which was first enacted in 1972 and modified in 1977, established three schedules of business enterprises. In Schedule I are enterprises preserved exclusively for Nigerians. Firms engaged, for example, in real estate, bread baking, poultry farming, and hair dressing are listed in this grouping. Operation of firms in this category is relatively non-capital intensive and does not involve a high level of technological input. In Schedule II are enterprises whose equity ownership must be at least 60 percent Nigerian. Operations such as mining and quarrying, banking, boat building and livestock feed production are listed in this schedule. Firms in this category generally employ more capital-intensive processes in production. The level of technology is also more sophisticated than in Schedule I operations. Schedule III lists business operations that must be at least 40 percent Nigerian owned. Business concerns in this grouping typically employ large inputs of both capital and technology. Business operations such as the manufacture of basic industrial chemicals, drugs and medicines, and engines and turbines appear in this schedule.

Provisions for Compliance

To ensure compliance with the provisions of the Indigenization Decree, the Nigerian government established the Nigerian Enterprises Promotion Board as a watch-dog agency. The board is responsible for the issuance of Certificate of Compliance to those firms that have met all requirements of the decree. To receive a certification, companies must submit several documents ranging from a list of directors of the business, two of whom must be Nigerians, to the submission of the firm's Tax Clearance Certificate. Several other provisions also control the establishment and operation of foreign investment in Nigeria. Among these are ceilings on the remittance of profits and dividends, residency permits, and a network of government bureaucracies the potential investor must deal with and answer to.

Thus far, the Indigenization Decree has had several beneficial effects on investment in Nigeria. First, it has increased and promoted indigenous investment in the economy. Second, it has provided Nigerian entrepreneurs with opportunities to operate joint businesses with private foreign investors, who bring additional capital, management techniques, and new technology. Furthermore, several provisions of the decree have been used to channel foreign capital and investment to sectors of the economy where they are most suitably needed for development.

On balance, however, the Nigerianization decrees and their statutes have also had several undesirable effects on investment and development in Nigeria. The most obvious of these is the increased cost associated with business establishment and compliance procedures. This can be quite prohibitive in a country such as Nigeria, where laws and decrees have not succeeded in reducing corruption among government officials. There is also the basic issue of capital mobility, arbitrage, and free competition, which are inhibited in the strictly-regulated language and spirit of the Indigenization Decree and the accompanying enforcement laws.

AN APPRAISAL OF MONETARY AND INVESTMENT POLICY

In spite of the elaborate structure of credit creation and control mechanisms outlined in the previous section, monetary policy is still only a part of the overall economic policy of Nigeria. Its successes must be viewed in the context of the larger political environment in which it is carried out and the degree of independence enjoyed by the policymakers. The subordinate status of the Central Bank to the Ministry of Finance potentially undermines the independence of the Central Bank. It is not clear whether the bank, if it had been less subordinate to political pressure, would have financed the huge government deficits during the late 1970 and early 1980s. It was, however, the expansionary monetary policy of this period that caused the inflationary spirals of the 1980s. And yet, there are several other factors that have limited the effectiveness of the monetary policy in the country. These include:

1. The limited number of bank offices in relation to the population (Nigeria's population is estimated to be about 120 million), as well as the size and effective demand for bank services in the country. It is pertinent to point out that banking still remains a seller's market in Nigeria. Frustrating and agonizing delays at bank counters are still key features of the country's banking environment.

2. The limited success of the Rural Banking Program designed by the Central Bank to bring banking services to the rural areas in order to mobilize the financial resources of these areas for economic development. Banks have been directed rather than encouraged through market-oriented incentives to establish in these areas. Further, the urban bank staff in these rural areas have been known to have little attachment and commitment to the development of these rural areas.

3. Noncompliance with Guidelines. Despite the detailed Guidelines and sanctions for noncompliance, banks still underlend to the preferred and overlend to the less preferred sectors, preferring in many instances to pay the penalties rather than comply with the Guidelines. This lack of compliance suggests that the opportunity cost of lending to the preferred sectors is high relative to the penalties for noncompliance. The net effect is that monetary policy is weakened since central the bank is ineffective in controlling and channelling bank credit to the preferred sectors of the economy.

4. The undermining of the efficacy of monetary policy by the widely-acknowledged prevalence of corrupt and fraudulent practices in the banking system and the lack of adequate cooperation between the CBN and other agencies of government.[7] Financial documents relating to foreign exchange transactions were known to have been successfully forged and processed through the banking system during the late 1970s. The Central Bank did not (and had no statutory power to) question the authenticity of financial documents that had been processed and approved by other agencies of the government such as the customs department, the import inspection agency, insurance companies, and commercial banks.

5. External factors relating to the instability and wide fluctuations in the world oil market. These factors played a major role in complicating and diminishing the effectiveness of the monetary policy in Nigeria. The heavy dependence of the Nigerian economy on oil for a disproportionate part of its foreign exchange earnings suggests a strong causal link between the monetary base and external reserves. Shortfalls in government revenues arising from low foreign exchange earnings would and did result in huge government deficit spending which was, in large part, financed by credit from the Central Bank. This accommodative monetary policy is largely responsible for the spiraling inflation of the late 1970s and early 1980s. Additionally, there has also been a significant crowding out of private domestic investment.

Table 13.3
Selected Major Economic Indicators in Nigeria, 1975–1984

Economic Variable	1975	1976	1977	1978	1979	1980	1981	1982	1983	1984
1. Money Supply (Naira mil)	2044	3293	4794.	5089.	6146.	9226.	9744.	10048	11282	122041
2. Balance of Payments	183.	–309.	–422.	–1364	1868.	2402.	–3020	–1398	–244.	362.12
3. Industrial Production Index (% Change)	–5.9	19.1	3.6	2	18.6	–1	–2.8	11.4	–4.1	–11.7
4. % Contribution of Petroleum to some Economic Variables:										
Export Earnings	92.7	93.6	92.7	89.1	93.8	96.1	96.9	98.6	96.4	96.8
Gross Domestic Product	20.4	22.9	22.6	22.7	26.2	30.2	24.5	21.8	19.7	20.3
Government Revenue	78.7	77.8	71.4	66.3	82.3	81.8	62.8	70.2	59.7	68.8

Sources: Central Bank of Nigeria Annual Report (various issues), and Federal Office of Statistics, Lagos.

Appraisal of Investment Policy

The investment policy pursued during the period under review yielded mixed results. While indigenization resulted in greater control of the development processes by the Nigerians themselves, it was not without economic costs. A cursory analysis of the performance of the macro-economic variables that appear in Table 13.3 suggests that the policies did not achieve their desired objective: partnership with foreign investors in the pursuit of self-sustaining growth and development.

The rise in the percentage contribution of oil to export earnings, government revenues and the gross domestic product dramatizes the heavy dependence of the economy on the single commodity, oil. The balance of payments, which was negative for most of the period, reflects the decline in revenues from oil that followed the steep decreases in the price of oil between 1976 and 1983. The expansionary monetary policy of the period undertaken to accommodate government deficit spending explains much of the inflationary spiral of the period. The index of industrial production, a key measure of the overall productive capability of the economy, shows that the economy contracted during the period.

SUMMARY

By the end of the 1970 decade, the optimism with which the Nigerian economy began the decade had faded and had turned into despair. The heavy dependence of the Nigerian economy on oil meant that the resulting shortfall in foreign exchange earnings which followed the declines in the price of oil would, and did, have a depressing effect on the level of economic activity.

To deal with these problems, the Central Bank initiated a number of policy actions that were designed to control imports and redirect domestic credit to predetermined preferred sectors of the economy. Because of several factors, however, the bank's efforts met with limited success. By the end of the decade, most industrial plants in the country were operating at very low production capacity. Further, some institutional factors operated to negate the anticipated beneficial effects of the monetary policy initiatives of the central banks. Notable among these was the subordination of the Central Bank to the Ministry of Finance, which undermined the efficacy and the efficiency with which the Bank conducted monetary policy. In addition, the use of administrative and bureaucratic directives in place of market incentives to channel bank credit resulted in the inefficient allocation of scarce economic resources in the economy.

NOTES

1. See ''The Budget Speeches Made by the Honorable Minister of Finance, Chief Fastus Okotie-Eboh During the Period 1958–1963,'' Federal Ministry of Information, Lagos, 1964.

2. First National Development Plan, 1962–68, Federal Ministry of Economic Development, Lagos, Nigeria.

3. The Marketing Boards act as wholesale buyers of export crops from the unit farmers. Their primary function is to provide small individual farmers with price and income stability. However, it has often been argued that the Boards' domestic pricing schemes lowered rather than raised the income of the farmers. For more information on this, see I. Livinstone and H.W. Ord, *Agricultural Economics for Tropic Africa* (1981), pp. 247–253.

4. See "The Nigerian Enterprises Promotion Decree, 1972," Federal Ministry of Information, Lagos, Nigeria.

5. See "Central Bank of Nigeria Decree 1969 (Amendment #3)" as amended by the Banking (Amendment) Decree, 1970.

6. The Guidelines constitute a formal policy statement by the Central Bank of the thrust of monetary policy for the beginning calendar/fiscal year. The Guideline is generally circulated to all the institutions with the Nigerian financial system. For a typical guideline, see "Central Bank of Nigeria Credit Policy Guidelines for 1986 Fiscal Year," by Ahmed Alhaji A in *The Bullion, Publication of the Central Bank of Nigeria*, Vol. No. 10, 1986.

7. It is widely acknowledged that during the hay days of the oil boom, several forged documents were passed through the Central Bank system as genuine. Central Bank officials lament their lack of legal authority to reject documents that had the authorization of other inspectorate agencies of the government, such as the Nigerian Customs Department, but that seemed suspect.

14

Southern Africa: Prospects for an Integrated Economic Community

KARL P. MAGYAR

South Africa and her neighboring states face two possibilities for the future: development as a result of competition with each other, or as a result of mutual cooperation. In the former case, the rhetoric of independence, self-determination, sovereignty and nationalism dominate—all symbols and traditional myths transposed from Europe's by-gone era to the African continent. Cooperation, on the other hand, requires a prudent policy of tolerance, some self-sacrifice, restraint, and a long-term vision. These are characteristics which do not frequently describe South Africa's regional diplomatic style. The predominant policy of competition has resulted in a twenty-year war in northern Namibia and in Angola, as well as repeated limited attacks by South Africa on selected targets in neighboring states. No permanent gains have been recorded by such measures. We may, therefore, make an early judgment that there is little choice for Southern Africa's future but cooperation.

Of the various conceivable scenaria for the future of the Southern Africa region, the eventual formation of an integrated economic community has been envisaged, but few detailed studies of this prospect have been undertaken.[1] A decade ago the proposal for an economic community, which was to have been comprised of Zambia, Tanzania and Mozambique, was made. Then a South African-dominated "constellation" was proffered. The Frontline States, in turn, formed the Southern African Development Coordination Conference (SADCC). And South Africa still manages the Southern Africa Customs Union. In this regard, it is evident that the idea of transnational cooperative efforts has been explored and in one or two cases implemented, but no wide-ranging integrated community on the scale and intensity of the European Common Market has been introduced.[2]

The entire phenomenon of economic integration in its narrow sense is only a few decades old.[3] But when integration is taken in a broad sense to encompass any intensified economic activities among two or more independent political entities who capitalize on each other's productive capacities, then economic integration is as old as the practice of international trade. There have existed customs unions at various times in Europe's history, but it was the European Economic Community, formally established in 1957, which provides us with the best available model for a very advanced degree of institutionalized economic interaction.

Europe's model is a good one for other advanced industrial societies, but it suffers innate limits in its relevance for the Third World. There, the phenomenon is as attractive as it is misunderstood and it has demonstrated only rare successes. The major reason for this is that the European Community is comprised of relatively well-developed industrial states that could realize the advantages of free trade, competition, and the development of complementarity among members of the community as they tend toward industrial specialization. Analysts were intrigued by this evolving economic form and sought to transfer its evident advantages to various Third World regions. There they soon discovered that the developmental environment was very different, as neither industrialization nor trade among Third World states is very advanced.[4]

Early theorists of integration emphasized the political advantages over the economic context.[5] Hence they saw the need for expanding trusting relationships and for a decline in nationalistic predominance. Not surprisingly, these theorists envisaged the formation of federal forms. An integrated community would comprise a regional grouping of states that would resolve their conflicts peacefully. Such intensified cooperation would command a shift in loyalties from national institutions to a new higher supra-national authority that could create and impose superior law in certain functional areas. This vision reflects, of course, the European context after World War II, when Europe's preoccupation concerned reconstruction along new political lines to prevent the recurrence of such devastation. In this regard, integration was biased heavily towards political objectives. In fact, when, in 1952, the European Coal and Steel Community was inaugurated, a major objective was to integrate the industrial capacities of Germany with those of neighboring states in order to prevent the prospects of German re-militarization again.

A federation in Europe has to date not been formed, nor should we expect one in the conceivable future. But what has emerged is a very advanced economic confederation that has, in fact, attained the objectives of mutual development and peaceful relations among its members. Therein lies the most important lesson for South Africa and for Southern Africa.

Where a Western European Union aspired to parliamentary authority, and an integrated defense force was contemplated as an attractive alternative to nationalistic competition, the Europeans were not prepared for such idealistic or radically new institutions. Instead, they focused on the one area of interest which promised visible improvement for all: the economic realm. If the whole could indeed become greater than the sum of the fragmented parts, then no one would lose and all would gain. These advances would accrue at the expense of the external countries, namely, the United States, Japan, and other members of the OECD. This formula, after only a decade of the European Community's existence, worked marvellously well. Economic interests now became the engine that pulled behind it the political train. Europe made great strides with each passing year, but in the process, the European Community became less relevant as a model for other regions. Yet as African countries became independent in the new era starting with Ghana in 1957, Europe's integration offered considerable logic to those early African realists who soberly assessed their newly-gained vulnerabilities. In 1963, Ghana's Prime Minister Nkrumah published his well-known book, *Africa Must Unite*.[6] A quarter of a century later Nkrumah's thoughts are revealed to have been impressively prescient in their anticipation of the African continent's predicament. He warned of Africa's impending poverty; of hostile external political and economic forces (labelled "neo-colonialism"); and becoming mired in the Cold War. His solution was unequivocal "unity."

Nkrumah must be credited with a realistic assessment of future prospects as he foresaw Africa's innate weakness in the face of a powerful "North." But, perhaps sadly, he grossly misassessed his persuasive abilities as he failed to motivate his fellow Africans to accept his conception of continental unity. At its center was his vision of an integrated community which went considerably beyond mere economic concerns, and his message addressed a full array of political questions. Nkrumah recommended continent-wide economic planning, the establishment of a unified military and defense strategy, and a unified foreign policy.[7] He was fully aware of Africa's need to develop its own model for economic integration, which contrasted with Europe's Common Market requirement of continent-wide integrated economic planning.

As a neo-functionalist, Nkrumah counseled the establishment of a "continental authority"; a common currency would be introduced; and he saw great advantage in the management of a common "selling policy" aimed at warding off external economic power. Strength was to lie in unity. By today's criteria, he was somewhat old-fashioned in that he relied too much on the export of primary products as the major source for capital formation, and he did not appreciate the impediments to Africa's industrialization. And, while warning of too-close ties to Europe, he admired the European Community—despite its irrelevance as a model for Africa. Nkrumah also sought to incorporate certain aspects of socialist economic structures, especially central economic planning of production and distribution. He was encouraged by China's impressive growth rates and he (rashly) predicted that China would "outstrip Japan and Britain in the not too-distant future."[8]

However, on attaining independence, Africans soon divided into two blocks: the more radical states led by Nkrumah formed the Casablanca group, while the more moderately inclined Francophone states and Nigeria organized as the Monrovia group. The former had more politically-oriented ambitions, while the latter were the functionalists who pursued cooperation in certain limited noncontroversial areas with the expectation that community-building would take place on a base of evolving common economic interests. Nothing remains of the radicals today, while the moderates survived to dominate the Organization of African Unity, and formed the Economic Community of West African States (ECOWAS).

From these—and other—early experiences, we see that ambitious and forced political integration across national lines has rarely succeeded quickly—if at all—and certainly not in the Third World. This lesson may be a valuable one for not only other international regions, but also for national communities within states—such as those in South Africa. In that country, federation may be a very useful structure rather than a coercive unitary political authority. And secondly, if people's democratic aspirations are to be respected, their more moderate inclinations towards the gradual attainment of communal interests will be realized mostly in the economic realm, once the advantages of integrating their resources and joint development planning are demonstrated to them.

Nkrumah is recalled because he was the first major African leader to have advocated economic integration for Africa and to offer an indigenous model.[9] However, Nkrumah was opposed at the outset by his fellow Africans, who resisted any encroachment on their sovereignties, which they had only recently attained. The major obstacle to integration was political—and that remains the case for integration in Southern Africa today. Much of what Nkrumah offered has great political relevance to Southern Africans. It is argued that economic integration of the region should be studied in order to prepare the groundwork for the day that political obstacles to such a move are eliminated, in which case it will be advantageous to have available a well-developed design. The rapid turn of events in Eastern Europe demonstrates that occasionally the international system is capably of rapid change.

The rationale for the need to form an economically integrated community in Southern Africa is easy to demonstrate.[10] At its most basic level, we may argue that if Europe, despite its relatively well-developed economic histories, foresaw in the early 1950s that alone, its countries could not survive and prosper in the competitive international climate at that time, is there any reason whatsoever to expect that the weak and unsophisticated economies of the Third World can progress as independent units in the much more competitive economic climate prevailing in the international system today?

For most of Africa, integration alone will hardly be the route to riches, as integration of these vulnerable economies may amount to little beyond the integration of poverty.[11] By eliminating the trade barriers and forming common external tariffs against imports into a Third World customs union, little trade will be created, nor will much trade be diverted from external to internal producers. The composition of Third World exports concerns similar primary products, while their imports are high tech manufactures and services which the Third World does not produce. This composition illustrates the inappropriateness of the European Community model to Africa's attempts at integration.[12] This is not to argue that improved trading relations cannot be expected in Third World customs unions. These organizations can benefit from increased market size, the introduction of more competition, the advantages of factor flows, and the greater opportunities for capital formation. Certain integrated communities have demonstrated measurable growth in the trade relations and hence improved economic welfare levels of members of Latin American and of Carribbean communities. But these countries generally had an established industrial base before the integrative process began. They were able to benefit from economies of scale, the saving of foreign exchange, and the use of low-cost labor.

Economic integration in the Southern African region would have one dominant feature, namely, the clear preponderance of South Africa, which alone, comprises 41 percent of the region's population and 77 percent of its GNP.[13] No such similar feature exists in the European Community. Nigeria enjoys this characteristic in ECOWAS, and Kenya represented a similar position in the East African community. Both countries, however, remain poor Third World nations. In the case of Southern Africa, we may at first sight argue that South Africa's domination would be the community's greatest weakness, yet this is only an unexamined assumption. In fact, the greatest weaknesses may be the underdeveloped economies and the political uncertainties of several potential member countries, and we may just as easily argue that South Africa's predominance could be the central pillar of strength for this economic community.[14] Perhaps this predominance is the only way in which Third World integration can succeed. We need to remember, above all, that there is no universal model for economic communities and that they must all be appropriately designed within their context of resources, geography, ideological framework, goals, levels of development, and in consideration of their unique features.

In a completely unrestricted common market, South Africa would naturally gain immensely at the expense of her partner by what Myrdal called the backwash effect,[15] that is to say, the tendency for the rich to get richer. South Africa has the infrastructure, capital, technology, and market size to attract most community and foreign investment capital. The goods produced in South Africa would be able to reach the wider community market unimpeded by restrictive tariffs. It would likewise be a magnet for whatever talent would exist in other member countries. This situation would, of course, be to the detriment of other members, whose economies could be expected to actually decline.

This negative effect could be overcome, however, if measures were to be introduced along the lines of some communities in Central and South America that stipulated that certain types of industries would be reserved for each respective member.[16] Such industries could be excluded from South Africa as the dominant member in a similar vein. Other member states could have their comparative advantage developed to the benefit of all members, e.g., Mozambique's harbors, Zambia's mines or Namibia's tourism potential. A community-wide development agency administered directly by the supra-national authority would undertake the establishment and management of decentralized growth points and a regional infrastructure not unlike those of South Africa today.

Under present circumstances, Lesotho, for example, will never realize a respectable industrial capability, but an economic community could ensure that certain low-technology, high-labor content industries such as textile manufacturers would be established there if prohibited elsewhere in the community. While such a procedure would not be in line with the optimal allocation of resources which a normal free market would prefer, and hence added costs would be encountered in the value of the finished product, this cost must be weighed against the fact of a much larger market than would otherwise be the case—to take advantage of the economy of scale. And the purely economic calculation must also be offset by the social benefits that would accrue to Lesotho's population as more jobs are created in that region. Additional jobs would enable more of her laborers to remain at home and not disrupt family lives as is the case presently with her vast male migrant labor force, which works in distant South African mines. Yet another argument suggests that communal restrictive measures would also be neutralized by the macro-economic growth rates of the integrated region as all economies improve. There would be more wealthy residents in the community who could afford to buy more textiles produced in Lesotho. Low-cost foreign imports would be restricted through the imposition of uniform tariffs in this customs union.

The community would enjoy another advantage in that it would attract greater private and public funds from the international community. Private investments would be greatly attracted to the large market of ninety-six million inhabitants and by the availability of a core of managerial, technical, and financial resources that exists in South Africa, but that would be available to all enterprises in the community. Namibia, for example, offers too small a market and resource base for it to ever aspire to even a modest degree of industrialization. Yet the free flow of production factors would offer positive prospects to such investment opportunities. Admittedly, South Africa would easily attract the greatest such investments but as noted, this could be regulated by the community authority, in line with social requirements.

Foreign public funds would not cease to flow into the community as integration would hardly ensure instantaneous wealth for everyone. Propects for foreign aid would be greatly encouraged because of the availability of communal resources to ensure that such funds would be used productively for development projects. Presently, for example, most aid flowing into Mozambique is emergency aid because of widespread starvation. Funds for specific developmental projects are in shorter supply as the meager resources of that country cannot sustain the establishment and maintenance of these projects. Or, as in the case of Mozambique's harbors, the international community may be reluctant to help rebuild them at very great cost because of insufficient domestic traffic and Mozambique's reliance on South Africa's goodwill to allow her commerce to pass through

Maputo. In an integrated community, this optimal usage of the regional infra-structure would be ensured; hence its expansion and improvement could be supported more easily by international aid agencies. In Mozambique, efforts are presently under way to revive the Limpopo line, which will enable Zimbabwe to ship goods directly to Maputo without passing through South Africa. This plan entails a very expensive and risky expenditure of funds motivated primarily by political considerations. Again, in an economic community, such waste would be obviated.

Controlling the distribution of certain industrial investments throughout the region in order to ensure benefits to all members of the community need not be done in a dictatorial fashion. Various methods may be employed to attain the ultimate objective. Existing industries could remain unmolested, but restrictions could be placed on new ones to encourage them to locate in certain pre-identified areas. Or, incentives could be offered to encourage the development of certain growth points. Still another technique is to allow the community's own entre-preneurs to locate where they wish, but to restrict foreign companies to certain areas. Depressed areas could also be made more attractive to investors by the communal extension of the infrastructural grid. All these techniques could be engaged in order to obviate the likelihood of South Africa's domination of the community and to ensure the spread of benefits to all members.

The community's success in achieving substantial progress from industrial coordination and trade relations will take some time due to the present low level of economic development in all countries other than South Africa. A Southern African integrated economic community would realize its early successes in the areas of joint development planning, infrastructural expansion and integration, the development of vital manpower resources, and the move towards regional industrial specialization. These areas pose substantial challenges that, if attained, would pave the way for the more advanced integrative functions as those of the European Community. A supra-national commission would undertake the plan-ning and coordination of development, the administration of community-originated projects, the training of technical and administrative personnel from all member states, the overseeing of the community-wide transport and com-munication links, and the initiation of integrative projects. All these activities would be authorized by a council representing the governments of the member states as is the case in Europe.

The political dimension of this enterprise also needs special consideration. Europe has demonstrated the advantages of having approximately similar political structures and economic ideologies for all members of the community. Ob-viously, an outright socialist member could hardly be accommodated in the planning mechanism, with others inclined toward free enterprise. Private and foreign investments would naturally gravitate toward the least-regulated and the best-developed states, but this problem could be overcome by the incentive system alluded to previously, as well as by an emphasis on the early stages of infrastructural integration, which tends to be dominated by the governments anyway. Hence, for example, community-wide airline or rail systems could easily serve the needs of states with disparate economic systems.

As the community would advance in its development, conflicting ideological bases would naturally moderate. Eastern Europe's Council for Mutual Economic Assistance (CMEA) could hardly have tolerated West Germany as a member. In Southern Africa, a socialist Mozambique or Angola would hardly attract the community's productive investments. An evening out of ideological differences would probably ensue naturally as peace came to this region and the member states began to realize the potential advantages of developing the community. The prevailing ideology would probably approximate a mixed economic system in all member states, including South Africa. The transport sector would, no doubt, remain in the hands of public enterprise, and a good argument could be made to include extensive public controls over the primary sector, including the exploitation of minerals. In agriculture a major land redistribution effort coupled with active governmental involvement in agricultural development could be expected. The secondary and tertiary sectors would do well to remain in private hands insofar as possible.

It is conceivable that advantage could be found in nationalizing all community-wide minerals production. The profits from this resource could form the base of the community's administrative funds and its investment capital for industrial diversification and job-creating enterprises. Such a mixed economic structure could go a long way toward satisfying the socialist-inclined members, who recognize the need for some public funds to be invested for the sake of promoting social welfare, and the more free enterprise-inclined, who could still enjoy the attractions of the free enterprise system (albeit in some agricultural and secondary and tertiary sectors). Such a pattern prevails in most of Africa already, and this pattern could be the basis for generating cooperative interest among the poorer members of the community.

South Africa in a Southern African community, just like West Germany in the European Community, would have to accept that there probably will be a modest degree of redistribution in an economic community, but that the economic cost would be offset by vital gains in the political realm. As Europe stabilized after the introduction of the Common Market, substantial savings were made in the military arena. South Africa has expended many billions of Rands in its war in Angola and Namibia—which would not be necessary in an integrated community. Redistributionist costs would also be offset by the expected general improvement in the welfare of the entire community, whose demand would generate further growth prospects for the dominant members. South Africa could thrive only in such circumstances.

For South Africa, such a regional community poses a dilemma, but also a challenging prospect. It would require a full commitment to throw in her lot with her fellow Africans in this area and to develop mutually together. White South Africans would not be in undisputed control of the community's institutions, although because of the established technical capability of the Whites, they would be welcomed as integral members. But the neighboring Africans will not embark on such a venture until fundamental political and administrative changes have taken place within the Republic. This situation should not deter studies of economic integration in anticipation of the day that South Africa is fully legitimized. Under the present circumstances, White South Africans face the prospect of turning over majority control of power to Blacks and, of course, a violent transition would not serve the immediate-term economic interests of either group—nor those of other members in the region.

Planning for integration presents an excellent opportunity to involve these neighbors in South Africa's reform process, lest the present unacceptable apartheid-based structure be replaced with one whose subsequent potentially turbulent rule would precipitate the destruction of the vital economic core that already exists and that could serve the needs of the entire sub-continental region.

NOTES

1. See Martin Holland's reference to South Africa and the EEC and to the "constellation" of states in *An Introduction to the European Community in the 1980s* (Cape Town: Juta and Company Ltd., 1983), chs. 7, 8. Also, Martin Holland, "A Rejoinder: The European Community and Regional Integration in Southern Africa—A Misplaced Analogy," *Politikon*, vol. 10, no. 2, 1983.

2. A more recent effort by South Africa has been established in the form of the "Economic Community of Southern Africa." Although ambitious, it is little more than a new version of the various attempts to link South Africa with her four "independent" homelands in a (hopefully) regionally-expanding pact through which South Africa hopes to attain international recognition for those homelands. *Sunday Times* (Johannesburg), May 14, 1989.

3. Jacqueline Matthews identifies 1950 as the start of theoretical inquiries, with the works of Viner, Bye, and Giersch. *International Economic Relations for South African Students* (Johannesburg: Southern Book Publishers, 1987), p. 62.

4. Peter Robson reviews the problems of integration among developing economies and judges progress and achievements in the last two decades to have been "less than satisfactory." *The Economics of International Integration* (London: George Allen and Unwin, 1980), ch. 10.

5. For two concise presentations referring to the political dimension of integration, see Roger Hanson, "Regional Integration: Reflections on a Decade of Theoretical Efforts," *World Politics*, vol. 21, no. 2, 1969, and Michael Hodges, ch. 11, in Trevor Taylor, ed., *Approaches and Theory in International Relations* (New York: Longman, 1978).

6. New York: Frederick A. Praeger, 1963.

7. Kwame Nkrumah, ibid., pp. 218–220.

8. Kwame Nkrumah, ibid., offers a concise statement of his formulation of appropriate integrative strategies in chapter 17.

9. Isebill V. Gruhn presents an interesting point that argues that Leopold Senghor's efforts with his philosophy of "Negritude" inspired the calls for Africa's unity–to tran-

scend Europe's borders, which meant nothing to Africans. *Regionalism Reconsidered: The Economic Commission for Africa* (New York: Academic Press, 1972), p. 281.

10. The last decade has produced integrative rhetoric referring to the potential ties between South Africa and her neighbors. Yet Andrew Lycett refers to a different conception, now lost in the obscure histories of the region. He reported on efforts to form a common market between Tanzania, Zambia and Mozambique during the mid-1970s. *African Development*, October 1975.

11. See the discussion on African economic integration by Ralph I. Onwuka, who presents a pessemistic prospect. Ch. 4, in Raplh I. Onwuka and Amadu Sesay, eds., *The Future of Regionalism in Africa* (London: Macmillan Publishers, Ltd., 1985).

12. Martin Holland states it bluntly: "Southern Africa can and should learn from the European model: but to blindly follow the example would be nonsensical." "A Rejoinder: The European Community and Regional Integration in Southern Africa—a Misplaced Analogy," op. cit., p. 49.

13. I addressed two articles on the topic of increased economic interaction in Southern Africa while residing in South Africa: "Federation vs. Confederation in Southern Africa: The Neglected Economic dimension," *International Affairs Bulletin*, vol. 7, no. 2, 1983, and "Southern Africa: Requirements for a Grand Strategy," South Africa Forum: *Position Paper*, vol. 8, no. 11/12, 1985.

14. With reference to the East African Community, Arthur Hazlewood recognizes that "the quest for equality can be pushed too far. Inequalities within an economic union will not be solely caused by union." *Economic Integration: The East African Experience* (London: Heinemann, 1975), p. 15.

15. Peter Robson, op. cit., p. 111.

16. G. Destanne de Bernies refers to Third World industrialization. He states: "The only real choice open to them is between industrialization in common and nonindustrialization." In Luis Eugenio Di Marco, ed., *International Economics and Development* (New York: Academic Press, 1972), p. 281.

Bibliography

Afonja, Simi. 1981. "Changing Modes of Production and the Sexual Division of Labor Among the Yoruba," *Signs*, Vol. 7, no. 2.

Africa Report, July–August, 1986, September–October, 1988, May–June, 1986.

African Development Bank. 1988. *Report by the Board of Directors of the African Development Bank, African Development Fund Covering the Period of 1 January to 31 December, 1987*, Abidjan (June 1–3).

Apraku, K. K. and Gyima-Brempong. 1986. "The Effects of Pricing Policy on Agricultural Production in Ghana," An Unpublished Paper Presented at the Twelfth Annual Convention of the Eastern Economics Association, Philadelphia, April 9–12.

Baker, Pauline H. 1983. *Obstacles to Private Sector Activities in Africa*, Unpublished, Prepared for the U.S. Department of State.

Balassa, Bela. 1984. "Adjustment Policies and Development Strategies in Sub-Saharan Africa," pp. 317–339 in Moshe Syrguin et al. (eds.), *Economic Structure and Performance*. New York: Academic Press.

Bates, Robert. 1981. *Markets and States in Tropical Africa*. Berkeley: University of California Press.

Beamish, P. W. 1987. "Joint Ventures in LDCs: Partner Selection and Performance," *Management International Review* 27 (no. 1): 23–37.

Berthelemy, J. C. and F. Gagey. 1987. "The Agricultural Supply Price Elasticity in Africa," *European Economic Review*, 31: 1493–1507.

Beveridge, A. A. and A. R. Oberschall. 1979. *African Businessmen and Development in Zambia*. Princeton: Princeton University Press.

Bonn, M. Mohs Ralf. 1988. "Structural Adjustment Programmes in Sub-Saharan Africa," *Intereconomics* 23 (Jan./Feb.): 25–28.

Boskin, Michael J. 1984. "The Fiscal Environment for Entrepreneurship," in Calbin A. Kent, *The Environment for Entrepreneurship*. Lexington, MA: Lexington Books.

Bourke, Gerald. 1988. "Cote d'Ivoire: Falling on Hard Times," *Africa Recovery*, Vol. 2, no. 1 (March): 10–11, 13.

Cable, Vincent and Mukherjee Bishakha. 1986. "Foreign Investment in Low-Income Developing Countries," in *Investing in Development: New Roles for Private Capital?* edited by Theodore H. Moran. Washington, D.C.: Overseas Development Council.

Caporaso, James. 1982. "The State's Role in Third World Economic Growth," *The Annals*, AAPSS, 459 (January): 103–111.

Chase, C. D., J. L. Kuhle and C. H. Walther. 1988. "The Relevance of Political Risk in Direct Foreign Investment," *Management International Review* 28 (no. 3): 31–38.

Cohen, M. John. 1987. *Integrated Rural Development: The Ethiopian Experience and Debate.* Uppsala, Sweden: The Scandinavian Institute of African Studies.

Coralie, Bryant and Louise G. White. 1982. *Managing Development in the Third World.* Boulder, CO: Westview Press.

Cornia, Giovanni Andrea, R. Jolly and F. Stewart. 1987. *Adjustment with Human Face,* Vol. 1, Oxford: Clarendon Press.

Curry, Robert L. and Donald Rothchild. 1974. "On Economic Bargaining Between African Governments and Multi-National Companies," *Journal of Modern African Studies* 12 (no. 2): 173–189.

Diamond, Larry. 1987. "Class Formation in the Swollen African State," *The Journal of Modern African Studies* 25, 4 (December): 567–596.

Dore, Ronald P. 1959. *Land Reform in Japan.* London: Oxford University Press.

dos Santos, Theotonio. 1984. "The Structure of Dependence," in *The Gap Between Rich and Poor: Contending Perspectives on the Political Economy of Development,* edited by Mitchell A. Seligson. Boulder, CO: Westview Press, pp. 95–104.

Dunning, John H. 1988. *Explaining International Production.* London: Unwin Hyman.

Economic Commission For Africa. 1985a. *Survey of Economic and Social Conditions in Africa, 1983–84,* Addis Ababa.

Economic Commission For Africa. 1985b. *Africa's Food and Agricultural Crisis, Prospects and Proposals for 1985 and 1986,* Addis Ababa.

Economic Commission For Africa. 1987. *Survey of Economic and Social Conditions in Africa, 1985–86,* Addis Ababa.

Economic Commission for Africa. 1989. *African Alternative Framework to Structural Adjustment Programmes for Socio-Economic Recovery and Transformation,* Addis Ababa: E/ECA/CM.15/6/Rev.3.

Economist, The. 1985. 294 (7382): 84.

Eicher, Carl K. 1984. "Facing up to Africa's Food Crisis," pp. 453–479 in Carl K. Eicher and John M. Staatz (eds.), *Agricultural Development in the Third World,* Baltimore: The Johns Hopkins University Press.

Evans, Peter. 1979. *Dependent Development.* Princeton: Princeton University Press.

FAO. 1988. *The Impact of Development Strategies on the Rural Poor.* Rome.

Financial Times of London. 1988. "Sub-Saharan Africa: Achievements of the Past 20 Years Eroded," Section III, p. IV (September 28).

Frank, Isaiah. 1980. *Foreign Enterprises in Developing Countries.* Baltimore: Johns Hopkins.

Galenson, Alice. 1984. *Investment Incentives for Industry: Some Guidelines for Developing Countries.* Washington, D.C.: The World Bank.

GATT. 1988. *International Trade 1987–88,* Vols. I and II. Geneva: GATT.

Ghai, Dharam and L. D. Smith. 1987. *Agricultural Prices, Policy, and Equity in Sub-Saharan Africa*. Boulder, CO: Lynne Reinner Publishers.

Gillis, Malcolm, Dwight H. Perkins, Michael Roemer, Donald R. Snodgrass. 1987. *Economic of Development*, 2nd Edition. New York: W. W. Norton and Company.

Godfrey, Martin. 1985. "Trade and Exchange Rate Policy: A Further Contribution to the Debate," pp. 168–179 in T. Rose (ed.), *Crisis and Recovery in Sub-Saharan Africa*, Paris: OECD.

Goldsbrough, David. 1985. "Foreign Private Investment in Developing Countries." Occasional Paper No. 33. Washington, D.C.: International Monetary Fund.

Gonzales-Vega, Claudio. 1984. "Cheap Agricultural Credit: Redistribution in Reverse," pp. 120–132 in Dale W. Adams, Douglas H. Graham and J. D. Von Pischke (eds.), *Undermining Rural Development With Cheap Credit*. Boulder, CO: Westview Press.

Green, Reginald H. 1981. "Foreign Direct Investment and African Political Economy." *Indigenization of African Economies*, edited by Adebayo Adedeji. New York: Africana Publishing Company.

Group of Thirty. 1984. *Foreign Direct Investment, 1973–87*. New York: Group of Thirty.

Guisinger, Stephen. 1987. "Host-Country Policies to Attract and Control Foreign Investment" in Theodore H. Moran et. al., *Investing in Development: New Roles for Private Capital*. New Brunswick, NJ: Transaction Books.

Gyima-Brempong, K. and K. K. Apraku. 1987. "Structural Change in Supply Response of Ghanaian Cocoa Production: 1933–1983," *Journal of Developing Areas*, Vol. 22 (1), October, pp. 59–70.

Gyima-Brempong, K. and K. K. Apraku. 1989. "Rationality of the Ghanian Cocoa Farmer: Supply Response to Government Policies, 1933–1983," an unpublished paper.

Hagen, Everett. 1962. *On the Theory of Social Change: How Economic Growth Begins*. Homewood, IL: Dorsey.

Hanke, Steve. 1987. *Privatization and Development*. San Francisco: ICS Press.

Hardwood, Edwin. 1982. "Sociology of Entrepreneurship," in Calvin A. Kent, et. al., *The Encyclopedia of Entrepreneurship*. Englewood Cliffs, N.J.: Prentice Hall.

Harris, John. 1971. "Nigerian Entrepreneurship in Industry," *Entrepreneurship and Economic Development*, edited by Peter Kilby. New York: Free Press.

Harris, John. 1967. "Industrial Entrepreneurship in Nigeria," Unpublished Ph.D. Dissertation, Northwestern University.

Hay, Margaret J. and Sharon Sticher. 1986. *African Women South of the Sahara*. New York: Longman Group.

Hayami, Yujiro, et al. 1979. *Agricultural Growth in Japan, Taiwan, Korea and the Philippines*. Honolulu: The East-West Center, University of Hawaii.

Hemming, Richard and Ali M. Mansoor. 1988. "Privatization and Public Enterprises," IMF, Occasional Paper No. 56, Washington, D.C., International Monetary Fund.

Helmboldt, Niles E. et al. 1988. "Private Investment and African Economic Policy." *Strategies for African Development*, edited by Robert J. Berg and Jennifer S. Whitaker. Berkeley: University of California Press.

Hirschliefer, J. 1957. "Economics of a Divisionalized Firm," *Journal of Business*, 30, no. 3, pp. 96–108.

Hirschmann, D. 1981. "Development or Underdevelopment Administration? A Furster Deadlock," *Development and Change* (July): 459–479.

Hyden, Goran. 1983. *No Shortcuts to Progress: African Development Management in Perspective*. Berkeley, CA: University of California Press.

Hyden, Goran. 1980. "The Resiliance of the Peasant Mode of Production: The Case of Tanzania," pp. 218–243 in Robert Bates and M. F. Lofchie (eds.), *Agricultural Development in Africa*. New York: Praeger.

International Labor Office. 1972. *Report on Kenya*.

International Monetary Fund (IMF). 1988. *International Financial Statistics Yearbook*, Washington, D.C.: IMF.

Islam, Azizula A., and Neema Majmudar. 1990. "Trends and Issues in FDI Laws in Least Developed Countries." *The CTC Reporter*, no. 30.

Jackman, Robert W. 1984. "Dependence on Foreign Investment and Economic Growth in the Third World," in *The Gap Between Rich and Poor: Contending Perspectives on the Political Economy of Development*, Mitchell A. Seligson, ed. Boulder, CO: Westview Press, pp. 211–231.

Johnson, Chalmers. 1982. *MITI and the Japanese Miracle*. Stanford: Stanford University Press.

Keen, Montague. 1988. "How to Attract Private Capital into LDCs," *Courier* (September–October): 100–101.

Kennedy, Paul. 1988. *African Capitalism: The Struggle for Ascendency*. New York: Cambridge University Press.

Kent, Calvin A. 1984. *The Environment for Entrepreneurship*. Lexington, MA: Lexington Books.

Kilby, Peter. 1965. *African Enterprise: The Nigerian Bread Industry*, Institute Studies, 8, Stanford University, CA.

Kilby, Peter. 1971. *Entrepreneurship and Economic Development*. New York: Free Press.

Kirzner, Isreal. 1973. *Competition and Entrepreneurship*. Chicago: University of Chicago Press.

Kirzner, Isreal. 1979. *Perception, Opportunity and Profit*, Chicago: University of Chicago Press.

Knight, Frank. 1948. *Risk, Uncertainty and Profits, Series of Reprints of Scarce Tracts in Economics and Political Science*, No. 16. London: London School of Economics and Political Science.

Krugman, P. 1983. "The New Theories of International Trade and the Multinational Enterprise," in C. P. Kindleberger and D. B. Audretsch (eds.), *Multinational Corporations in the 1980s*. Cambridge, MA: The MIT Press.

Landau, Daniel. 1984. "Government and Economic Growth in the Less Developed Countries," pp. 17–41 in *Report of the President's Task Force on International Private Enterprise: Selected Papers*. Washington, D.C.: U.S. Government Printing Office.

Lele, Uma. 1984. "Rural Africa: Modernization, Equity, and Long-Term Development," pp. 436–452 in C. K. Eicher and J. M. Staatz (eds.), *Agricultural Development in the Third World*, Baltimore: The Johns Hopkins Press.

Mabawonku, A. 1979. "An Economic Evaluation of Apprenticeship Training in Western Nigerian Small-Scale Industries," *Africa Rural Economy Paper*, #17, Michigan State University.

MacGaffey, Janet. 1988. "Economic Disengagement and Class Formation in Zaire," in Rothchild and Chazan, *Precarious Balance: State and Society in Africa*. Boulder, CO: Westview Press.

Manu, J. E. A. 1974. "Cocoa in the Ghanaian Economy," in Kotey, et. al., *The Economics of Cocoa Production and Marketing*, Accra, Ghana: ISSER.

Marceau, Ian. 1987. "Privatization of Agriculture and Agribusiness," pp. 141–148 in Steve H. Hanke (ed.), *Privatization and Development*, San Francisco: The International Center for Economic Growth, Institute for Contemporary Studies Press.

McClelland, David. 1961. *The Achieving Society*, New York: Van Nostrand.

McClelland, David, et al. 1969. *Motivating Economic Achievement*. New York: Free Press.

McNamara, Robert S. 1973. *Address to the Board of Governors, Nairobi, Kenya, September 1972*, Washington, D.C.: World Bank.

Mkanawire, Thandika. 1988. "The Road to Crisis, Adjustment and De-Industrialization: The African Case," *African Development*, Vol. 13, no. 1: 5–31.

Moran, Theodore H. 1988. "Shaping a Future for Foreign Direct Investment in the Third World," *Washington Quarterly* 11 (Winter 1988): 119–130.

Morgan, Robin, ed. 1984. *Sisterhood Is Global*. New York: Anchor.

Morgan, T. 1974. *Copper in Chile: The Politics of Dependence*. Princeton: Princeton University Press.

"Mozambique: The Economic Rehabilitation Programme One Year On." 1988. *Africa Recovery*, Vol. 2, no. 1 (March): 8–9, 12.

Myrdal, Gunnar. 1968. *Asian Drama: An Inquiry into the Poverty of Nations*. New York: Twentieth Century Fund and Pantheon Books.

Nair, Govindan and Anastasios Filippides. 1988. "How Much Do State-Owned Enterprises Contribute to Public Sector Deficits in Developing Countries—and Why?," World Bank Working Papers, Washington, DC, World Bank.

Nafziger, Wayne E. 1977. *African Capitalism: A Case Study of Nigerian Entrepreneurship*, Stanford, CA: Hoover Institution Press, 1977.

Ndegwa, Philip. 1989. "Increasing FDI in Africa," *The CTC Reporter*, no. 27.

Nelson, M. Joan. 1989. *The Politics of Economic Adjustment: Fragile Coalitions*. Washington, D.C.: Overseas Development Council.

Nelson, Nici. 1979. "How Women and Men Get By . . . ," *Casual Work and Poverty in Third World Cities*. New York: Wiley.

Norton, D. Roger. 1987. *Agricultural Issues in Structural Adjustment Programs*, Rome: FAO Economic and Social Development Paper No. 66.

Nyang'oro, Julius. 1989. *The State and Capitalist Development in Africa: Declining Political Economies*. New York: Praeger.

Nyerere, Julius. 1980. "No to IMF Meddling," *Development Dialogue* 2:7–9.

Okereke, Okoro. 1975. *Agricultural Development Programmes of African Countries*, Research Report No. 28. Uppsala, Sweden: The Scandinavian Institute of African Studies.

Oman, Charles P. 1987. "New Forms of Investment in Developing Countries" in Theodore H. Moran et al., *Investing in Development: New Roles for Private Capital*. New Brunswick, NJ: Transaction Books.

Onimode, Bade. 1989. *The IMF, the World Bank and the African Debt: The Economic Impact*. London: Zed Books.

Organization for Economic Cooperation and Development (OECD). 1987. *International Investment and Multinational Enterprises: Recent Trends in International Direct Investment*. Paris: OECD.

Organization for Economic Cooperation and Development (OECD). 1990. *Financing and External Debt of Developing Countries: 1989 Survey*. Paris: OECD.

Osirim, Mary J. 1986. "Characteristics of Entrepreneurship in Nigerian Industries: Some

Preliminary Findings,'' *Perspectives in International Development*, edited by Mekki Mtewa. New Delhi: Allied.

Page, Sheila A. B. 1986. *Relocating Manufacturing in Developing Countries*. London: NEDO EWP 25.

Page, Sheila, A. B. and Roger C. Riddell. 1989. "FDI in Africa: Opportunities and Impediments," *The CTC Reporter*, no. 27.

Pearce, Ivor. 1980. "Reforms for Entrepreneur to Serve Public Policy," in Arthur Seldon, ed., *Prime Mover of Progress: The Entrepreneur in Capitalism and Socialism*. London: Institute of Economic Affairs, p. 132.

Perry, M. 1978. "Vertical Integration: The Monopsony Case," *American Economic Review*, 68, pp. 561–570.

Pfefferman, Guy and Dale R. Weigel. 1988. "The Private Sector and the Policy Environment," *Finance and Development* 25 (December): 25–27.

Picard, Louis A. 1986. "Self-Sufficiency, Delinkage, and Food Production: Limits on Agricultural Development in Africa," in *World Food Policies: Toward Agricultural Interdependence*, William P. Browne and Don F. Hadwiger, eds. Boulder, CO: Lynne Reinner, pp. 121–136.

Popkin, Samuel L. "Public Choice and Peasant Organization," in *Towards a Political Economy of Development*, Robert Bates, ed. Berkeley: University of California Press, pp. 245–271.

Press, Robert. 1989. "Africans Seek Homegrown Solutions," *The Christian Science Monitor* (July 26): 6.

Ravenhill, John. 1985. *Collective Clientelism: The Lome Conventions and North-South Relations*. New York: Columbia University Press.

Rhazaoul, Ahmed. 1986. "Foreign Direct Investment in Africa," *The CTC Reporter*, no. 21.

Robinson, Joan. 1980. *Collected Economic Papers*, Vol. 4, Cambridge, MA: The MIT Press.

Robinson, Richard D. 1976. *National Control of Foreign Business: A Survey of Fifteen Countries*. New York: Praeger.

Root, Franklin R. and Ahmed A. Ahmed. 1979. "Empirical Determinants of Manufacturing Direct Foreign Investment in Developing Countries." *Economic Development and Cultural Change*, Vol. 27.

Roth, Gabriel. 1987. *The Private Provision of Public Services in Developing Countries*. New York: Oxford University Press.

Rweyemamu, Justinian. 1973. *Underdevelopment and Industrialization in Tanzania*. Nairobi: Oxford University Press.

Sanday, Peggy. 1974. "Female Status in the Public Domain," *Women, Culture and Society*, edited by Michelle Rosaldo and Louise Lamphere. Stanford: Stanford University Press.

Scandizzo, Pasquale L. and Dimitris Diakosawas. 1987. *Instability in the Terms of Trade of Primary Commodities, 1900–1982*, Rome: FAO Economic and Social Development Paper, No. 64.

Schatz, Sayre. 1977. *Nigerian Capitalism*. Berkeley: University of California Press.

Schneider, Friedrich and Bruno S. Frey. 1985. "Economic and Political Determinants of Foreign Direct Investment," *World Development* 13, no. 2 (1985): 161–175.

Schumpeter, Joseph. 1936. *The Theory of Economic Development*. Cambridge, MA: Harvard University Press.

Sender, John and Sheila Smith. 1984. "What's Right with the Berg Report and What's Left of Its Critics?" *Discussion Paper* (June): 1–21.

Services Group, The. 1989. *The Experience of Export Processing Zones in Developing Countries*. Arlington, VA: The Services Group.

Shafer, M. 1983. "Capturing the Mineral Multinationals: Advantage or Disadvantage," *International Organization*, Winter.

Speare, A., Jr. 1974. "The Relevance of Models of Internal Migration for the Study of International Migration," in G. Tapinos, ed., *International Migration* (Proceedings of a Seminar on Demographic Research), Paris.

Stoever, William A. 1981. *Renegotiations in International Business Transactions*. Lexington, MA: Lexington Books.

Sudarkasa, Niara. 1981. "Female Employment and Family Organization in West Africa," *The Black Women Cross-Culturally*, edited by Filomina Steady. Cambridge: Schenkman.

Swanson Daniel and Teferra Wolde-Semait. 1989. "Africa's Public Enterprise Sector and Evidence of Reforms," World Bank Technical Paper Number 95. Washington, D.C.: World Bank.

Tiewul, Sylvanua A. 1986. "TNCs in African Development: Some Policy Issues," *The CTC Reporter*, no. 2.

UNCTAD. 1988. *The Least Developed Countries: 1987 Report*. New York: United Nations.

United Nations Center on Transnational Corporations (UNCTC). 1985a. *Transnational Corporations in World Development: Third Survey*. London: Graham and Trotman.

United Nations Center on Transnational Corporations (UNCTC). 1985b. *Trends and Issues in Direct Foreign Investment and Related Flows*. New York: UNCTC.

United Nations Center on Transnational Corporations (UNCTC). 1988a. *Transnational Corporations in World Development: Trends and Prospects*. New York: United Nations.

United Nations Center on Transnational Corporations (UNCTC). 1988b. "Recent Trends in FDI 1975–1985," *The CTC Reporter*, no. 26.

United Nations Center on Transnational Corporations (UNCTC). 1988c. "The Process of Transnationalization in the 1980s," *The CTC Reporter*, no. 26.

United Nations Center on Transnational Corporations (UNCTC). 1989. "FDI Flows in the Mid-1980s," *The CTC Reporter*, no. 27.

United Nations Center on Transnational Corporations (UNCTC). 1990. "TNCs in the World Economy: Overall Trends and Foreign Direct Investment." *The CTC Reporter*, no. 29.

United Nations Center on Transnational Corporations (UNCTC), Economic and Social Council. 1990. "Foreign Direct Investment in Africa and Strategies to Encourage TNCs to Respond Positively to the Improved Investment Climate." A Report of the Secretary General (E/C.10/1990/9).

United Nations General Assembly. 1988. "Mid-Term Review of the Implementation of the United Nations Programme of Action for African Economic Recovery and Development 1986–1990: Investment of Transnational Corporations in Africa" (A/43/5—/Add.2).

Vengroff, Richard and Ali Farah. 1985. "State Intervention and Agricultural Development in Africa: A Cross-National Study," *The Journal of Modern African Studies* 23, 1 (March): 75–85.

Vernon, Raymond. 1988. *The Promise of Privatization: A Challenge for American Foreign Policy.* New York: Council on Foreign Relations Press.

Vickers, John, and George Yarrow. 1988. *Privatization: An Economic Analysis.* Cambridge, MA: MIT Press.

Vukmanic, F. 1983. "The Outlook for Foreign Direct Investment in Developing Countries." Paper Presented at the Annual Meeting of the Allied Social Sciences Association, San Francisco.

Wallerstein, Immanuel. 1981. "Dependence in an Interdependent World," in *From Dependency to Development.* Boulder, CO: Westview Press, pp. 267–293.

Washington Times, February 28, 1986.

Weber, Max. 1958. *The Protestant Ethic and the Spirit of Capitalism.* New York: Scribners.

Whitaker, Jennifer S. 1988. *How Can Africa Survive?* New York: Council on Foreign Relations Press.

World Bank. 1983. *Accelerated Development in Sub-Saharan Africa: An Agenda for Action*, Washington, D.C.: World Bank.

World Bank. 1986. *Financing Adjustment with Growth in Sub-Saharan Africa, 1986–90*, Washington, D.C.: The World Bank.

World Bank 1987. *World Development Report 1987.* New York: Oxford University Press.

World Bank. 1988. *World Debt Tables 1988/89*, Washington, D.C.: The World Bank.

World Bank. 1989a. *Africa's Adjustment and Growth in the 1980s*, Washington, D.C.: The World Bank.

World Bank. 1989b. *The World Bank Annual Report 1988*, Washington, D.C.: The World Bank.

World Bank. 1989c. *The World Bank Annual Report 1988*, Washington, D.C.: The World Bank.

World Bank. 1989d. *Sub-Saharan Africa: From Crisis to Sustainable Growth: A Long-Term Perspective Study.* Washington, D.C.: The World Bank.

World Bank. 1989e. *World Development Report 1989*, New York: Oxford University Press.

World Bank. 1989f. *World Bank Watch.* Washington, D.C.: The World Bank (July 17).

Young, Crawford, 1982. *Ideology and Development in Africa.* New Haven, CT: Yale University Press.

Appendix A
Africa: Foreign Direct Investment Inflows, 1970–1985 (millions of dollars)

Country/Region	1970	1975	1980	1981	1982	1983	1984	1985	Annual Average/2		
									1970-74	1975-80	1981-85
OIL EXPORTERS	424.0	169.8	-499.0	1102.3	976.2	1116.1	1083.0	1657.1	455.1	267.8	1190.1
ALGERIA	47.0	119.0	348.8	13.0	-54.1	-14.0	1.0	-2.0	125.3	165.8	-8.0
ANGOLA	2.0	0.1	37.4	49.0	115.8	104.3	42.5	19.9	*	6.7	66.3
CAMEROON	16.0	27.1	129.8	135.4	111.4	213.8	17.6	317.3	9.2	47.4	159.1
EGYPT	*	8.5	547.9	752.3	293.7	489.6	728.8	1177.8	*	376.1	688.4
GABON	-1.0	166.9	31.5	54.6	131.8	111.8	8.1	11.1	25.5	63.9	63.5
LIBYA	139.0	-614.4	-1089.4	-744.0	-391.9	-327.1	-17.4	-315.8	-21.8	-659.2	-359.3
NIGERIA	205.0	417.7	-739.3	546.0	429.5	353.8	188.6	341.2	285.3	163.3	371.8
TUNISIA	16.0	44.9	234.3	296.0	340.0	183.9	113.8	107.6	31.6	103.8	208.3
NON-OIL EXP./1	*	305.9	742.2	668.7	681.0	478.8	414.8	386.7	175.6	515.6	525.3
BENIN	7.0	1.9	4.0	2.0	-5.0	-5.0	-5.0	-	-	*	*
BOTSWANA	-	-38.2	111.5	88.4	21.1	23.8	62.1	53.6		44.3	49.8
BURKINA FASO	0.4	0.2	0.0	2.5	2.0	2.0	1.7	0.0	1.5	1.3	2.1
BURUNDI	*	0.3	4.6	11.1	0.9	3.0	1.2	0.2	*	0.9	3.3
CENTRAL AF. REP	1.0	5.6	5.3	5.8	9.2	4.5	5.1	2.4	*	6.8	5.4
CHAD	1.0	20.3	-0.4	-0.1	-0.1	-0.1	9.2	53.6	4.1	17.0	12.5
CONGO	25.0	15.4	40.1	30.9	35.3	56.1	35.0	13.0	50.9	13.2	34.1

Appendix A (continued)

| Country/Region | 1970 | 1975 | 1980 | 1981 | 1982 | 1983 | 1984 | 1985 | Annual Average/2 | | |
									1970-74	1975-80	1981-85
Cote d'Ivore	31.0	69.1	94.6	32.8	47.5	37.5	3.0	29.2	29.9	63.5	30.0
ETHIOPIA	4.0	19.3	*	*	*	*	*	*	15.9	4.9	0.0
GAMBIA	*	0.1	*	2.1	*	*	*	*	*	*	*
GHANA	68.0	70.9	15.6	16.3	16.3	2.4	2.1	5.6	27.2	15.7	8.5
KENYA	14.0	17.1	79.0	62.7	79.2	58.3	62.8	87.7	-	52.9	70.1
LESOTHO	*	*	4.6	4.8	3.9	4.5	4.7	3.1	*	*	4.2
LIBERIA	*	80.7	*	0.0	34.8	49.1	38.8	-16.2	*	*	26.6
MADAGASCAR	20.0	4.9	-7.0	*	*	*	*	*	13.6	-1.3	*
MALAWI	9.0	8.6	*	1.1	*	*	*	0.5	11.7	6.9	*
MALI	*	2.7	2.3	3.7	1.5	3.1	4.1	4.5	*	1.6	3.4
MAURITANIA	1.0	-122.8	27.1	12.5	15.0	1.4	8.5	7.0	*	-4.0	8.9
MAURITIUS	2.0	3.9	1.2	0.7	1.8	1.6	4.9	8.0	1.6	2.8	3.4
MOROCCO	20.0	*	89.8	59.0	79.5	46.0	47.2	20.3	6.9	54.0	50.4
MOZAMBIQUE	*	6.7	4.4	0.4	1.9	2.5	-3.2	0.3	*	0.5	0.4
NIGER	1.0	22.6	49.1	-6.1	28.3	1.2	3.9	*	0.9	30.7	6.8
RWANDA	-0.2	3.0	16.4	18.0	20.8	11.1	15.1	14.6	1.2	7.9	15.9
SENEGAL	5.0	22.6	14.4	20.0	10.0	-33.0	27.0	*	7.8	17.6	6.0
SEYCHELLES	*	*	9.5	10.1	10.0	9.2	9.9	11.7	*	4.6	10.2
SIERRA LEONE	8.0	10.1	-18.6	7.5	4.6	1.7	5.8	-31.0	6.3	7.6	-2.2
SOMALIA	5.0	6.7	*	*	-0.8	-8.2	-15.0	-0.7	2.7	*	-4.9
SUDAN	*	*	*	*	*	*	8.8	-2.8	*	*	1.2

228

SWAZILAND	*	14.4	25.6	40.2	2.6	-14.0	7.6	24.7	*	24.1	12.2
TANZANIA	*	-0.9	4.6	18.9	17.3	1.5	-3.7	1.7	*	4.5	7.1
TOGO	1.0	5.2	42.3	10.1	16.1	1.5	-9.9	*	-6.0	35.1	4.5
UGANDA	4.0	2.1	*	*	*	*	*	*	-0.6	1.3	*
ZAIRE	42.0	15.8	56.0	255.9	176.6	137.9	7.2	*	*	64.3	144.4
ZAMBIA	-297.0	37.6	61.2	-38.9	38.6	25.7	17.4	*	*	36.9	10.7
ZIMBABWE	*	*	1.6	3.8	-0.7	-2.0	-2.5	2.9	*	*	0.3
TOTAL	424.0	475.7	243.2	1771.0	1657.2	1594.9	1497.8	2043.8	630.7	783.4	1715.4

Minus sign indicates debit.

*indicates that the figure is zero or close to zero or data are missing.

1/Totals may not sum to column totals because of missing data or data indicated as close to zero.

2/For some countries the annual averages are calculated based on 4-year averages derived from IMF (1988).

Sources: The primary source of data is UNCTC (1988a). The UNCTC figures were updated by using data from IMF (1988). Data for 1970–74 were derived from UNCTC (1985a).

Appendix B
Annex Table: Recent Changes in Regulations Relating to Transnational Corporations

Country	Law/Regulation	Coverage
AFRICA		
Benin	Law No. 82-005 of 20 May 1982 (Investment Code).	Contains general guarantees, specifies four categories of investment in regard to different sectors and forms of investment; contains approval procedures and incentives for selected enterprises.
Botswana	Industrial Development Policy of October 1984 (Gov. Paper No. 2).	Provides financial incentives, protective measures and a local preference scheme. Established the Trade and Investment Promotion Agency (TIPA). Maintains a liberal policy on foreign exchange procedures in relation to foreign investors and skilled manpower.
Burkina Faso	Order No. 84-051, PRES/CNR of 7 August 1984 (Investment Code).	National and foreign investments. General guarantees and special incentives (three categories according to enterprise activities).
Burundi	Law No. 1-005 to 14 January 1987 (Investment Code), superseded Decree-Law No. 1-001-86 of 10 July 1986.	Contains general guarantees for domestic and foreign investors. Established the National Commission on Investments. Contains provisions for different investment regimes with respect to their preferential treatment.
Cameroon	Law No. 84-03 of 4 July 1984 (Investment Code). Replaced the Investment Code of 27 June 1960.	National and foreign investments. General guarantees. Four priority regimes (according to size of investment, localization, activities, etc.).
Central African Republic	Order Nos 82/039 of 17 August 1982, 82/019 of 4 May 1982 and 80/039 of 2 May 1980, which supplement and modify Lay No. 63/355 of 9 February 1973 (Investment Code).	Applies to both foreign and domestic investors. Contains provisions on approval procedures and a special regime for large development projects.

Source: United Nations Center on Transnational Corporations (1988a).

230

Appendix B (continued)

Country	Law/Regulations	Coverage
Comoros	Act No. 84-005/P.R. of May 1984 (Investment Code). Replaced Act No. 80-009 of 1980.	Conatins general guarantees and provisions on four preferential regimes.
Cote d'Ivoire	Law No. 84-1230 of 8 November 1984 (Investment Code). Replaced Law No. 59-134 of 3 September 1959.	National and foreign investments. General guarantees. Two special regimes (priority enterprises and establishment agreements).
Djibouti	Law No. 88/AN/84/1 of 13 February 1984, Amended Law No. 494/6 of 24 May 1968 and Law No. 117/8 of 27 May 1975.	Contains general guarantees for investors, provisions on approval procedures, reinvestment, condition for preferred treatment of investors (2 categories).
Egypt	The Companies Law No. 159 of 1981. Replaced Law No. 26 of 1954.	Intended to rationalize the treatment of all private investors and to remove former disincentives for expanding existing businesses. Foreign majority ownership in joint ventures is allowed, no limit on foreign ownership exists except banks, contracting companies and consultant services (49-51 per cent limit).
Equatorial Guinea	Law No. 1 of 17 November 1979 (Investment Code).	Basic law on admission procedures and repatriation of capital and profits.
Ethiopia	Proclamation No. 235 of 1983 (published 22 January 1983).	Formation of joint ventures between Ethiopian public capital and foreign public or private capital.
Ghana	Law No. 116 of 13 July 1985 (investment Code) as enacted by the Provisional National Defence Council Law. Replaced Law No. 437 of 11 August 1981.	National and foreign investments. General guarantees. Special incentives in priority areas.
Guinea	Ordinance No. 001/PRG/87 of 3 January 1987. Amended Order No. 239/PRG/84 of 3 October 1984 (Investment Code).	Contains general guarantees for foreign investors, provisions on the transfer of capital, conditions and incentives for preferential regimes (small and medium-size enterprises, export industries, which use domestic resources or are located in rural areas), approval procedures.

Appendix B (continued)

Country	Law/Regulation	Coverage
Guinea Bissau	Decree Law No. 2/85 of 13 June 1985 and Regulating Decree No. 25-E/85 of 13 June 1985 and annex.	Defines foreign investment, contains general guarantees, regulates the approval procedure and grants several incentives to foreign investors.
Kenya	Foreign Investment Protection Act 1981. Revised Act No. 35 of 15 December 1965.	Protection to certain approved foreign investments and related activities (Certificates, import of assets, ptransfer of profits).
Liberia	Law of 1980 (Investment Code). Amended the Investment Code of 1973.	Incentives to new, approved investments (tax holidays, exemption from customs duties); priority of labour-intensive industries which utilize local raw material.
Madagascar	Act No. 85-001 of 18 June 1985 (Investment Code); Decree No. 86-153 of 21 May 1986 implementing Act No. 85-002. Replaced Law No. 62-024 od 9 September 1962, as amended.	Contains general guarantees for foreign investment, indicates restricted areas (for example, banking, insurance, mining), sets a preferential plan for national development, contains provisions on small and medium-size companies and sets obligations of privileged enterprises.
Mali	Law No. 86-39/AN-RM (Investment Code) of 8 March. No. 76-31/CMLN of 30 March 1976.	Contains regulations ofpreferential regimes (for example, small and medium-size enterprises, enterprises in rural areas, enterprises which use new technologies, export industries) and contains list of incentives offered.
Mauritius	Export Services zones Act No. 8 of 23 June 1981.	Investment law for the service industry.
Morocco	Law of 1987 (not yet published) Amended the Industrial Investment Code No. 17-82 promulgated by Decree No. 2-82-623 of 17 January 1983.	Contains provisions relating to duty and tax exemptions, registration, small and medium-size industries, land, energy and environmental protection.
	Real Estate Investment Code No. 15-85 pf 17 August 1985. Replaced Law No. 2-80 promulgated by Decree No. 1-81 -207 of 8 April 1981.	Concerns investment in the construction industry (Urban and suburban areas). Grants tax incentives.

232

Appendix B (continued)

Country	Law/Regulation	Coverage
Morocco (continued)	The Tourism Investment Code No. 20-82 of 3 June 1982.	Establishes incentives for investment in tourism.
	The Maritime Investment Code No. 1-83-107 of 5 October 1984.	Incentives for investment in marine fisheries, shipping and sea services (50 per cent limit for foreign ownership)
Mozambique	Law on Foreign Investments No. 4 of 18 August 1984.	Foreign direct investment. Prior authorization. Established the Office for the Promotion of Foreign Investment. Guarantees and discal incentives.
Nigeria	Nigerian Enterprises Promotion Order os 1981. Amended the Nigerian Enterprises Promation Decree No. 3 of 12 January 1977 A/63. (Indigenization Act) Control of Public Corporations Act, 1981.	Act to enhance the role of Nigerians in local business activities. Restricts industrial sectors to foreign enterprises.
Rwanda	Law Nó. 21/1987 of 5 August 1987 (Investment Code). Replaced Decree No. 30/77 of 21 September 1977 (Investment Code).	Contains provisions on approval procedures, on general guarantees for foreign investors, on preferential regimes (for example, decentralized or small enterprises, joint ventures) and on incentives.
Sao Tome and Principe	Decree-Law No. 14/86 of 18 March 1986 (Investment Code). Revoked Decree Laws No. 13/76 of 30 April 1976 and No. 30/80 of 23 July 1980/	Grants different incentives to large companies, small and medium-sized companies, to investors in preferred sectors and to joint ventures between the Government and private entities.
Senegal	Law No. 87/25 of 18 August 1987. Replaced Act No. 81-50 of 10 July 1981 (Investment Code).	Covers both foreign and domestic investment; contains eligible sectors of activity, guarantees on free transfer of capital and reciprocal treatment, provisions on preferenital regimes and incentives.
Sudan	The Encouragement of Investment Act P.O. Nr. 17 of 26 April 1980. Superseded the Encouragement of Investment in Economic Services Act 1973, the Development and Encouragement of Industrial Investment Act 1974, and the Development and Encouragement of Argicultural Investment Act of 1976.	Aims at encouraging investments in the livestock, mining, industrial, transport, tourism, storage and housing fields; classified into incentives and privileges protection and guarantees, and administration.

Appendix B (continued)

Country	Law/Regulation	Coverage
Togo	Act No. 85-03 of 29 January 1985 (Investment Code); abrogated Act No. 65-10 of 10 July 1965 (Investment Code) as last amended by Order No. 73-6 of 1 February 1978.	Contains guarantees, incentives and approval procedures; established the Commission for Investment.
United Republic of Tanzania	Law of 16 April 1986	Transfer of technology. Estblished the Centre for the Transfer and Development of Technology. Authorization and registration of technology transfer agreements.
Zaire	Order No. 86-028 of 5 April 1986 (investment Code).	Aimes at encouraging local and foreign investment; established three preferential regimes applicable to both new and existing investment; contains transfer guarantees (including limitations on capital, dividends, royalties, etc,).
	Ordinance-Law No. 83-008 of 21 February 1983. Amended Ordinance-Law No. 81-010 of 2 April 1981.	Created a Free-Zone Regime for Industrial Development to, inter alia, encourage foreign capital investment, export trade, transfer of technology to Zaire and industries using preferably raw materials produced in Zaire.
	Ordinance-Law No. 83-060 of 21 February 1983. Modified Ordinance-Law No. 81-066 of 30 April 1981.	Administration of the INGA Free Zone Regime (ZOFI).
Zambia	Investment Act of 28 February 1986. Replaced the Industrial Development Act No. 18 of 30 August 1977.	National and foreign investments Registration of manufacturing enterprises and transfer of technology agreements. Established the Investment Council.
Zimbabwe	Policy, Guidelines and Procedures on Foreign Investment by the Ministry of Finance, Economic Planning and Development of September 1982.	Contains provisions on approval procedure. Provides guarantees on the remittability of the proceeds of divestment.

Index

About the Contributors

REXFORD A. AHENE is Associate Professor of Economics and Business at Lafayette College. He is the founder and president of AHEAD Consulting Services, an international business management consulting firm specializing in sub-Saharan Africa. He has done extensive research on international strategic management, investment feasibility analysis, cross-cultural management education, and has served as a consultant on export production and management to UNDP and ITC. His work has been published in a number of books and journals.

BERNARD S. KATZ is Associate Professor of Economics and Business at Lafayette College and has served as a consultant to Bank of America International on foreign exchange trading, interest rates, and country analysis. He is also an expert consultant on economic loss and service wage disputes.

Dr. Katz is a prolific writer with books and articles in a wide range of disciplines. His research interests are in the areas of international finance and management of organizations in Europe, Latin America, and Africa.

KOFI APRAKU is Associate Professor of Economics at the University of North Carolina at Asheville.

CATHERINE BOONE is Assistant Professor of Government, with a special interest in politics and political development in Africa, at the University of Texas at Austin.

ADHIP CHAUDHURI is Assistant Professor of Economics at Georgetown University in Washington, D.C.

MYLES F. ELLEDGE is a consultant with Development Alternatives Inc., an economic development consulting firm in Washington, D.C.

JON KRAUS is Professor of Political Science and a member of the faculty at the State University of New York College at Fredonia, New York. Dr. Kraus is a regular contributor to the African Studies Program and the Foreign Policy Institute seminar series offered by the Johns Hopkins Nitze School of Advanced International Studies.

KARL P. MAGYAR is a member of the faculty and Professor of Economics at the Center for Aerospace Doctrine, Research, and Education (RIP) at Maxwell Air Force Base in Alabama. Dr. Magyar was the economic advisor to the president of Bophuthatswana in Southern Africa in 1982 and served as an International Trade Specialist at the African Institute of International Studies and Training in Fujinomiya, Japan, in 1980.

KIDANE MENGISTEAB is Associate Professor of Political Science and Geography at Old Dominion University, Norfolk, Virginia.

FELIX NDUKWE is an economist responsible for market demand modelling and analysis for AT&T and a part-time instructor of economics and business at Lafayette College, Easton, Pennsylvania.

MARY J. OSIRIM is Assistant Professor of Sociology and Coordinator of the Africana Studies Program at Bryn Mawr College in Bryn Mawr, Pennsylvania.

GANGA PERSAD RAMDAS is Associate Professor of Economics and Business at Lincoln University, Philadelphia, Pennsylvania. Dr. Ramdas has received a number of scholarships and awards including the Nissan-HBCU Fellow in Finance in 1989 and the Lily Grant Foundation Summer Research Stipend in 1990.

LOUIS A. PICARD is Associate Dean of the Graduate School of Public and International Affairs and Director of the Public Management Program at the University of Pittsburgh in Pittsburgh, Pennsylvania.

ERNEST J. WILSON III is the Director of the Center for Research on Economics and Development at the University of Michigan in Ann Arbor, Michigan. Dr. Wilson has done extensive research on public enterprise reform in Africa, and has served as a consultant on privatization to the World Bank, UNDP and USAID.

MULATU WUBNEH is Associate Professor of Planning and Coordinator of the African Studies Program at East Carolina University, Greenville, North Carolina. He has taught at Florida State and Florida A&M University. He is the author of *A Spatial Analysis of Urban-Industrial Development in Ethiopia* (1982), and co-author of *Ethiopia: Transition and Development in the Horn of Africa* (1988). In addition, he is the author of several articles and papers on planning and economic development in Africa.